DIAMONDS
IN THE DUST

Other titles by Joni Eareckson Tada
available from Marshall Pickering

JONI . . . THE START OF A JOURNEY
A STEP FURTHER
CHOICES . . . CHANGES
ALL GOD'S CHILDREN
WHEN IS IT RIGHT TO DIE?

DIAMONDS IN THE DUST

366 meditations on finding the
extraordinary in the ordinary

Joni Eareckson Tada

MarshallPickering
An Imprint of HarperCollinsPublishers

Marshall Pickering is an Imprint of
HarperCollins*Religious*
Part of HarperCollins*Publishers*
77–85 Fulham Palace Road, London W6 8JB

First published in Great Britain
in 1993 by Marshall Pickering

1 3 5 7 9 10 8 6 4 2

A catalogue record for this book is
available from the British Library

ISBN 0 551 02655-3

Printed and bound in Great Britain by
HarperCollinsManufacturing Glasgow

❧ CONTENTS ❧

FOR JUDY BUTLER
AND
FRANCIE LOREY

THANK YOU FOR BEING MY "HANDS"
TO HELP ME PICK UP
DIAMONDS IN THE DUST

Before You Begin

I've seen plenty of babies handle a bottle of milk with their hands and feet. But this two-year-old didn't need her hands. Her mother, sitting next to me in the prayer circle, had placed little Melissa on the floor and, as we prayed, the eyes of this child held my gaze.

Melissa *had* to use her feet. She was partially paralysed from large tumours. And so she gingerly picked up the bottle with her toes and placed it neatly to the side of her head. Her eyes darted to me and I smiled. This was now a game of skill, and so Melissa reached again for the bottle, tightened her toes around it, and set it down on her other side.

Melissa was pleased with herself. Her eyes sparkled and the game continued. After prayer time her mother, Sue Burke, told me Melissa also enjoys using her feet to play with toys and turn pages of books. "She can't walk and doesn't have much use of her hands," commented Sue as she lifted her daughter into a wheelchair, "but she loves to go to the park to watch the children. She gets as much of a charge watching as the kids do from playing."

I believed it. I also believed I saw tears in Sue's eyes, making them glisten with pride for her daughter. I felt Sue's long and silent struggle watching her two-year-old suffer pain and loss and I had to finally ask, "Please, I must know. How do you . . . do it?"

Sue reached for her husband's hand and, with the other, stroked her daughter's head, made bald by chemotherapy. "God has taken us down a rough and rocky road, but we always make time to stop, reach down, and find a few diamonds in the dust."

Diamonds in the dust. Precious jewels we might pass over. Just a sliver of Scripture, but packed with power. Just short words from the Lord, but cutting and convincing. A fragment from a proverb. A snippet of a psalm. Small treasures that sometimes blind us with their brilliant truth. In fact, I brushed off a dusty diamond when I listened to Sue describe her daughter's joy at watching children play. That toddler gave new meaning to the word "vicarious". She experiences the joy of play through others. For her, it's enough. And we experience joy unspeakable through the vicarious death of our Lord. For us, it is enough, more than enough.

Sue might not want you to know this, but she and her husband have always had a rough and rocky road. They get tired. At times, over-whelmed. Income is tight and help is not easy to find. Hope is hard to come by when you know your child has only a short time to live. Yes, they get down. But sometimes, looking down gives the best view of diamonds in the dust.

The book you hold in your hands is my treasure trove of diamond chips I've collected over the years. I've carefully selected favourite gems, ones I've often held to the light, turned this way and that to admire their beauty, diamonds that have made me rich in faith and wealthy in hope.

But I'm not the only one. Look down at your feet. The path sparkles. God has placed diamonds in the dust of your road, too!

Joni Eareckson Tada
Summer 1993

JANUARY

A New Thing

Cymbals clashed. Kettledrums boomed. The orchestra swept into its closing crescendo and the final chord was struck. The audience rose to its feet and clamoured, "Encore!" The scene was the Los Angeles Pavilion, the occasion was a recent holiday symphony, and I, too, called for an encore. The musicians came back on stage and launched into a final number.

You don't have to hold a season ticket for the best box seat at the symphony in order to appreciate encores. You know all about them. Remember that special weekend retreat last year with your Christian friends? The fellowship was fantastic, the speaker was super and, oh, how you wish the blessings could go on and on. And now, this year, you want God to do an encore.

God, however, may not give it. But don't take it hard. For although it's true the Lord will never do exactly the same thing a second time around, He will do something better. A new thing. A new way. God specializes in things fresh and firsthand. He is not satisfied with the updated and revised version – He's always quick to create something new.

"Forget the former things; do not dwell on the past. See, I am doing a new thing! Now it springs up; do you not perceive it? I am making a way in the desert and streams in the wasteland . . . (for) the people I formed for myself that they may proclaim my praise." ISAIAH 43:18–19, 21

≈

His plans for you this year may outshine those of the past. His blueprint is hot-off-the-press and He's prepared to fill your days with reasons to give Him praise. That's why you can begin the year with hope and expectancy.

Lord of beginnings, I'm ready to have you do something new in my life this year. Thank you for leading me into the untouched days ahead. I'm ready to follow.

Heartfelt, Honest Prayers

"God is spirit, and His worshippers must worship in spirit and in truth."
JOHN 4:24

The most powerful prayer I ever offered was the shortest. After three depressing years of suicidal despair over my paralysis, I prayed, "God, if I can't die, show me how to live, please!"

Things didn't change overnight, but with that simple prayer my outlook began to change. I realized I had to take responsibility and face reality head on. With God's help, I would have to learn how to do the impossible – handle life in a wheelchair.

And did God help! It's been said that faith may move mountains, but prayer moves God. I'm convinced the Lord was touched deeply by my short, simple prayer. Why? Because I pushed myself out of the way in order to rely on His spirit; and I told Him the honest truth about my desperate desire to live.

You might not have the strength to say much more to God than a simple prayer like mine. God is not looking for a lot of fancy words. He simply wants you to approach Him in spirit and in truth. That means heartfelt honesty.

❧

You may not change overnight after you offer a prayer in heartfelt honesty, but change, you will. When we approach God in spirit and in truth, we touch His heart and move Him in a special way.

When you offer your earnest prayer to Him, mean it! Then watch your outlook change. You just might start living the impossible.

Lord of the impossible, I come to you with an open heart. I want to be honest and truthful with you. I expose my life, I share with you my need. Please glorify yourself through all the situations and problems I will face today. And thank you for caring about my prayers.

Grow in Grace

And we, who with unveiled faces all reflect the Lord's glory, are being transformed into His likeness with ever-increasing glory . . .

II CORINTHIANS 3:18

I received a letter from an old school friend the other day. After twenty-five years of friendship, it was good to read that she is still growing in the Lord. But I was especially touched with her closing salutation, "Grow in grace". That was certainly a lot nicer than "Yours sincerely".

Her note made me think: Just *how* have I grown in God's grace over the last year? Is it something that can be measured?

Bishop J. C. Ryle puts it this way, "When I speak of growth in grace, I mean an increase in the degree, size, strength, vigour and power of the graces which the Spirit plants in our hearts. When I speak of a person growing in grace, I mean simply this – that his sense of sin is becoming deeper, his faith stronger, his hope brighter, his love more extensive and his spiritual-mindedness more marked. He feels more of the power of godliness in his heart. He manifests more of it in his life. He goes on from strength to strength, from faith to faith, and from grace to grace."

Is your sense of sin deeper than it was last year? Is your hope brighter? Do you sense more of the power of godliness in your heart?

We can be transformed into His likeness; something fundamentally different can happen in our lives from year to year. Change is possible and a new and improved you is within reach. This is how it happens: Behold the Lord's glory and you will grow in grace.

Lord Jesus, I behold you today in all of your majesty and splendour, your excellence and purity. Transform me into the person you want me to be as I grow in your grace.

Exchange the Meaning

Then the Lord said to Moses, "Raise your staff and stretch out your hand over the sea to divide the water so that the Israelites can go through the sea on dry ground" . . . Moses said to Joshua, "Choose some of our men and go out to fight the Amalekites. Tomorrow I will stand on top of the hill with the staff of God in my hands."   EXODUS 14:15–16; 17:9

Look closely at today's verses. When God parted the Red Sea, He told Moses to "raise *your* staff". After the glorious miracle occurred, Moses was careful to refer to it as "the staff of God". It was just an ordinary stick of wood, but when the Lord chose it for His tool, the staff took on new ownership and meaning.

God can exchange the tragic meaning behind accidents or injuries for something new and positive. The cross is a good example. What was once a symbol of torture and pain now represents hope and salvation. My wheelchair which once signified tragedy and confinement, is the very thing that now gives me freedom and mobility.

When God uses for His glory the most ordinary things – such as a staff, or a cross, or a wheelchair – He gives each one unique and special meaning.

◅

What are the symbols of tragedy in your life? A crutch or hearing aid? Where you live? Your appearance or abilities? God can exchange the meaning of the heartbreak for something hopeful and positive. God did it at the cross, and He can do it for you.

Father, I present to you today the disappointing things in my life which hold sad or tragic meaning. Turn my darkness into light. Exchange the sadness for hope. Let me see these things as symbols of your loving and sovereign touch. I will praise you for you are the God who turns weeping into joy.

Do Not Forget

Then Moses and the Israelites sang this song to the Lord: "I will sing to the Lord, for He is highly exalted. The horse and its rider He has hurled into the sea. The Lord is my strength and my song; He has become my salvation. He is my God, and I will praise Him, my father's God, and I will exalt Him."

EXODUS 15:1–2

What a song of praise! The entire chapter of Exodus 15 is a glorious praise song to the Lord after He opened a path through the Red Sea. You can imagine the Israelites' amazement when they saw the water parted like giant glass skyscrapers. Little wonder they sang on for twenty-one verses in music and melody.

But a few verses later, their joy turned sour. Their song gave out. After three days of travelling in the desert without finding water, they grumbled, saying, "What are we to drink?" The songs faded all too quickly when they ran into a little bit of trouble. The irony is, they grumbled about water! Didn't they remember God's miracle with water? They had just watched Him part a whole sea of it.

But we can't point fingers. Our songs of praise fade all too quickly when we forget how God protects and provides for us. We need to take the advice God gave those Israelites in Deuteronomy 4:9:

Only be careful and watch yourselves closely that you do not forget the things your eyes have seen.

The next time you're tempted to grumble or complain, think of your favourite praise song and then . . . sing it. It will be God's way of helping you not to forget His protection and provision in your life.

Lord, forgive me for having such a short memory of all the marvellous ways you've protected and provided for me. I thank you for all that you've done in the past and all you'll do in the future. I'm grateful to you.

Magnificent Vision

One of my favourite songs begins with these words:

Glorify the Lord with me, Let us exalt His name together . . .

It's the third verse of the 34th Psalm. When I read the story of the Epiphany, it is as if David wrote the words as an invitation to the three wise men. The three kings came to Christ and did exactly what David commanded. They fell at the Lord's feet. They worshipped Him and gave Him gifts.

How could they do that to a small toddler in poor surroundings? Because Christ the King was magnificent and, as King, demanded devotion. Too often we approach God differently. We approach Him as if by our actions or words we could make Him more magnificent or more kingly, as if God needed a boost in self-esteem.

Such thinking never entered David's mind or the minds of the wise men. When you magnify an object under a microscope, you don't make the object any bigger. What you magnify is your vision.

Likewise when you exalt a king you do not pronounce him as king. He already is. Magnifying and exalting God are functions of our vision and humility, not of His revelation or His promotion. He already *is* who He is.

The wise men did not bring gifts to enhance Christ's power on earth. Nor did they come as heralds of heaven's court to place a crown on Jesus' head. His coronation had been held before time began. The wise men came with one thought in mind. To see the King. To accept His rule. And that, my friend, is worship worthy of our God.

Glorify the Lord with me . . .

∽

Lord, enlarge my vision of you. Clarify my hazy notions of your power. Sharpen my focus on your holiness. Empower me with a picture of your majesty. And when I see you, may I accept you as King of my life.

Feed on Him

"I tell you the truth, unless you eat the flesh of the Son of Man and drink His blood, you have no life in you . . . For my flesh is real food and my blood is real drink. Whoever eats my flesh and drinks my blood remains in me, and I in him. Just as the living Father sent me and I live because of the Father, so the one who feeds on me will live because of me . . ." On hearing it, many of His disciples said, "This is a hard teaching. Who can accept it?"   JOHN 6:53–60

The Lord Jesus wants us to know Him in an intimate way, to realize a deep, personal union with Him. In order to press home the point about intimacy, Jesus shared this emphatic analogy with His disciples, after which, many deserted Him.

The disciples were right about one thing: This was a hard teaching. Jesus asks us to feed on Him or, as Psalm 34:8 invites us, *"taste and see that the Lord is good."* And when it comes to drinking His blood? Song of Songs 1:2 says, *"His love is more delightful than wine."* In other words, we must abide in Him and let His Word abide in us if we are to know Christ in a deep and intimate way.

⚜

Deep devotion to the Lord Jesus energizes service that is tiring or rigorous. Affection for Him that is warm and heartfelt gives boundless joy to every task. Fervent love for Jesus takes the squeamishness out of every duty that seems distasteful.

This sort of life which sustains and invigorates service can only be realized through an intimate fellowship with Him.

Sometimes, Lord, I expect intimacy with you without taking time to feed on and drink in your life. This day, I want to abide in you and have your Word abide in me.

Seated with Christ

And God raised us up with Christ and seated us with Him in the heavenly realms in Christ Jesus, in order that in the coming ages He might show the incomparable riches of His grace, expressed in His kindness to us in Christ Jesus.

EPHESIANS 2:6–7

In your mind's eye, where is your place when you pray? Do you see yourself coming to God with cap in hand to beg? When you pray, do you feel a little out of place in the divine throne room? Perhaps you picture yourself at a distance from God, timid, shy, and imploring the Lord to work.

There may be times when it's appropriate to go to God as a beggar. Times when you need to seriously mourn over some terrible transgression. But mostly, God wants you to understand your glorious position in prayer. For when you come before God to praise and intercede, it is your privilege and pleasure to join with Christ where He is seated at God's right hand. And that's no place for a beggar, it's a place for a child of the King.

As today's reading says, it is God who has raised you up to be seated with Christ in the heavenly realms. It's a place not only of privilege, but of serious responsibility, for as you pray, you do so alongside your Lord and from an exalted position. You are a partner with Jesus Christ in spiritual warfare. Because Christ lives to intercede, you live to intercede, as well.

❧

When you pray, seated next to your Lord in the heavenlies, remember that your most feeble and faint prayer shakes the hearts of the people for whom you intercede. It's a privilege. It's a responsibility.

You, Lord, live to intercede. Thank you for giving me life so that I might intercede alongside you in the heavenlies.

Sorry, Devil!

The devil is constantly looking for people he can tempt to blame God for their circumstances. But the Lord is constantly ahead of the devil, giving His unique grace to every Christian facing unique problems.

It's as if the devil says to God, "Look, if a woman lost her mother, her husband got fired, her house got robbed, all in the span of one week, I bet such a person would curse you." Then God would say, "You're wrong, devil. Mrs Brown went through that very set of circumstances and she trusted me. The victory is hers and the glory is mine."

Then the devil, slightly miffed, would drum up another scenario. "Okay," the devil argues, "let me get my hands on a young missionary. You give me permission to slap him with a strange illness. At the same time, take away his financial support. Surely, such a man would curse you, God." Then God would say, "Wrong again. Mr Smith went through that very thing, and a few more problems at that. He gained victory by my grace. The glory is mine."

"Does Job fear God for nothing?" Satan replied. "Have you not put a hedge around him and his household and everything he has? You have blessed the work of his hands, so that his flocks and herds are spread throughout the land. But stretch out your hand and strike everything he has, and he will surely curse you to your face." The Lord said to Satan, "Very well, then, everything he has is in your hands, but on the man himself do not lay a finger." JOB 1:9–12

You could be sitting by the bedside of a dying loved one. In a courtroom answering unjust charges. Sweeping up glass on your kitchen floor. Whatever the circumstances, they are yours and they are unique. How will you respond? And to whom will you give the glory?

A Sacrifice of Praise

I don't like blood. And when I picture animals being slain in the Old Testament, I cringe at the thought that our God who created cute woolly lambs would use them in sacrifices. But that has nothing to do with why I'm glad Christ came to earth to die as the final and complete sacrifice. (Although it sure does allow me to eat a hot bowl of lamb stew a whole lot easier.)

My relief is minor compared to those who lived under the ceremonial law. Imagine their sigh of relief. At last, the Messiah had come and banished every drop of animal blood from every act of worship from then on until eternity. The Jews who came to Christ must have been overjoyed.

But a bit mystified. After all, sacrifices were such an integral part of life. Without the need for a temple or an altar, what were they to do now? Hear these words as a Jewish Christian:

Through Jesus, therefore, let us continually offer to God a sacrifice of praise — the fruit of lips that confess His name. And do not forget to do good and to share with others, for with such sacrifices God is pleased.   HEBREWS 13:15–16

What great news! Our penchant to do something is provided with an outlet! And rather than the sacrifice being burned and the blood poured out on the floor, our sacrifices have a destination. Our thanks lifted up to God and our doing good affects the lives of those around us.

Praise be to God for His Son, the Lamb that was slain. And praise be to God for giving us the privilege of presenting a new and joyful sacrifice of praise.

❧

Lord, thank you for your gift of salvation and for your precious Son. May my lips and my hands be ever ready to sacrifice a praise offering.

A Heavenly Perspective

Jesus answered him, "I tell you the truth, today you will be with me in paradise."
LUKE 23:43

My friend Debbie, a polio quadriplegic, recently died and went to be with the Lord. I said to a woman in church, "Just think, she's free of her paralysis and pain!" The woman shook her head "no" and reminded me that Debbie is "asleep" and won't join the Lord until the dead are resurrected.

She's right. But her frame of reference is limited. We operate within the confines of time and space in this world, but God exists outside of time. It's mind-boggling to think that He lives as the great "I Am", always in the present tense, always observing the past and present *now*. We hear Him laugh at the confines of time when He shares His frame of reference: *"A day, to the Lord, is as a thousand years and a thousand years, is as a day."*

Probably that's why the Lord Jesus could say to the thief on their dying day, *"This* day you shall be with me in paradise."

Yes, that woman is correct (and right in line with God's Word) when she says that Debbie is asleep. But Debbie doesn't know that. She, along with the thief on the cross, is today with the Lord in paradise. A twinkling of an eye, for her, has already passed. Time, for Debbie, is removed. When she and King David, Adam and Eve, you and I (if we die before He comes), awake from our sleep, we will all think that only a flash of a moment has passed.

❧

It takes faith to have this heavenly perspective. Faith that is the *substance* of things hoped for. Faith removes all intervening time. Exercise this kind of faith next time a believing friend dies and goes to be with the Lord.

Lord of time and space, give me your heavenly perspective.

When Scripture Hurts

For the word of God is living and active. Sharper than any double-edged sword, it penetrates even to dividing soul and spirit, joints and marrow; it judges the thoughts and attitudes of the heart.　　　　HEBREWS 4:12

Have you ever read a verse scores of times and then suddenly, on the sixty-fifth reading – zap! – the verse nails you squarely between your soul and spirit? Verses such as *"Follow me"* or *"Flee youthful lusts"* sharply rebuke you for that lustful fantasizing you've been wallowing in lately. Any other time you would have skimmed right over those verses. But now, it hurts.

That's what happens when the Word of God slices through that thin line between your soul and spirit. Your soul, clouded by emotions and excuses, is not prone to conviction. Your spirit, however, bears witness with the Spirit of God as His truth, painfully revealing, hits home.

Often you may reread the verse, double checking to make certain you heard God right. But if you are honest, the verse still pierces and stings your conscience. You have been wounded by the Word of God.

Andrew Murray has put it this way: "Jesus has no tenderness toward anything that is ultimately going to ruin a man in service to Him. If God brings to your mind a verse which hurts you, you may be sure that there is something He wants to hurt."

We must not view our disobedience as a vague generality, as when we say, "God, forgive me, a sinner." What sins? Specifically, how have you disobeyed? Try making a list of at least ten specifics. Having trouble? Then ask God to wound you with His Word.

You, Lord, are the judge of my thoughts and my heart. Place the sword of your Word between my soul and spirit and reveal to me today things in my life that displease you.

A Dozen Ways to Be Miserable

"Therefore I will not keep silent; I will speak out in the anguish of my spirit, I will complain in the bitterness of my soul."   JOB 7:11

There are some people who need no help at all when it comes to being miserable. For them, it comes naturally. But in case you're looking for a few suggestions on how to be more miserable, take this advice:

Worry every single day about something. It won't add a cubit to your stature, but it will give you plenty to think about. Count your troubles. Do it preferably at the breakfast table so you can make everyone else miserable, too. Pity yourself. Do this especially if no one else is pitying you.

Don't be compassionate. Don't dare get involved in the lives of people who spill their troubles all over you. If you do, you may end up neglecting your own troubles and that would be a waste. Don't let Bible reading and prayer get in the way of what's really relevant. After all, focusing your sights on things unseen is too eternal; rather, be relevant and get caught up in the here and now. Finally, devise skilful ways to serve both God and the world. Show everyone that Christians can be in the world and of the world.

There are people around you for whom misery is a way of life. The world has enough misery of its own without Christians adding to it. We are to be *in* this world, not *of* it. Do you know someone for whom misery comes naturally? Lift his sights, jar his thinking, give him hope beyond his misery by showing him at least a dozen ways to trust in the Lord of Joy.

Lord, I want to reverse the plea of Job. I give you any anguish in my spirit and I confess any bitterness in my soul. I will not complain. And if I'm to speak out, I will sing and shout your praises.

Hunger

Remember how the Lord your God led you all the way in the desert these forty years, to humble you and to test you in order to know what was in your heart, whether or not you would keep His commands. He humbled you, causing you to hunger and then feeding you with manna, which neither you nor your fathers had known, to teach you that man does not live on bread alone but on every word that comes from the mouth of the Lord. DEUTERONOMY 8:2–3

Humans get hungry, and not just for food, but for a whole range of desires and dreams. Hunger to have hopes fulfilled and longings answered seems to be built into us.

Sometimes our hunger get us into trouble and we wish we could curb our appetites. But in Deuteronomy 8:2, you'll be surprised to learn who gives us these longings. The Lord is the one who *causes* us to hunger. He is the one who has put within us our desires and yearnings. At first, this seems odd. Doesn't God know the "hungries" often get us into trouble?

God has good reasons for giving us such large appetites. He has placed within us desires and dreams in order to test us and humble us, to see what is in our heart, to see whether or not we would follow Him. According to Deuteronomy, He causes us to hunger so that we might learn to feed on the Bread of Heaven, to live on every word that comes from the mouth of the Lord.

To hunger is to be human, but to hunger for God is to feed on Him. Hunger and thirst after His righteousness and feed on Him in your heart. Taste and see that the Lord is good, it is He who will fill you to satisfaction.

Prone to wander, Lord, I feel it. I'm prone to leave the God I love. Here's my heart, please take and seal it, seal it for thy courts above.

Prescription for Weariness

Cast all your anxiety on Him because He cares for you.　　　I PETER 5:7

That verse kept echoing in my mind as I powered my wheelchair through the group of disabled residents in a home for people with cerebral palsy. I clunked wheels with a boy in a bulky, oversized chair while trying to listen to a mentally handicapped girl explain her testimony. Another patient was leaning against the wall, whining to go back to his room.

A nurse wanted me to come and talk to a quadriplegic who was confined to his dormitory. I smiled, nodding at the nurse, and tried to keep my focus on the girl's testimony. It was useless. The nagging whine of the man against the wall shattered what little concentration I had left.

I was far from home and slightly irritated that my sponsors had overloaded my schedule. I had been up all day touring and talking at a rehab centre, leading a disability workshop with pastors, and now I was bone-tired. I wanted to scrap the evening, head out the door and get back to the hotel before they closed the restaurant.

I had to stop. I had to remember that Jesus was with me, moving ahead of my wheelchair and delighting in the smiles of the faces of each disabled resident. In the midst of the clamour, I discovered his voice, whispering, "Come to me, Joni, you are weary and burdened. Let me give you rest." I paused and prayed silently, asking God to give me His rest. I Peter 5:7 was all the reminder I needed.

When weariness or anxiety threaten to overtake you, place your cares in the arms of Jesus. I Peter 5:7 was a simple prescription for weariness penned almost twenty centuries ago and no one has improved on it since!

Thank you, Lord, for carrying my cares today!

A Kick in the Pants

The kingdom of Judah needed a kick in the pants, a shot in the arm, a knock on the head. They had rebelled against God for which God plainly and directly judged through the prophet Isaiah and through foreign nations.

They deserved to be kicked, shot, and knocked, but God was as wise then as He is now. He simply opened their eyes.

"Enlarge the place of your tent, stretch your tent curtains wide, do not hold back; lengthen your cords, strengthen your stakes." ISAIAH 54:2

"Your vision is too small because of your pain," He said. "You've focused on your lack – lack of a nation, lack of power, lack of unity, lack of an army. Hang it all! Expand your tent pegs out a few notches and live as if you have it all. Because you do! You have my prophecy of a mighty nation. You have my undying love. My forgiveness. My power. You have me!"

There are days when I need such a vision. I tire easily at times. And when I tire I want to go into my "tent" of pity and frustration and anger. My small tent is comfortable. Though it's dark and cramped, I feel a sense of comfort.

But not for long. My Maker is my husband, God tells me. And He desires my company under a larger tent that I might expand His kingdom with Him. And as I do so, I find the fresh breeze of new strength to deal with my pity, frustration, and anger. I am renewed.

Lord, expand my vision today. Let me see the light of day from your perspective. Drive home the tent pegs of hope deep and far. Stretch my life to conform to the potential you see.

The Enemy's Strategy

I praise you because I am fearfully and wonderfully made; your works are wonderful, I know that full well. PSALM 139:14

This morning I was having a rough start getting out of bed. My paralysis was giving me fits. I shook my head and growled, "This body is a pain . . . I hate it!"

Why was that so awful? Because the enemy has a deep hatred of my flesh and blood and all I was doing was agreeing with him. He gets a charge when I bad-mouth my body. And he would like to get you to do the same.

Why? Because your body, even underneath wrinkles or fat, and despite the ravages of illness or old age, is made in the image of God. Your heart, mind, hands, and feet are stamped with the imprint of the Creator. Little wonder the devil wants you to do your body in!

This morning I had to, once again, plug my ears against the lies of the tempter and remember that I am *"fearfully and wonderfully made"*. I rehearsed the old, familiar truth that God has a plan for this flesh and blood of mine. That's why the devil considers my body a threat – he understands that when I yield to God my body, albeit paralysed, my feet and hands are powerful weapons against his forces of darkness.

❧

By the way, the devil would have you believe a couple more lies. He wants to convince you that he is either a powerless elf-gone-bad in a red suit with a funny tail, or an evenly-matched and almost-as-mighty opponent of God. Neither is true.

The devil is only a fallen angel. He is a deceiver. He is doomed for destruction. And until then, he has one goal in mind: your spiritual defeat, emotional malignment, and physical frustration. If he tries to get you to agree with him today . . . don't.

I praise you because I am fearfully and wonderfully made, O Lord.

Jeremy

M iss Miller had taught many students at the Christian school, but none so exasperating as Jeremy. He was twelve years old, slightly retarded, and had not progressed beyond the second grade. Miss Miller had repeatedly tried to place Jeremy in a special class, but the boy's parents wanted him to stay with his classmates. This frustrated her as she had eighteen other youngsters to supervise.

After teaching about the resurrection one day, Miss Miller gave the class an assignment. Each child was given a large plastic egg and told to bring it back the next day with something inside that showed new life. All the kids were enthusiastic except for Jeremy. Miss Miller wasn't certain the boy understood.

The next morning the children arrived in class with their eggs, laughing and discussing their surprises inside. In one egg a child had placed a flower. In another, a plastic butterfly. One concealed a rock with moss. When Miss Miller opened Jeremy's egg, it was empty. She reasoned that he must not have understood the instructions. Because she did not want to embarrass the disabled boy, she quietly set the egg aside.

'Miss Miller," Jeremy spoke up, "aren't you going to talk about my egg?" The teacher replied that it was empty. "Yes, but the tomb of Jesus was empty, too."

While the other children ran out to the schoolyard, Miss Miller stayed behind, wiping her tears. Here she had thought it was a waste of time trying to teach Jeremy, but all the while, he had cultivated a wisdom far beyond that of his classmates. Three months later, Jeremy died. And those who paid their respects at the funeral home were surprised to see nineteen eggs on top of his casket. All of them, empty.

"Do you hear what these children are saying?" they asked him. "Yes," replied Jesus, "have you never read, 'From the lips of children and infants you have ordained praise'?" MATTHEW 21:16

∾

Supernatural Encouragement

The Sovereign Lord has given me an instructed tongue, to know the word that sustains the weary. He wakens me morning by morning, wakens my ear to listen like one being taught.   ISAIAH 50:4

I admire people who always know what to say, when to say it, and where. These are folks who encourage with thoughtful words straight from the heart. For them, it comes naturally.

But for you, it can come supernaturally. If you weren't born with the gift of encouragement, God can teach you. There's no better instructor than the Lord Himself because He wrote the lesson in Isaiah 50:4.

God, the all-time great Encourager, says He will give you His words to sustain those around you. He even wants to show you, first thing in the morning, those who may need an encouraging word. He'll teach you who to be on the lookout for, such as a neighbour who just received a bad medical report, a co-worker who didn't get the promotion, or a family member who feels hurt and neglected.

And what does God required of you, His student? *"Listen like one being taught."* That means active listening, not passive. It means cooperating with the Lord when He nudges you to say a kind word to an unsuspecting friend. Folks all around you are facing failure; you can add richness and meaning to their lives as you offer supernatural encouragement.

Ask God to show you today that special person who needs a word of hope. Ask the Lord to give you His words and then keep your eyes open through the morning and afternoon. It may be someone who is discouraged about his job – remind him of past successes. It may be your spouse who feels overwhelmed with the workload – how about an extra hug? Encouraging others costs no more than a bit of time and effort, yet who can put a price on its value?

Sovereign Lord, please give me an instructed tongue. Awaken me and teach me how to listen. Help me to look for those who need your help.

How Much Will It Cost?

"And anyone who does not take his cross and follow me is not worthy of me. Whoever finds his life will lose it, and whoever loses his life for my sake will find it."
MATTHEW 10:38–9

Jesus, with eyes full of love and compassion, extends His hand and offers us life abundant and joyful, here and for eternity. "But how much will it cost?" you ask. The answer is short, simple and painful. "It will cost you everything," the Lord replies.

Ouch. That's what the rich young ruler must have said when he asked Jesus how he could have eternal life. The Lord commanded the young man to sell everything he had, give the money to the poor, and follow Him as Lord. The man couldn't bear the cost and he walked away the loser.

Is it worth taking up your cross, losing your life, and following the Lord? Jesus wraps His loving arms around us, reminding us:

"Everyone who has left houses or brothers or sisters or father or mother or children or fields for my sake will receive a hundred times as much and will inherit eternal life."
MATTHEW 19:29

What was true for the rich young ruler is true for us. God seems to always be pointing to one more area of our life that needs to come under His domain. "Ouch," we reply, "Lord, haven't you asked enough of me?" You can be sure that at whatever point you resist, God will persevere.

Lord, what area of my life still needs to come under your rule? Please show it to me, and then help me to place it under your domain. May I look to the apostle Paul who counted everything a loss in order to know Jesus. Please help me to understand that I have everything to gain when I lose my life for your sake.

Law and Liberty

So the law was put in charge to lead us to Christ that we might be justified by faith. Now that faith has come, we are no longer under the supervision of the law.   GALATIANS 3:24–5

Sometimes the sins we commit are not moral ones, but spiritual. We cultivate a legal attitude towards God, and that's wrong. Christians start out in the Spirit, but when it comes to daily living, we try to perfect ourselves by the flesh.

The law says *do* these things and you shall live, but the Gospel says *live* and these things you will do. The law commands us to love the Lord our God with all our heart, soul and mind; the Gospel says that this is love: Not that we have sought God, but that He loved us and sent His Son to atone for our sins.

The law *demands* holiness but the Gospel *gives* holiness. The law makes blessings the result of *obedience*, but the Gospel makes obedience the result of *blessings*. Under the law, the old man was *restrained*, but with the Gospel, the new man is given *liberty*. And one more thing: Salvation was *earned* under the law, but under the Gospel, salvation is a *gift*.

If we are right in our inward being, we shall certainly do right in our outward actions. This is what Christian liberty is all about.

Picture a woman who is a servant in a house and under the law of her master whom she tries to please. She's paid a wage. She does her duty. But then, the master offers her his love and lifts her up from her place of service to be his bride and share his wealth. She may continue to do the same things, but now she does them with a different motive – love, not duty!

Lord, my old sense of duty is now lost in my new sense of love.

Jesus, My Friend

"Oh the comfort, the inexpressible comfort of feeling safe with a person. Having neither to weigh words nor measure thoughts but pouring them all out like chaff and grain together – certain that a faithful hand will keep what is worth keeping, and with a breath of kindness, blow the rest away."   GEORGE ELIOT

If you have a friend like that, you have a treasure. Someone with whom you can peel back the layers of your heart, knowing that he or she will handle tenderly and loyally everything that's revealed.

That's why I consider Jesus my friend. Of course, there used to be times in prayer when I would get tongue-tied over whether or not I was praising Him properly. I would measure far too carefully my words, wondering if my prayer was progressing the way it should in a tidy order of adoration, confession, thanksgiving and supplication. Sometimes I just gave up in frustration.

All the while, Jesus must have been waiting for me to simply peel back the layers of my heart, and openly share a tumble of thoughts and confessions, like chaff and grain. He wanted to assure me that with His faithful hand He would keep what was worth keeping in my prayer and gently blow the rest away.

Jesus is a friend with whom you can feel safe.

A friend loves at all times . . .   PROVERBS 17:17

～

Oh, the comfort of feeling safe with you, Jesus. Thank you for inviting me to pour out my thoughts to you in a tumble of praise and confession, thanksgiving and petition. I praise you for being a true friend who loves at all times.

Things Above

Since, then, you have been raised with Christ, set your hearts on things above, where Christ is seated at the right hand of God. Set your minds on things above, not on earthly things. COLOSSIANS 3:1–2

In this verse, we are twice commanded. First, we are to set our hearts, and then second, set our minds on things above. In other words, things above are to capture our imaginations, emotions, thoughts, feelings, ideas, and on and on.

Most of us consider this command to be not as necessary as other mandates in Scripture. But it is! When you consider that the first and greatest commandment is to love the Lord with all your heart and mind, it follows naturally that we should set our hearts on things above *"where Christ is seated at the right hand of God"*.

C. H. Spurgeon once said, "Some of you, right now, could not be happy if you were allowed to enter heaven. Shall I tell you why? It is because heaven is a land of the spirit and you have neglected your spirit."

It is the *spiritual* person who can most readily set his heart and mind on heaven. So live in the Spirit, walk in the Spirit, abide by the Spirit, pray in the Spirit, and you can't help but glean a real and deep longing for heavenly glories above.

I want to be a truly spiritual person, Lord, so help me to keep in step with your Spirit today. May my flesh diminish and my spirit increase as I set my heart and mind on things above.

What enriches your spirit? Filling your heart and mind with whatever is true, noble, right, pure, lovely, admirable or anything excellent or praiseworthy. *What enriches your spirit?* Accessing the means of grace through prayer, worship, the reading of God's Word, and fellowship. *What enriches your spirit?* Trusting and obeying your Lord.

Heavenly Citizenship

Their destiny is destruction, their god is their stomach, and their glory is in their shame. Their mind is on earthly things. But our citizenship is in heaven. And we eagerly await a Saviour from there, the Lord Jesus Christ, who, by the power that enables Him to bring everything under His control, will transform our lowly bodies so that they will be like His glorious body.

PHILIPPIANS 3:19–21

Christians who think the most of the next world are usually those who are doing the most good in this present world. It is the person whose mind is only on earthly things who, when it comes to earth, does little good. C. S. Lewis expands on this, saying, "Aim at heaven and you get earth thrown in. Aim at earth and you get neither."

Our verse today highlights what happens when your heart and mind are set on things above. Unlike the person whose mind is on earthly things, you begin to see yourself as a sojourner, a pilgrim on earth. You begin to appreciate your citizenship in heaven. You also begin to eagerly await the Lord's return and you anticipate the joy of having Him transform your body into one like His.

Those whose destiny is destruction may say that being so heavenly minded makes you no earthly good. Not so! Those whose minds are on heaven do earth a world of good.

❧

When you realize your citizenship is in heaven, you begin acting as a responsible citizen should. You begin to invest wisely in relationships. Your conversations, goals and motives become more pure and honest. And all of this serves you well not only in heaven, but on earth. Heavenly minded people are for earth's highest good.

Help me to understand, Lord, what it truly means to have my citizenship in heaven. And may I act as a heavenly citizen should while I temporarily reside here on earth.

Who's Stronger?

You, dear children, are from God and have overcome them, because the one who is in you is greater than the one who is in the world.   I JOHN 4:4

In our less consistent moments, we almost unconsciously see the conflict between God and Satan as an arm-wrestling match. Their wrists go first this way, then that; God's arm is on top one moment, Satan's the next. We remind ourselves that God will win in the end because He's slightly stronger and can hold out longer. But, we reason, it's going to take much time, effort, and a few close calls. We almost think Satan's schemes throw a monkey wrench into God's plans, catch Him off guard, and present Him with problems He wishes wouldn't happen.

That's silly. The truth is that God is infinitely more powerful than Satan. God, the one who is in you, is greater than Satan, the one who is in the world. Why, Satan owes his very existence to God – he is a created being, an angel, and a fallen one at that. Satan had to receive God's permission before afflicting Job, and even then he was under definite restrictions. Satan's demonic hordes feared Jesus and obeyed Jesus' commands. And the Bible is clear that when our Lord is ready, He will crush the evil one for ever.

No, Satan doesn't sneak out and cause pneumonia and cancer while God happens to be looking the other way listening to the prayers of His saints. He can only do what our all-powerful and all-knowing God allows him to do.

Lord Jesus, I have nothing to fear knowing that you are in control. There is no accident, injury, or circumstance that can happen beyond your sovereign will. I recognize that the devil cannot touch my life, he cannot even tempt me without gaining your permission. Help me to realize just how great and powerful you really are!

The Plan behind the Cross

"Indeed Herod and Pontius Pilate met together with the Gentiles and the people of Israel in this city to conspire against your holy servant Jesus, whom you anointed. They did what your power and will had decided beforehand should happen."

ACTS 4:27–8

Satan clearly played the leading role in instigating the crucifixion. He entered the heart of Judas Iscariot, the betrayer of Jesus. Satan-sponsored evil was working in the hearts of the Jewish mob who clamoured for Jesus' crucifixion. The devil puffed up Pilate with pride and intimidated him with fear so that he would condemn an innocent man in order to gain political popularity. Finally, Satan-sponsored sin provoked the cruel soldiers to ridicule Jesus with spit and slaps in the face.

And how did the early Christians view it all? They praised God that the men responsible for Christ's death had only done what divine power and will had decided beforehand should happen. In his most daring attempt to frustrate the plan of God, Satan cut his own throat and performed the deed which was God's provision for man's redemption.

Suppose God the Father had taken the view many modern Christians take – the view which says that anything Satan wants must be bad for God's people? It's the same view which implies that if Satan wants one thing to happen, God must want the exact opposite to happen. The result? God would have cancelled the crucifixion. If God had done that, none of us would be saved!

The truth is, Satan and God may want the exact same event to take place – but for different reasons. Satan's motive in Jesus' crucifixion was rebellion; God's motive was love and mercy.

⤳

Lord, I realize that although Satan was a secondary cause behind the cross, it was the Father who ultimately willed it and allowed the devil to carry it out. It's a mystery . . . and I praise you for your mysterious ways . . . we have salvation because of it!

There's No Place Like Home

Let the word of Christ dwell in you richly as you teach and admonish one another with all wisdom, and as you sing psalms, hymns and spiritual songs with gratitude in your hearts to God. COLOSSIANS 3:16

My mother just sold our childhood home on the corner of Poplar and Birch Drives in the little town of Woodlawn. Somebody else owns it now and they will change the wallpaper and put a new sink in the kitchen. I guess it happens to most families. And it feels like I'm losing a good friend.

You see, I know that house like the back of my hand. I know how the linoleum tile squeaks by the washing machine. I know the way the rafters creak on a windy night. I recall exactly how long my sister could be in the shower before the hot water would run out. I know the smell of the cedar closets and the way the dining room looks in the moonlight.

Home is wherever your heart resides. That's why many people call heaven or the arms of Jesus, home. But God's Word is home, too. When the apostle Paul says, *"Let the word of Christ dwell in you richly,"* he is reminding us that Scripture should find a home in our hearts. We should dwell in it. Richly. For like any home, we should know God's Word like the back of our hand.

Do you consider God's Word a "dwelling place"? Do you reside with its promises, live with its commands? Or is Scripture something you visit only for occasional refreshment, like a vacation spot?

God wants His Word to find a home in your heart. For you, it can be a strong refuge, or a restful sanctuary from a pressure-filled world. Wherever life takes you, home can be as close as your heart, as close as that Bible next to you.

Father, teach me to live comfortably in your Word. When it comes to knowing Scripture, I want to feel at home.

Explanations

"Even to your old age and grey hairs I am he, I am he who will sustain you. I have made you and I will carry you; I will sustain you and I will rescue you."

ISAIAH 46:4

Warren Wiersbe once said, "Nothing is harder to heal than a broken heart shattered by experiences that seem so meaningless. But God's people don't live on explanations; God's people live on His promises."

A grocery list of biblical reasons explaining the "whys and wherefores" behind suffering doesn't always help when you're hurting. What does help are the promises of God. Even though God's promises are usually devoid of standard explanations and don't always detail the blueprint behind His plan, they *do* point to the loving character of our good and kind Lord.

Take Isaiah 46:4. Even for someone bent over with old age and arthritis, God's explanation is simple and powerful, *"I am he, I am he who will sustain you."* God wants us to understand that He alone is the source of help and hope. God owes us no explanations. He did enough explaining on the cross to show that His love is sufficient to meet each and every need.

Look again at our verse for the day. In one short sentence, God promises that He will rescue, carry, and sustain you. How? At least six times, God uses the personal pronoun to point to Himself. His promises are signed, sealed and delivered on the basis of who He is. And He is faithful. He is loving. He rescues you and carries you. It's a promise.

Lord, I don't survive because you roll out in front of me the blueprint behind my painful experiences. I don't live on reasons why. I live on your promises. Draw me to them today and help me to lean on your loving faithfulness. This will be enough.

Worry

"Therefore I tell you, do not worry about your life, what you will eat or drink; or about your body, what you will wear. Is not life more important than food, and the body more important than clothes? Look at the birds of the air . . . Are you not much more valuable than they? Who of you by worrying can add a single hour to his life?

"And why do you worry about clothes? See how the lilies of the field grow . . . so do not worry, saying, 'What shall we eat?' or 'What shall we drink?' or 'What shall we wear?' . . . But seek first His kingdom and His righteousness, and all these things will be given to you as well. Therefore do not worry about tomorrow, for tomorrow will worry about itself. Each day has enough trouble of its own."

MATTHEW 6:25–34

Try this. Go back over these verses and count how many times the Lord uses the word "worry". You'll discover in the span of these few short verses that the Lord Jesus repeats six times, "Do not worry." Talk about driving home a point!

The Lord was wise in repeating His warning so many times. He knows the devastating effects of worrying, how it can corrode your faith like acid. Worry robs you of joy, it steals your hope.

What is worrying you today? A deadline or a diet? A car payment or a gloomy medical report? Repeat one more time your reading of Matthew 6:25–34 and personalize it by putting your name after each time the Lord commands (notice it's not a suggestion) "Do not worry."

Lord, I admit that I'm so prone to worrying about things that happen in my life. Help me today to trust you. Receive glory as I turn from my anxiety and turn to you. Thank you that Jesus has given me this solemn warning not to worry.

Grieving God's Heart

A young friend of mine, who is usually mild-tempered, exploded in anger when her mother meddled in her relationship with her boyfriend. Afterwards she shook her head and said, "I don't know what came over me. I'm not like that at all. That's not me."

I looked directly at my friend and warned, "I'm afraid you're wrong. That *is* you. You *are* like that." I could understand the look of surprise on her face for we both knew that she was not one usually given to outbursts of anger. I went on to explain. "All of us, at any moment, are capable of the most vicious sins against others and against God. In fact, we could all say 'yes, we *are* like that.' "

Jerry Bridges in his book *The Pursuit of Holiness* says, "We are more concerned about our own victory over sin than we are about the fact that our sins grieve the heart of God. We cannot tolerate failure in our struggle with sin, chiefly because we are success-oriented, not because we know it is offensive to God."

Against you, you only, have I sinned and done what is evil in your sight, so that you are proved right when you speak and justified when you judge.

PSALM 51:4

How many times have you said after a moment of disobedience, "I don't know what came over me, I'm usually not like that at all." It's true. We like to think of ourselves as above-average sinners, not quite as wretched as those who commit truly ugly offences against God. But every disobedience is ugly, no matter how great or small. Our problem is that our attitude toward sin is more self-centred than God-centred.

My Lord, I realize that all of my sin grieves you. Thank you for helping me today live a life that pleases you and does not grieve your heart.

Taking Sin Seriously

Have mercy on me, O God, according to your unfailing love; according to your great compassion blot out my transgressions. PSALM 51:1

There are countless times when I get impatient with my husband, Ken, over little things. Like when he uses my good pair of scissors to trim his fishing line. Small irritations like that build until I snap at Ken. I get mad at him, but I also get mad at myself for failing to hold my tongue. Soon the spat is forgotten and God, I feel, has hardly entered into it.

We have a way of sweeping small sins under the carpet of our conscience without ever considering how they affect God. A spat with a friend. A slip of the tongue in gossip. A white lie. An impatient response. An insincere word. A snide comment.

We almost ignore them, thinking God is there only to handle the big offences. It's up to me and my self-control to handle the small sins, we think.

You might say that small offences such as white lies or silly spats do not actually offend God, that He is quite content to have you sweep little things under the carpet. But not so. Perhaps half our problem is that we do not take sin seriously enough. When we line up all of our offences, major and minor, against a holy God, we are then able to say with the psalmist, *"Against you, you only, have I sinned."*

You, O God, are holy and sin is a great offence to you. You hate sin because it cost you the life of your precious Son. It has marred and stained your beautiful creation, including all of the human race. Today I refuse to sweep small sins out of my conscience without bringing them before you in sincere confession. Help me to take sin . . . seriously.

FEBRUARY

Faith

Now faith is being sure of what we hope for and certain of what we do not see.
HEBREWS 11:1

According to this verse, faith is a sort of substitute for sight and possession. Faith gives to invisible things a substance. Spiritual concepts which previously had no form, suddenly become embodied through faith. That which was once invisible becomes concrete and tangible.

But faith does more than give hard, fast reality to that which we do not see. It also makes us look differently at visible things around us. Through faith's eyes, the concrete world in which we live becomes drained of substance and importance. Things around us no longer possess the glow of excitement when we look at life through the lens of faith.

Faith enables us to realize our true positions as sojourners on this planet. As a friend of mine once said, through faith we understand that we are not physical beings having a spiritual experience, but spiritual beings having a physical experience.

Little wonder the world cannot understand a Christian's faith. We have nothing, yet we possess everything. We are sorrowful, yet we are able to rejoice. We are poor, but we are rich. Such is life when, through faith, we ascribe substance to invisible things.

The New English Bible renders Hebrews 11:1 this way: *"And what is faith? Faith gives substance to our hopes, and makes us certain of realities we do not see."* Faith is what will enable us to see God as a God of love at work through hurt and hardship in our lives.

How do we cultivate such faith? Faith comes by hearing, and hearing by the Word of God. If we would find the faith that gives invisible things substance, that enables us to live triumphantly, then we must find it by hearing the Word of God.

Lord Jesus, increase my faith as I behold you, the Word of God.

A Cure

The cords of death entangled me, the anguish of the grave came upon me; I was overcome by trouble and sorrow. Then I called on the name of the Lord: "O Lord, save me!" PSALM 116:3–4

February, they say, is the time of year when many people suffer from depression. Whether it's the cold, damp days or the long, dreary nights, this seems to be a season when people are easily overcome by trouble or sorrow. And what better words describe the living death of deep depression than Psalm 116?

There was a time during the early years of my paralysis when I could not even bring myself to talk about the depression that overwhelmed me. I did nothing, I said nothing. The look on my face was one of sullen, numb despair. I felt strangled by the cords of a living death, just like it says in the Psalm. I didn't even care if there was a cure for my depression.

Thank God, there was a cure. Several friends met with my church youth leader every week to pray specifically and committedly for me, asking God to push back the darkness in my life. Changes did not happen overnight, but slowly my countenance began to brighten. God was using the prayers of my friends to sever the cords of deathly despair which entangled me. Praise God for friends who are willing to call on the name of the Lord on my behalf.

If you are feeling slump-shouldered today, call on the name of the Lord and ask Him to save you. Remember, you may feel overcome by trouble and sorrow, but He who has overcome the world can deliver you.

Gracious Lord, I praise you for offering peace and hope in the midst of depression. Save me from deadly feelings which entangle and pull me down into a grave of defeat and despair. Your powerful name saves!

Dreams

I don't know much about interpreting dreams, but I do know the Lord used a few weird and wonderful dreams in days gone by to reveal His plans for the future. Take the prophet Isaiah. He lay down one night and had a very strange dream. He found himself in the middle of a desert with nothing but sand stretching to the horizon. He felt depressed in the dream, just like the bleak landscape. He felt hungry and thirsty and very unsatisfied.

Just then, the dream took an exciting turn. Out of the sand pushed one small flower and then another. Soon grass sprouted and then trees loaded with fruit. Just before Isaiah woke up, he hurried to write down a fantastic description of the abundant paradise blooming and budding all around him.

You can read about this strange and exciting dream in Isaiah 35. It's a marvellous chapter for anyone with a fearful, faint heart because it talks about going from gloom to glory, from depression to ecstasy. The good news is that Isaiah forecasts this for all of God's people! So . . .

Strengthen the feeble hands, steady the knees that give way; say to those with fearful hearts, "Be strong, do not fear; your God will come, he will come with vengeance; with divine retribution he will come to save you." ISAIAH 35:3–4

*Is your spirit dried up like a parched desert? Has the joy and singing gone out of your life? Then ask God to replace the endless stretch of your dry days with the Living Water. Soon, out of the sand in your life, will push the beautiful Rose of Sharon.

Lord of joy, strengthen my feeble hands and steady my fearful heart so that I can praise you today. Come soon, Lord, to open the eyes of the blind, to make the burning sands a pool, to crown our heads with everlasting joy and to make sorrow and sighing flee away.

Empowerment

When this became known to the Jews and Greeks living in Ephesus, they were all seized with fear, and the name of the Lord Jesus was held in high honour. Many of those who believed now came and openly confessed their evil deeds.

ACTS 19:17–18

Power is let loose when Christians start living out the Gospel on a grass roots level. Just read Acts chapter 19. The early Church unlocked the power of God's Word as they turned upside down their local communities. Neighbours in Ephesus were gripped with an awesome fear of God as they gathered to openly confess their waywardness. It even says they held the name of the Lord Jesus in high honour. Can you imagine such a thing in your community?

Because first-century Christians lived out the Gospel on a local level, God got people's attention. And the same can happen today. The Lord wants to use this time of social unrest and political change as an unprecedented opportunity for the local church to demonstrate the power of God to change a situation, to change people's lives, to change a community.

Empowerment is when the people closest to a problem learn how to solve it themselves. Need a few ideas? Just open your eyes. Elderly people in dilapidated houses. Suicide among teenagers. Lonely widows in busy neighbourhoods. Abused wives and battered children. Girls with unwanted pregnancies. Disabled people needing housekeeping help. Drug abuse in schools.

These are the problems you live close to. And when believers begin living out the Gospel on a grass roots level, God will get people's attention.

❧

God's life-changing power shakes a community when a church directly addresses the needs in the streets, schools and homes. The Gospel is best declared when it is demonstrated toward the people closest to you.

Empower my church, Lord, to make a difference in my community. And please begin with me!

Who's behind Suffering?

The Lord said to him, "Who gave man his mouth? Who makes him deaf or mute? Who gives him sight or makes him blind? Is it not I, the Lord?"
EXODUS 4:11

Does God cause blindness or does He allow it? Does He plan for a person to be born deaf or does He permit it? In short, does God *want* disease? The key here is how we use the word "want". God doesn't want disease to exist in the sense that He *enjoys* it. He hates disease just as He hates all the other results of sin – death, guilt, sorrow, and so on. But God must want disease to exist in the sense that He *wills* or *chooses* for it to exist, for if He didn't He would wipe it out immediately.

God chooses to allow sickness for many reasons. One of those reasons is to mould Christian character. In this way God uses one form of evil, that is sickness, to help remove another form of evil, personal sin.

But most importantly, God is delaying closing the curtain on suffering until more of the world can have the chance to hear the Gospel. For if God erased all disease today, He would also have to erase sin, the general cause of disease, and that would mean the destruction of all people. It is God's mercy which delays His judgment!

Though He brings grief, He will show compassion, so great is His unfailing love. For He does not willingly bring affliction or grief to the children of men.
LAMENTATIONS 3:32–3

Does God ordain? Permit? Plan? Allow? The verb is not so much the important thing as the noun: God. And God is love.

Your ways are higher than mine, Lord, and your thoughts unsearchable. I praise you that one day you will give us the key which will unlock sense out of seemingly senseless suffering.

God Allows Suffering

"Yours, O Lord, is the greatness and the power and the glory and the majesty and the splendour, for everything in heaven and earth is yours. Yours, O Lord, is the kingdom; you are exalted as head over all."   I CHRONICLES 29:11

This verse resounds of God's sovereignty and power. God is exalted as head over all – including peace and war, light and darkness, health and sickness, prosperity and calamity.

Someone once said that Satan may power the ship of calamity, but God steers it to serve His own purposes. And when it comes to God's purposes we have His promise that nothing will be allowed in our lives which is not for our good or which is too hard for us to bear (Romans 8:28; I Corinthians 10:13).

But when we say that God allows Satan to do the things he does, it isn't as if Satan twists God's arm and God hesitantly grants permission. Nor are we to imagine that once God grants permission, He then nervously runs behind Satan with a repair kit, patching up what the devil has ruined. The Lord is never forced into a corner. The Lord is never backed against a wall. No. Not only is God not frustrated or hindered by Satan's schemes, but God actually uses the devil's deeds to advance His kingdom and bring glory to Himself.

⋐

"Suffering is . . . an opportunity to experience evil and change it into good," quotes Saul Bellow. We can do that when we trust our sovereign God who works all things for our good and His glory.

I bow before your sovereign majesty, O Lord, praising you that all power and glory and splendour is yours. Only you can reach down into what otherwise would be evil, and pull out of it good for your children and glory for yourself. So be it!

The Twenty-third Psalm

Even though I walk through the valley of the shadow of death, I will fear no evil, for you are with me; your rod and your staff, they comfort me.

PSALM 23:4

What one of us hasn't faced fright and fear head-on by softly quoting the Twenty-third Psalm? We repeat those old familiar verses time and again to soothe our souls and break the suffocating grip of fear.

I'm particularly fond of the fourth verse. Even though I walk *through* the valley of the shadow of death, I will fear no evil, for you are with me. The psalmist doesn't focus his attention on the dark valley and he's not distracted by the shadows. He sees through the valley, past the darkness, and looks with confidence towards the other side.

The dark valley is a place to go through, not a place to stay in.

Are you in the middle of a dark valley? It could be a bad financial report. Perhaps you just discovered drug abuse in your family. Your son is to be sent overseas. You are facing two weeks of bedrest. Your reputation has been stained by gossip.

It may look dark and gloomy right now, but please remember that God does not intend for you to stay in those shadows. The valley He has led you into is the same valley out of which He will lead you. You will, by His grace, go *through* it. There is, thanks to our Shepherd, a smile on the other side.

Lead me, Shepherd, through the dark times. I promise to follow you closely and to stay on the path, to remember your rod is with me and your staff is there to comfort and guide. Thank you for that little word, "through" in this beautiful Psalm . . . I trust that you will lead me to the other side of the dark times to safety, rest, peace and joy.

The Book of Philippians

I thank my God every time I remember you . . . it is right for me to feel this way about all of you, since I have you in my heart. PHILIPPIANS 1:3, 7

When it comes to different styles of writing, the apostle Paul was a versatile author. When writing to the Galatians, Paul sounded fighting mad as he told them in no uncertain terms they were way off track. When he wrote to the Romans, he came off sounding like a theology professor. When he addressed Christians in the book of Thessalonians, Paul sounded like a youth leader.

But Paul's letter to the Philippians is different from the rest. Philippians is not a theology lesson or a manual on how to solve problems. Philippians is a thank you letter and, because of that, Paul doesn't watch his words but writes an endless stream of joyful remembrances and encouragements. You can tell he had fun with his pen and paper.

How poignant that Paul wrote his thank you letter from a dark, stinking prison cell. That he can say *"be anxious about nothing"* and *"I've learned to be content"* while in bruising chains, makes the book of Philippians all the more joyful.

❧

You may not be in an actual prison, but like the apostle, you may feel chained to a few unpleasant circumstances. If so, are you still able to write a thank you letter to God? If you need help composing your words, take time to flip open to the book of Philippians and peruse the finest thank you letter ever written.

Lord, I want to thank you for every good and perfect gift with which you've blessed my life. For friends and family . . . for smiles and sunny days . . . for the promise of heaven . . . for your grace which gives joy and peace . . . and most of all, for the example of people like Paul whose example inspires us all.

Gifts Are to Be Shared

Each one should use whatever gift he has received to serve others, faithfully administering God's grace in its various forms.　　　I PETER 4:10

So what's your gift? Before you give me a theological list or a shrug of the shoulder, let me share a story with you about a six-year-old little girl. Her daddy serves as a pastor in the United States. Daddy was busy studying at the dining room table for a sermon the next morning on the chapter from which today's verse is taken. He looked up to see Bethany watching him with a smile.

"What are you doing, Daddy?"

"I'm studying for tomorrow's sermon."

"Well, when you get done, I'll give you a big hug."

With that, Bethany wrapped her arms around her father and squeezed the biggest hug she could muster. "Why did you do that?" my friend responded, "I'm not finished yet." "I know," said Bethany, "I just wanted you to know what it would feel like when you do get done."

What a wonderful picture this little girl provided for her father's sermon the next day. *"Each one should use whatever gift he has received to serve others."* The pastor was employing his gift when he sat down to study and stood up to preach. But do you see the employment of yet another gift? Bethany put her arms to work and exhorted her father with comfort and the promise of reward. Now that's what I call teamwork.

❧

Our time is so short here. Our chances to put our gifts to work are fleeing fast. The question of the day is not how to find your gift. It's where and when you use it. Only in that way will we be *"faithfully ministering God's grace"*.

Lord, I know my gift. Let me use it. Place me into paths of oncoming problems or new opportunities that I might exhibit the manifold grace of God.

The Joy of the Lord

Stop and muse for a moment on the joy of the Lord. Consider His gift of Spirit-inspired fruit of joy. His oft-repeated command was, "Rejoice!" Fullness of joy is to be found in Him. Finally, for the joy that was set before Him, Jesus endured His cross. In other words, if you're looking for joy, it can only be found in one place or, that is, one Person.

Now place yourself back in time. The sun is warm on your shoulders and through the golden glow of history in the making, watch this Lord of Joy. He laughs as He holds a neighbour's newborn baby. He smiles while bouncing a three-year-old on His knee. He tousles the hair of a rowdy little boy. Picture His joy to watch a puppy at play, to hear a funny story, to taste a hot and savoury stew. Feel His joy when the disciples listened and obeyed. Think of the joy that seized Him at the sight of a glorious sunset . . . and the joy to know He created it. And finally, Jesus' joy at seeing His Father's dream fulfilled.

When you meditate on God's smile, His joy will be yours.

". . . for the joy of the Lord is your strength."   NEHEMIAH 8:10

᪥

It is not possible to always be happy. It *is* possible to always have the joy of the Lord. Some have described it as a calm-centredness that tickles at the edges. It's a solid assurance that laughs, if given the chance. It is unwavering confidence that can't help but look on the bright side. My friend Tim Hansel once said that joy is peace dancing.

Think of all the things which make up the joy of the Lord, and your smile can't help but last.

If I need a reason to smile today, Lord, it will be found in you!

Betrayal

"Simon, Simon, Satan has asked to sift you as wheat. But I have prayed for you, Simon, that your faith may not fail."   LUKE 22:31–2

They say that betrayal cuts deeper than any other kind of pain. Probably that's because only a friend can betray you. An enemy can't. And the fact that Judas, someone from the Lord's inner circle of closest friends, stabbed Him in the back, is very unsettling for those of us in His circle of friends today.

It's scary to think that we have the potential to betray our Lord. We will sing "What a Friend We Have in Jesus" in one breath, and then act like He's anything but a friend. We end up behaving like a real Judas when we dishonour the Lord's name and discredit His reputation. It should concern us all that Judas, one who knew the Lord so intimately, could fail Him so completely.

This is why we can appreciate the intercessory prayers of Jesus. He knows all about those times when we are tempted to betray Him with an act of stubborn disobedience. Jesus knows very well that our faith can fail. That's why He prayed for Simon Peter . . . that's why He prays for you.

Enemies of the Lord may mock Him, agnostics may scorn Him and atheists may laugh at Him. But only you, His friend, can betray your Lord. In short, don't you dare. One backstabbing is enough. Lean on your Lord's intercessions for you and that will give you all the resource you need to love and obey.

Great Intercessor, I praise you that you are living to intercede on behalf of your children that they might remain strengthened by your grace and obedient to your will. Thank you for including me in your prayers . . . for praying that my faith today may not fail. You are all the resource I need to make that happen!

Security and Significance

"God did this so that men would seek Him and perhaps reach out for Him and find Him, though He is not far from each one of us. 'For in Him we live and move and have our being.' " ACTS 17:27-8

A woman recently asked me, "Joni, you seem so confident. Have you always been that way?" Inwardly I smiled. If she only knew the knots I feel in my stomach before I speak to a crowd or the times I'm scared stiff to sit in front of a blank canvas with a paintbrush.

They call it insecurity and, for me, it started in my early scramble to keep up with three older, more athletic sisters. As a four-year-old, I would cling to the saddlehorn as my sixteen-hand-high horse galloped behind the steeds of my sisters. I didn't dare tell them how scared I was!

My life journey has been to put aside those insecurities. My wheelchair has helped. At first, it made me feel more insecure, but over the years God has used the chair to force me to sit still, quit competing, and be quiet before Him. That was all I needed! People are only as secure as the source of their security; if we are secure in Christ, then we have every reason to be confident.

❧

Christian psychologists say that good mental health springs from two things: security and significance. Security in *who we are* and significance in *what we do*. Since Christ is the source of peace, joy, strength and rest, and in Him we live and move and have our very being, we can be secure and feel significant when we place our trust in Jesus.

Lord, there are so many times when I feel afraid and insecure. Today I recognize that in you I live, move, and have my being — my life is secure and significant because I am your child and your servant.

What Does God Ask of You?

And now, O Israel, what does the Lord your God ask of you but to fear the Lord your God, to walk in all His ways, to love Him, to serve the Lord your God with all your heart and with all your soul.　　　　　DEUTERONOMY 10:12

Not long ago I was forced to lie in bed flat on my back for a month in order to heal a couple of stubborn pressure sores. That meant cancelling a few important appointments and missing some critical deadlines. It meant days of the same old routine: A bed bath. Dressing the wounds. Leg exercises. Breakfast. Waiting. Lunch. Napping. Dinner. Being read to. Prayers and then sleep.

At times it was hard to hold depression at bay and I was tempted to think, "Now come on, God, none of my Christian friends seem to be faced with these faith-challenging tests. Aren't you asking a bit much?"

Just what does God ask of us? Deuteronomy 10:12 sums it up neatly. All God asks for is . . . everything. if we feel like a martyr faced with heart-wrenching trials, perhaps we're concentrating too much on what God asks of us, and not enough on what God has given us.

Is "everything" too much? Think about what God has given you. How much did He hold back? Anything? Of course not. In fact, He gave more than everything. He who did not spare His own Son, but gave Him up for us all, will He not also, along with Him, graciously give us *all* things?

❧

If we're fainthearted, remember that God has promised us power to help us do all that He asks of us. Even if it *is* everything.

Lord, you gave your life! You ask me to do the same. Bless you for giving me the power to love and serve you with all my heart and soul. Take my life and let it be consecrated, Lord, to Thee.

Love Has Got to Grow

Love is patient, love is kind. It does not envy, it does not boast, it is not proud . . . love does not delight in evil but rejoices with the truth. It always protects, always trusts, always hopes, always perseveres. I CORINTHIANS 13:4, 6–7

Love must grow. It can't stand still and it certainly cannot go backwards. Love must flourish or else it withers and dies. In fact, growth in a relationship is very much like growth in a tree or flower. If a flower doesn't bloom, if a tree doesn't sprout leaves, it signals a problem.

Our love for the Lord Jesus is also a living thing. We are intimately united with Him in His body. Remember, love between you and your Lord, like anything that lives, must grow. Just think, I Corinthians 13 is how God feels about you!

We can always come up with good excuses as to why our relationships do not progress and increase in love. But instead of blaming others, ask yourself a couple of direct questions about love. Do I protect my loved one's reputation? Are my expectations unrealistic? Do I pray committedly? Does my love cover a multitude of the other's sins? Do I keep Christ at the centre of our relationship?

Lord, help me to be patient and kind toward others. Help me not to envy those who seem to be enjoying tremendous progress and increase in their marriages. Help me not to boast when I'm right, or be proud when others are wrong. Help me not to be rude to my husband . . . wife . . . or friend. I don't want my love to be self-seeking or easily angered. And, Lord, convict me if I start keeping a record of wrongs, for I desire that my love will always rejoice with the truth. Help me to have faith, hope and love ever increasing, ever growing.

Would You Like to Be Handicapped?

Someone once asked me, "If you had the power, would you go back and choose your life in a wheelchair?" In one sense, I knew what he meant. After all, God has taught me much through my wheelchair. But would I want to do it over again? I don't think so.

I can't think of anyone who desires to be paralysed. Who would be foolish enough to choose not to have use of his legs and hands? Can you imagine someone wanting to be blind, choosing darkness over the brilliance of a clear blue sky? Who would want to deliberately shut his eyes against the sight of a glorious rainbow?

I find it hard to believe that anyone would want to be deaf in order to close out the sounds of birds chattering and friends laughing. What silly person would desire dead silence over the beauty of a waltz or the soothing voice of a loved one?

Yet there are people who choose to be handicapped. If you challenged them, they wouldn't have it any other way. They deliberately determine to be disabled. Theirs are very serious disabilities, not physical ones, but spiritual handicaps. Jesus even talked about such people:

" 'You will be ever hearing but never understanding; you will be ever seeing but never perceiving. For this people's heart has become calloused; they hardly hear with their ears, and they have closed their eyes. Otherwise they might see with their eyes, hear with their ears, understand with their hearts and turn, and I would heal them.' " MATTHEW 13:14–15

O God, it's foolish to think someone would choose a physical handicap. I certainly wouldn't. But forgive me when I foolishly close myself off from you and your Word. Help me to open my eyes and ears. To look for you and listen to you today. I choose not to be paralysed by indifference or doubt.

Fearlessness

Pray also for me, that whenever I open my mouth, words may be given me so that I will fearlessly make known the mystery of the gospel, for which I am an ambassador in chains. Pray that I may declare it fearlessly, as I should.

EPHESIANS 6:19–20

The apostle Paul may be considered one of the most bold and courageous ambassadors of the Gospel, but even he got butterflies in his stomach. In one paragraph, he twice asks for prayer for courage in sharing the truth of the Gospel. How odd to think that even the great apostle felt fear.

We can identify with Paul's struggle. When it comes to declaring the Gospel, whether pointing an unbeliever to Christ, or exposing sin in the life of a fellow believer, many would rather drop broad hints and hope the Holy Spirit would do the rest. Often we are an emotional mixed bag, fearful of saying the right thing in the wrong place or the wrong thing in the right place.

Sometimes we are fearful of not only declaring the Gospel, but demonstrating it. Compassion may have suited our Lord, but perhaps we would rather drop coins in a Salvation Army bucket and remain at an arm's-length distance from people with real hurts.

Fear is natural for humans. Fearlessness is a supernatural grace God gives when we, like Paul, pray and ask for courage.

◆§◆

We may fumble with what to say, when and how to say it; we may struggle with what to do, when and how to do it. That's why prayer is the best preface to either declaring or demonstrating the Gospel. The Lord is our resource for courage.

Lord, I need your courage today. Help me to look for opportunities to make known your Gospel. And when I open my mouth, please give me words so that I can fearlessly declare and demonstrate your Gospel of love.

Saying Yes to Jesus

"Choose for yourselves this day whom you will serve . . ."   JOSHUA 24:15

Do you remember when you said "yes" to Jesus? How long ago was it? A few months, maybe years? I said "yes" to the Lord in November of 1964 when I was a teenager. But I also said "yes" to Him just the other day.

After a row with Ken, I escaped to the shopping mall with a friend to get my mind off the quarrel. While meandering past a sales rack of blouses, I could no longer contain my self-pity. I began sobbing right next to a couple of mannequins. I couldn't hide my face in a tissue and my wheelchair was too big for me to escape behind several clothes racks. All I could do was sit there, cry, and stare at the mannequins with the plastic smiles.

Whiel wiping my eyes with the back of my hand splint, I knew what I had to do. In between sobs, I said out loud what I've said so many times before, "Yes, Jesus, I choose you. I don't choose self-pity or resentment. I say 'yes' to you!"

Even though my face was still wet, my heart filled with peace. Nothing about my husband had changed. Shoppers on the other side of the store still picked through the racks . . . teenagers still ambled by, giggling and eating popcorn . . . but *everything* was different because of my peaceful heart. Because I said "yes" to Jesus.

For the grace of God that brings salvation has appeared to all men. It teaches us to say "no" to ungodliness and worldly passions, and to live self-controlled, upright and godly lives in this present age . . .   TITUS 2:11–12

◈

Dear Lord, I choose you right now. I will be faced with many challenges today and so in the power of your Spirit, I say "yes" to following you each moment.

Crocuses

It was good for me to be afflicted so that I might learn your decrees.

PSALM 119:71

The crocuses in my back yard are fragrant and beautiful, even for the dry, warm climate of southern California. I don't know how to account for such a profusion of flowers except to say we had a couple of weeks of hard frost back in January. I'm only an amateur gardener, but I'm convinced the freezing cold forced a lot of beauty out of my crocuses.

A theologian who also knew something about gardening once said, "The nipping frost of trial and affliction are ofttimes needed, if God's trees are to grow. They need the cold to revive and bud." What is true for crocuses is true for people.

It's interesting to note that David, who wrote our Psalm for today, was not a hard-headed sort who needed to be pushed into line. He was not the type who required a little affliction in his life to get him to appreciate God. Rather, the psalmist was a man after God's own heart. But David's afflictions were not intended to slap him into shape, they were God's way of helping to create something beautiful in his life.

Do you feel the nipping frost of loneliness? Are you experiencing the biting cold of persecution? For you, it could be the icy sting of rejection or the numbing chill of heartache. Just as flower bulbs need the nipping frost to revive and blossom, hardships have a way of helping peace and joy blossom in your life. Patience can flower out of failure and self-control or kindness can bud out of brokenness.

I'm grateful that you, heavenly Father, know exactly how much affliction to permit in my life in order that fruit of joy and peace may blossom. The biting cold hurts, but I look forward to the beauty that you will bring forth in my life.

At a Loss for Words

Above the expanse over their heads was what looked like a throne of sapphire, and high above on the throne was a figure like that of a man. I saw that from what appeared to be His waist up He looked like glowing metal, as if full of fire, and that from there down He looked like fire; a brilliant light surrounded Him.

EZEKIEL 1:26–7

How would you describe God the Father? Try groping for the right words and you'll fall short because He's not exactly like anything or anybody.

The prophets strained to come up with words to describe what they saw. A. W. Tozer puts it this way, "When the Spirit would acquaint us with something that lies beyond the field of our knowledge, He tells us that *this* thing is *like* something we already know . . ."

Even when Ezekiel hunted through his dictionary for adequate nouns and adjectives to describe God, he had to fall back on language that was old and familiar. Thus he talks about something that looks like a throne or someone who looks like fire. In fact, read the first chapter of Ezekiel and you'll discover that the nearer the prophet approached God, the less sure his words!

≈

When you read a book like Ezekiel, Daniel, or even the book of Revelation, please don't be put off by the strange and mysterious descriptions of God or heaven or terrifying accounts of the last days. These descriptions are man's best effort to explain the unexplainable. Instead of avoiding those books, rejoice that your God is high and lifted up, and will never be reduced to terms that we can manage.

Great and Sovereign Father, I acknowledge that your glory and majesty cannot be reduced to mere words. Yet I feel I must offer up words about how great and grand you are. Teach me to know what I cannot know and let my faith take over when words fail me.

Word of the Father

Philip said, "Lord, show us the Father and that will be enough for us." Jesus answered: "Don't you know me, Philip, even after I have been among you such a long time? Anyone who has seen me has seen the Father . . ."

JOHN 14:8–9

God has placed within our hearts a yearning, a longing for Himself, a desire to know Him and understand what He is like. After all, despite the stain of the Fall, we are stamped in His image, we are created as a kind of reflection of God. And every soul feels the void and the emptiness until it connects with its Maker. Yet God is incomprehensible. How then can our longing for Him be satisfied? How can we know Him?

Thankfully, our longings are satisfied in Jesus, for He has said, *"Anyone who has seen me has seen the Father."* We can know God's love when we look at the love of His Son. We can understand something of mercy and compassion when we look at the way Jesus demonstrated the same.

The Father, through the Son, does not permit us to know Him by scrutiny and rationale. Tozer says, "That God can be known by the soul in tender personal experience while remaining infinitely aloof from the curious eyes of reason constitutes a paradox best described as 'Darkness to the intellect but sunshine to the heart.' "

FABER

The Son is the radiance of God's glory and the exact representation of His being, sustaining all things by His powerful word.

HEBREWS 1:3

Jesus, to Thee be all glory given! You are the Word of the Father now in flesh appearing. I sing a hymn of praise, saying, "O come, let us adore Him, O come, let us adore Him, O come, let us adore Him, Christ the Lord!"

Whose Side Are You On?

So, I say, live by the Spirit, and you will not gratify the desires of the sinful nature.
For the sinful nature desires what is contrary to the Spirit, and the Spirit what
is contrary to the sinful nature. They are in conflict with each other . . .
GALATIANS 5:16–17

Remember that old game of Tug-of-War? Line up the strongest guys on your side, wait for the signal, then dig your heels in, strain hard and pull till it hurts.

I think of Tug-of-War when I consider what the average Christian goes through every day. It's like two forces that wrench you in a fierce contest of push-and-pull – the Holy Spirit pushes you up and the flesh pulls you down. It's a constant struggle to crucify the flesh and keep walking in the Spirit. To starve the old man and feed the new. To reckon yourself dead to sin and alive to God.

And who wins? It depends on whose side you choose to be. In this contest, you are either on one side or the other and never in the middle. Every day you're either rejecting the claims of your fallen nature or disbelieving the promises of God. Who prevails in this contest depends on the attitude you adopt toward either side.

Every moment of the day, each decision you make, every choice and every thought is a chance to crucify the old and encourage the new. Remember, you can't be neutral, you can't remain in the middle. You are either walking in the Spirit or you're not.

Lord, as I begin this day, I want to choose you and your promises. And as each
hour, each moment passes, help me to keep choosing to walk in your Spirit and
thereby starve the desires of my sinful nature. I praise you for the difference you
will make in my life.

Redefine Happiness

Some people are never going to be happy.

I'm not being cynical because the very folks about whom I'm speaking would agree. They would be the first to say that they are in a dead-end marriage, that they see no end to the constant irritation of their supervisor at work, that they will never lose those ugly twenty-five pounds. Life, to them, seems to be a never-ending drudgery of the same, sad routine.

Are you this way? Does happiness, like a butterfly, almost flutter within reach but just when you think you grasp it . . . it's gone? Or perhaps you feel your marriage is okay, your weight is so-so, your job is acceptable. Yet you feel like something's missing. Perhaps, you think, it's real happiness.

Well, I'm here to say that life is hard. For some, it is downright hard. Unhappiness seems to be here to stay. But it doesn't have to be this way because the answer is not to get rid of unhappiness, but to find a new definition for it.

My friend Elisabeth Elliot has suggested that we redefine happiness as duty and honour, sacrifice and faithfulness, commitment and service. Happiness is fleeting and elusive, but joy is an overflow of the perseverance and hope which comes from demonstrating faithful sacrifice and committed service.

And we rejoice in the hope of the glory of God. Not only so, but we also rejoice in our sufferings, because we know that suffering produces perseverance; perseverance, character; and character, hope. ROMANS 5:2–3

❧

Lord of joy, will you help me redefine happiness in my life? You promise joy in the midst of our suffering, so please let me know your joy today as I persevere in faithful service and as I demonstrate true commitment in my tasks. Give me your smile, let me feel your peace dancing in my heart . . . that, for me, will be true joy.

The Lowliest Servant

"But after me will come one who is more powerful than I, whose sandals I am not fit to carry."
MATTHEW 3:11

In the days of John the Baptist, rich households employed various levels of servants for different responsibilities around the home. Yes, there was even a servant who had the lack-lustre job of untying a guest's sandals and carrying them aside.

John the Baptist couldn't think of a better way to humble himself before the Lord than to say he would carry his Saviour's sandals. To him, it was a vocation of humility.

But Jesus demonstrated a more amazing model of humility when He placed Himself lower than even a sandal-carrying slave. Jesus not only untied the sandals of His disciples and placed them to the side, but He went further and washed their dirty feet – a responsibility of the lowest servant on the household totem pole.

John the Baptist extolled the power and greatness of the Lord Jesus. But Jesus was the One who glorified His power by divesting Himself of it in order to wipe clean the filthy feet of common men. And in so doing, Jesus showed us what power there is in sacrificial love and humble service.

❧

A job description for a lowly servant can be found in Philippians 2:3–4 which says:

Do nothing out of selfish ambition or vain conceit, but in humility consider others better than yourself. Each of you should look not only to your own interests, but also to the interests of others.

How appropriate that a couple of verses later we are told that Jesus took on this job description, made Himself nothing and became a servant. Your attitude today should be the same as that of Christ Jesus.

Lord, I want to be your servant. May I serve others today as you would, always considering my brothers and sisters as better than myself. Give me your servant's heart, please.

Two Mountains

You have not come to a mountain that can be touched and that is burning with fire; to darkness, gloom and storm . . . but you have come to Mount Zion, to the heavenly Jerusalem, the city of the living God. You have come to thousands upon thousands of angels in joyful assembly, to the church of the firstborn, whose names are written in heaven. HEBREWS 12:18–23

My spirit soars when I sit at the base of the snow-capped Sierras. Even though they're grand and glacier-scarred, their beauty makes them approachable. I don't feel that way about Mount St Helen's, the volcano at the northern edge of the same range. That mountain blew its top years ago and an eerie plume of smoke still rises from the crater. There's nothing approachable about Mount St Helen's.

The twelfth chapter of Hebrews reads like a topography of mountains. Mount Sinai burns with fire and is surrounded in darkness and lightning. Even Moses was afraid of it. But then there's Mount Zion, a place of angelic joy and happy assembly. This mountain is one glorious destination.

Two mountains. Two views of life. One depicts a God of gloom and doom. The other represents a God of joy and forgiveness. How often we find ourselves living in the frightening shadows of Mount Sinai, confronted by our inability to live up to the demands of a Holy God, consumed by guilt and backsliding in despair. That kind of lifestyle paralyses you with failure after failure.

Don't pitch your tent at the foot of that fearful mountain. Brush up on your topography and walk in the direction of Zion today.

May the Lord bless you from Zion all the days of your life. PSALM 128:5

∽

Lord of Mount Zion, I give you my striving and straining. I give you my defeat and despair. May I place my trust in you and discover along the way that your dwelling place, Zion, is where I long to be.

Don't Miss the Obvious

Aware of their discussion, Jesus asked them: "Why are you talking about having no bread? Do you still not see or understand? Are your hearts hardened? Do you have eyes but fail to see, and ears but fail to hear? And don't you remember? When I broke the five loaves for the five thousand, how many basketfuls of pieces did you pick up?"   MARK 8:17–19

Sometimes we need to be hit over the head to see what's right in front of us. We're sure the keys are lost but then we discover them in plain view on the table. We're certain we're out of milk until a second look in the refrigerator reveals an unopened pint. We do it all the time: We miss the obvious.

We also miss the obvious when it comes to God. Even though His presence is with us, His promises as clear as day, we don't always see the Lord in the events of our lives. But we're not the only ones. The disciples in Mark chapter 8 worried over where they could buy bread for lunch. Silly disciples. Hours earlier the Lord had whipped up a miracle lunch and fed seven loaves of bread to four thousand people.

Still, they missed the obvious. Even though the Lord was standing right there, they did not recognize him as the Bread of Life. If Jesus had fed four thousand, could He not also feed them?

Read again Mark 8:17–19. Notice the Lord's dismay over the unbelief of the disciples. He inasmuch says, "Are you deaf? Blind? Has your memory failed you? Or is it that your hearts are hardened?!" Jesus could scarcely believe that His disciples failed to see what was right in front of their nose.

The same is true for you. Jesus, the source of help and hope, is in the midst of every circumstance in your life. Period.

Bread of Life . . . Lord of Peace . . . Father of all comfort . . . I acknowledge now that you are always with me. Please remind me should I forget.

Considering Others

The ugly old woman sat slumped in her wheelchair, her dirty terrycloth robe twisted underneath her. Her hair was mussed, her teeth missing. Most of the group visiting the nursing home made a right-hand turn down the hallway in order to avoid the woman. But my friends, Bev and Carolyn, made straight for her.

As Bev approached, she expected the crotchety-looking woman to snarl a nasty remark. Instead, the old lady smiled and said, "My, my, look at you two in those bright and lovely sweaters. And aren't you sweet to come here and visit us. Thank you!"

Bev told me later that the woman made her feel so at ease, so appreciated, so . . . beautiful. Here they had visited the nursing home to cheer up others! That nursing home resident had developed the art of Hebrews 10:24. She may have only been able to offer her smile and short greeting but, oh, the difference it made not only in the lives of others, but in the way people perceived her.

And let us consider how we may spur one another on towards love and good deeds.
HEBREWS 10: 24

Considering others is not the art of doing something extraordinary. It's the art of doing a common thing extraordinarily well. The most trivial action, the slightest smile, the briefest greeting may be considered a service not only to others, but to God. The least thing – the shutting of a door gently, the walking softly, speaking quietly – all can be a part of the art of considering others.

Lord Jesus, you refined the art of considering others when you walked the earth. Help me to model myself on you today. Help me to lighten someone's burden, or look for a way to lessen someone's cares. Help me to find someone whose little pleasures I can help promote, whose wants and wishes I can gratify. May Hebrews 10:24 be my guide.

Forgiven and Forgotten Sins

If you, O Lord, kept a record of sins, O Lord, who could stand? But with you there is forgiveness; therefore you are feared. PSALM 130:3–4

Somewhere in the back of my memory, I have a list. It's called "Forgiven Sins That I Can't Forget." The list isn't long, but it contains a handful of personal transgressions that, in my estimation, tend towards the vile and disgusting. In my lower moments, these old sins flash in front of my thinking in neon lights. I cringe, recalling those awful things I am capable of doing. Against my own conscience, I am unable to stand.

Thankfully, my conscience does not render the final judgment. Christ does. And oh, how I praise the Lord that He keeps no lists. To be sure He takes notice of every sin. But does He keep account? No. For one thing, God is love and I Corinthians 13 says that love *"keeps no record of wrongs"*. For another thing, Psalm 103:12 reminds us that *"As far as the east is from the west, so far has he removed our transgressions from us."*

When we confess our sin, we acknowledge that Christ paid the penalty for it on the cross. He wipes the slate clean. He washes away the guilt and cleans our conscience. In other words, He erases the list. When it comes to the sin of His truly repentant children, God forgives and forgets.

That's the nature of His grace.

≈

Wonderful grace of Jesus, reaching to all the lost,
By it I have been pardoned, saved to the uttermost;
Chains have been torn asunder, giving me liberty,
For the wonderful grace of Jesus reaches me.

I know you've already forgiven me for past sins, Lord, but today I'm reminded to thank you for your grace that covers it all!

Winter's End

He has made everything beautiful in its time. He has also set eternity in the hearts of men; yet they cannot fathom what God has done from beginning to end.
ECCLESIASTES 3:11

I'm getting tired of winter. But not the winter *you* are used to. In southern California, the season is one long stretch of balmy, sunny days. Oh, how I miss the cold, wet winters back in my home state of Maryland.

I've been nagging Ken to drive me up to Lone Pine, California, a little town on the edge of the high desert near the base of the snowy Sierra Mountains. The road is one long, straight line across the desert and you can see Lone Pine long before you come to it. When you arrive, it's just a couple of Victorian houses, a few stop lights, and a corner café called BoBo's Bonanza. But the highlight is the awesome view of the towering Sierras at the edge of town. An icy downdraught from the mountains takes your breath away . . . and I love it!

I'm longing for a change of seasons. And just like I'm wishing for snow, you are most likely pining for the caress of a warm, sunny day. How good of God to make us such "seasonal" people. We enjoy change, and having been imprinted with the image of the Creator, we love variety. God has set eternity in our hearts and we simply must move forward like the changing of seasons.

So hang in there until spring. I may get my drive up to Lone Pine before the snow melts off the peaks. You may see warmer, sunnier days on the horizon. There's a time for everything and God promises that your days will be beautiful . . . in His time.

❧

Lord of winter and spring, I praise you for making everything beautiful in its time. Give me patience to wait for change in my life.

Catching Up with Our Calendars

Whoever of you loves life and desires to see many good days, keep your tongue from evil and your lips from speaking lies. Turn from evil and do good; seek peace and pursue it.   PSALM 34:12–14

Scientists tell us we need February 29th to make up for the difference between the way we calculate our year and the length of time it actually takes for the earth to revolve around the sun. It seems our planet is just a tad behind our calendars.

I agree. Our days often seem to outrun the planet which spins through space at 107,200 km per hour. At 7:00 a.m. we're gulping down a cup of coffee to catch the train or shoving a bottle into the little tyke while we drive to nursery school before a committee meeting. Our weekends rush by in a frenzy of cleaning (who's got time for cleaning!) and shopping and cooking and . . .

David, the psalmist, did not have to catch trains or change diapers. And I suspect he didn't have a single committee meeting to attend. But his calendar was no less stressful. In Psalm 34 he's being chased by a rat, King Saul. (That's the first rat race ever recorded in history!) There was hardly time to think. Plus, he had a band of discontented castaways to protect in a dingy cave.

But his outlook on the day is worthy of attention. He tells us in verse 12 that if we want to have a life (not activity, but life) and enjoy our days and the length of them, there are four things we must do:

Keep your tongue from deceit
Depart from evil
Do good
Seek peace

❧

This list represents a life of simplicity, devoid of deadlines and calendars. Take today, this extra day, and cultivate the habit of placing David's list on your agenda.

Lord, my life is so hectic and I feel I've outrun your will, at times. Slow me down to do that which is good in your sight. Fill my calendar with faithful appointments.

MARCH

The Good Fight

I have fought the good fight, I have finished the race, I have kept the faith.
II TIMOTHY 4:7

My husband, Ken, is a World War II buff, especially when it comes to knowing types of aeroplanes and ships. But I couldn't care less why the Army Air Corps used B-29 rather than B-17 bombers in the Pacific theatre. I'm just not interested in war. I agree with the person who said, "There's no such thing as a bad peace or a good war."

However, I'm reminded of one war that is emphatically good. I read how the apostle Paul, near the end of his battle-scarred life, laid down his weapons of warfare and said, "I have fought the good fight."

The good fight of a Christian is the one battle to wipe out all evil, espeically in our lives. We choose our weapons, either a bullet-sized verse or bulletproof prayer. We may grieve over lost territory because of disobedience, but we can rally to reclaim lost ground. Sometimes we have to tighten a tourniquet on wounded pride or step back for reconnaissance into God's Word.

Every day you and I go into war against an ensnaring world, a corrupt flesh and a busy devil. The front lines are a risky and ruggedly demanding place to be. But the battle prize is for all of us who reckon the fight to be . . . good.

For you, the front lines of the good fight may be drawn against an extra minute or two of an indecent TV programme. Or when you battle a surge of self-pity. Your fight may be against immoral thoughts that linger in your mind, or phrases that manipulate others. Choose your weapons, for your warfare is real.

As the Captain of the Lord's Army, I thank you for the shield of faith and the sword of the Spirit. Help me to fight the good fight.

Come before God in Purity

"Say to Aaron: 'For the generations to come none of your descendants who has a defect may come near to offer the food of his God. No man who has any defect may come near: no man who is blind or lame, disfigured or deformed . . .'"
LEVITICUS 21:16–18

When I was struggling to understand God's view of my disability, it didn't help matters when I stumbled across Leviticus 21:16–18. I slammed shut my Bible. I knew it – God *did* have a problem with my handicap. It seemed my impairment offended Him in the same way my wheelchair offended waiters in restaurants!

But then I discovered the true meaning behind these verses. Leviticus 21 is a strict list of do's and don'ts for men entering the priesthood of Aaron. A priest had to be pure, with no physical defects, because he was a physical symbol of a future spiritual reality – an important type of the coming Messiah. God was looking for a physically perfect man as a priest to represent the spiritually perfect man, the Lord Jesus.

This passage speaks to you, whether you're disabled or not. As part of a "royal priesthood" (I Peter 2:9), God welcomes you into His presence, accepting you no matter what your limitations. But when you come before Him in worship, make certain you are not harbouring a blemish of pride or defect of impurity. You may not be tied to strict do's and don'ts, but if God wanted Old Testament people to be pure when they came before Him, surely He expects the same of us.

How I praise you, God, that you accept me with all of my deficiencies and limitations. However, I want to rid my life of those sins that keep me from you, confessing those hidden handicaps that are a blemish on my life. I want to be pure and whole before you.

A Farm Road in Spring

Trust in the Lord with all your heart and lean not on your own understanding. In all your ways acknowledge Him, and He will make your paths straight.
PROVERBS 3:5–6

Call it late winter storms or early spring rains. When the sky breaks open this time of year, it makes for plenty of wet and muddy earth.

On our farm in Maryland, heavy rains were great for our furrowed fields, but disaster for the dirt road leading from the county highway to our farmhouse. Our truck would spin out on the wet earth, splattering gravel everywhere. The road was normally easy to drive, a straight line between our house and the highway. With rain, the road may have been straight, but it wasn't easy!

Journeying down that farm road is much like travelling the path ahead of you. When you trust in the Lord, He promises the road will take you directly to the destination He plans. He will make your path straight and you will arrive in His perfect timing. But your path, although straight, will *not* be smooth. It's direct, but you'd better expect storms along the way.

Don't be like the Israelites who, when they forgot about God, wandered around in circles for forty years. Their path to the promised land was anything but straight. Trust in the Lord and He will take you directly to where He wants you to go. It's worth the few bumps, potholes, and uncomfortable places along the way.

Lord, I need to confess that I haven't always trusted in you with all my heart. Forgive me for leaning on my own understanding when the road gets rough. I acknowledge today that I am not promised an easy path, just a straight one, if I trust entirely in you. Lord, with every pothole, rut or barrier I may come across, help me to remember to lean on you.

Take a Longer Look

"You will seek me and find me when you seek me with all your heart. I will be found by you," declares the Lord . . .   JEREMIAH 29:13–14

I love looking at paintings. Actually, I stare at them. When you take time to actually observe, you see so much more.

The other day I wheeled into a gallery and spotted a framed print by a favourite artist who is known for "hiding" secrets in her paintings. You have to examine her work closely in order to find her little surprises. This particular print was a mountain scene of a trapper and his pack horse fording a river.

At first glance, it was just another Western picture, but the frightened look on the trapper's face clued me in that there was more to the painting than met the eye. I wheeled closer. Camouflaged behind the rocks were shapes of Indians. A few more minutes of observation revealed more Indians behind the trees. Branches of pine became outlines of bows and arrows. Boulders turned into the angry faces of warriors. The more time I spent in front of the painting, the more I discovered. And the more I discovered, the greater my delight with the painting. Finally, I had found what the artist wanted me to see!

The point? The Master Artist wants you to discover the hidden treasures of His heart. And that requires more than a passing glance.

So often we read Scripture in a one-dimensional way, never venturing beyond the surface. God wants to surprise us with His Word and so He invites us to look longer and search harder. The more time you spend with Him, the more you will discover. And the more you discover, the greater your delight in Jesus.

Today, Lord, help me not to pass quickly over this devotional thought. Open my eyes so I can truly see what you want me to see.

Love's Opposite

What would you say is the opposite of love? Would you answer, "hate"? Many would agree that hate is the antonym of love, but consider this: Lust is love's opposite.

Love can always wait to give, but lust can hardly wait to get. Love is never self-seeking, but lust always places its selfish desires first. Love is patient and kind, but lust burns with impatience. Love does not delight in evil but rejoices with the truth. On the other hand, lust twists the truth and delights in whitewashing evil to make it look acceptable.

In fact, if you're looking for a definition for lust, flip to I Corinthians 13 and replace the words "lust is not" for "love is". You will discover its character traits include insensitivity, sensuality, impurity and a continual desire to indulge.

Having lost all sensitivity, they have given themselves over to sensuality so as to indulge in every kind of impurity, with a continual lust for more.

EPHESIANS 4:19

Is there someone whose time, attention and affection you crave? Perhaps it's not a person that you grasp for, but position, or power. Desire for someone or something becomes inordinate when it becomes consuming. So ask yourself this honest question, "How much time in a day do I spend thinking about this person? or this thing? or this position?" Also, "Where or to whom do my thoughts drift when my mind is relaxed?"

If an extraordinary amount of time is spent seeking this person or thing in your thoughts, then take the advice of Colossians 3:5:

Put to death, therefore, whatever belongs to your earthly nature . . . impurity, lust, evil desires . . .

Lord, I purpose to set my mind on things above, not on earthly things. Reveal those things in my life after which I lust, and then help me to mortify them in my flesh. May my life reflect love, pure and truthful.

Footsteps

And how can they preach unless they are sent? As it is written, "How beautiful are the feet of those who bring good news!"   ROMANS 10:15

Funny how certain sounds make you feel so good, so warm inside. The crackling of a fire. The whistling of a tea kettle. Chimes tinkling in a breeze. The steady breathing of a sleeping infant.

When I think of heartwarming sounds, I recall the sound of familiar footsteps coming down the hospital hallway – visitors! Friends and family brightened up those dreary days; and I even got to the point when I could recognize their footsteps. My sister's brown loafers would go click-click on the linoleum floor. The soft padding of my mother's tennis shoes. The flip-flop of my boyfriend's thongs. Diana who was slightly overweight had a heaviness in her step.

These dear ones brought sunshine into my room. Smiles and hugs. Sometimes a plate of freshly baked cookies. Maybe their Bibles and a time of prayer together. How beautiful were the feet of those who brought good cheer and good news. As Romans 10:15 says, I'm convinced they were sent by God Himself.

❧

How beautiful are those who bring good news. Are your footsteps pleasantly familiar to someone you know? When you walk through the front door of your office in the morning, what do people think when they hear you enter? When you climb the stairs to wake your husband after a nap, what do you believe comes to his mind when he hears you? Do your footsteps carry a smile or a happy hello? Try it and feel the pleasure of having beautiful feet.

My Lord, may I see the real beauty behind sharing simple words and gifts of encouragement. Help me to understand that the smallest of graces lifts the spirit, strengthens the heart, and glorifies you.

Beyond Your Limitations

For we do not have a high priest who is unable to sympathise with our weaknesses, but we have one who has been tempted in every way, just as we are — yet was without sin. HEBREWS 4:15

I woke up this morning thinking, "Here we go again. Another day of someone giving me a bed bath, getting me dressed, and plopping me in my wheelchair." No sooner did that irritating thought escape than Hebrews 4:15 came to mind. Jesus tasted the boredom of routine. He knew the pain of limitations. In short, He sympathizes. He understands. He's been there. And Jesus was the one who brought to my mind that little verse in order to quiet my frustrations and give me a brighter perspective on the day.

Look closer. It says that Jesus can sympathize with our weaknesses *in every way*. The Lord did not share only partially in our weaknesses, but fully. There's not an emotion with which you wrestle that Christ has not first felt its sting. And He did it for a reason. Jesus took on our limitations so that you and I could break beyond them.

≈

Jesus deserved glory, but He humbled Himself. He deserved love, but He took the full blow of people's hatred. Jesus deserved comfort, but He hardly had a place to call home. This is good news for anyone who feels humiliated and rejected. It's even good news for someone who's homeless! For this is the extent to which Jesus sympathized with our weaknesses.

You are Lord over every one of my weaknesses, whether they are emotional, physical, mental or spiritual. That's why I boast in my weaknesses for I know that your power rests upon me when I present to you all my shortcomings. Thank you for giving me the grace to delight in my limitations, for through them, I am drawn closer to you.

What's in a Look?

Peter replied, "Man, I don't know what you're talking about!" Just as he was speaking, the cock crowed. The Lord turned and looked straight at Peter. Then Peter remembered the word the Lord had spoken to him: "Before the cock crows today, you will disown me three times." And he went outside and wept bitterly.

LUKE 22:60–62

The eyes can give looks that love or looks that kill. When someone you love holds your eyes with his, you're enraptured. But when that same person looks at you in deep disappointment, it cuts to the core.

Suppose right now, your eyes met the Lord's. What would you see? Compassion and tenderness, yes. But suppose if, in a thoughtless moment of self-centred sin, you slapped the Lord? In that horrible instant, what would you read in His eyes?

This once actually happened. Peter angrily denied Jesus. At that instant, Scripture says the Lord looked straight at Peter. Perhaps Jesus caught Peter's eye through a window, or as He was being led through the court. Whatever, this much is sure: their eyes met.

It's impossible to say what was in the Lord's eyes. I would like to think the look Jesus gave was not cutting or judgmental. I choose to believe that He gave a look of hurt and disappointment, a sad yet tender expression in His eyes. And perhaps, for Peter, it was the look that both loved and killed.

☙

Jesus always loves. That's why it's safe to say that the Lord was probably more concerned for Peter's pain and anguish than He was for His own plight. Like Peter who wept bitterly, that fact alone should make us grieve all the more over our sins and offences.

As you look into my eyes today, Jesus, I hope you will see my love and deep affection. May the light in my eyes be a reflection of your light in my life.

For Ever Friends

"From one man He made every nation of men, that they should inhabit the whole earth; and He determined the times set for them and the exact places where they should live." ACTS 17:26

Did you catch that? It's no mistake that you are living in this century, this decade, and this very year. It's no accident that you are residing in your town, living on the street you live, and with the neighbours you see every day. And is your circle of friends just coincidence? No way. God has determined it.

Just think. You could have easily been born in another time, another place. You could have been raised on the other side of the country – think how different your life would be growing up with a whole new set of childhood friends and neighbours.

Of all the billions of possibilities, of all the millions of people with whom you could have been best friends, God determined the exact time and place where you should live. When you consider this amazing fact, your friendships take on a new and profound significance. God has a special reason, a unique design in each friendship. He chose to surround your life with these certain and treasured dear ones for good reasons.

As Christians, these are the people with whom you will live for eternity, enjoying an even greater dimension of friendship. Because God has placed you together on earth at this time and in this place, you and your friends have a chance to get a head start on God's eternal plan.

Father, I stand in awe at your wisdom and ways. You could have placed me anywhere on this earth, but you determined that I should live here and now. Teach me what this means. Show me your special design for my friends and family. And thank you that each person you put in my life is precious in your eyes.

The Secret of Contentment

I know what it is to be in need, and I know what it is to have plenty. I have learned the secret of being content in any and every situation, whether well fed or hungry, whether living in plenty or in want. I can do everything through Him who gives me strength.   PHILIPPIANS 4:12–13

I saw a man in the supermarket yesterday using a new sporty wheelchair. When he zipped down the aisle, his chair didn't make a squeak. I looked down at my big clunky twenty-year-old model with dirt on the frame and threadbare padding. Little wonder I looked with envy at his high-tech wheels.

I'd like a trade-in on my wheelchair, but perhaps you would like a trade-in on your old car. Perhaps the grass seems greener down the street where they are building brand new homes. Sometimes when we compile our desires up against God's desires for us, I wonder how many match.

The apostle Paul says that he has learned the secret of remaining content despite either plenty or poverty. What was the secret Paul had learned? He gave it away in his next breath when he said that he was ready for anything *through the strength of the One who lived inside him.*

Contentment is found not in circumstances. Contentment is found in a Person, the Lord Jesus.

It requires a special act of grace to accommodate ourselves to every condition of life, to carry an equal temper of mind through every circumstance. Only in Christ can we face poverty contentedly, that is, without losing our comfort in God. On the other hand, only in Christ can we face plenty and not be filled with pride.

Lord, there are many things I desire, but I really don't need. Subtract my desires and keep me from adding my own wants. Help me to find satisfaction in you for only then will I find real and lasting contentment.

Double Standards

But when he asks, he must believe and not doubt, because he who doubts is like a wave of the sea, blown and tossed by the wind. That man should not think he will receive anything from the Lord; he is a double-minded man, unstable in all he does.
JAMES 1:6–7

D ouble standards. Why is it we make requirements of others which we don't keep ourselves?

Some Christians work hard to wipe out social evils like pornography, abortion and homosexuality. But at the same time their personal morality leaves a lot to be desired. Then there are others who are personally righteous, watching their P's and Q's at church and at home, but when it comes to their social ethic, it's another story: racism and prejudice abound.

We cannot have one kind of ethic for ourselves and another for society. We cannot demand a strong morality in our culture and yet carry on with a personal morality – or immorality – which dishonours God.

~

What we do in private deeply affects what happens in public. The man who is faithful to his wife while exercising bigotry toward his neighbour is no better than the adulterer who crusades for social justice. What God requires is morality with a capital "M", both personal and social. God calls for an ethic that is consistent. No matter how you look at it, nobody can have their ethical cake and eat it, too . . . without getting moral indigestion.

Father, reveal to me when I say one thing and do another. Show me the double standards in my life. I want you to be Lord of my thoughts and actions, who I am in private, and what I'm like in public.

The Person God Uses

Whatever you give unreservedly to God, He will take. Whatever God takes, He will cleanse. What He cleanses, He fills and what He fills, He will always use.

God will always take what we give Him – when we give to Him without strings attached. If you offer to Him a special friend, He will set about the business of purifying that relationship and filling it with His power and purpose. If you offer God your thought life, He will take that as well, helping you to cleanse your mind and fill it with thoughts that are noble and praiseworthy.

Do not offer the parts of your body to sin, as instruments of wickedness, but rather offer yourselves to God, as those who have been brought from death to life; and offer the parts of your body to Him as instruments of righteousness.

ROMANS 6:13

Who wouldn't want to be the vessel God reaches for when He has a job to do? Wouldn't it be wonderful to so win His favour that He delights in choosing you for special purposes? It's the desire of every Christian to be handpicked by God for a unique task He has in mind. So if you desire to be used in the Lord's service, take heart. He wants to use you.

When you offer yourself to God, as one who has been brought from death to life, He knows you mean business. He is then free to cleanse you and fill you with His power. And remember, the person He fills is the person He uses.

Lord, I want to be someone that you delight in using for your glory. When you desire to accomplish a certain task, I want you to think of me. That's why I offer myself unreservedly to you. Please take me and cleanse me. Fill me and use me. That's all I ask.

No Sea?!

Then I saw a new heaven and a new earth, for the first heaven and the first earth had passed away, and there was no longer any sea. I saw the Holy City, the new Jerusalem, coming down out of heaven from God, prepared as a bride beautifully dressed for her husband. REVELATION 21:1–2

The first time I read these verses, I whined, "Oh no, you mean in the new heaven and new earth there won't be any sea? Heaven's centrepiece will be a city? I've always preferred country landscapes, not cities. It doesn't sound very appealing!"

C. S. Lewis long ago addressed my fears when he wrote, "Our notion of heaven involves perpetual negations: no food, no drink, no sex, no time . . . Against all these, to be sure, we set one positive: the vision and enjoyment of God . . . The negative have an unfair advantage. We feel that the vision of God will come not to fulfil but to destroy our nature. We must not allow this to happen. We must believe that every negation will be only the reverse side of a fulfilling."

I agree with Lewis. My desire for a new earth to include oceans and country landscapes is so limited by my human perceptions. Heaven won't be less than my natural experience here on earth, it will be more. And it will be far better!

How? Lewis sheds more light on this. "Our natural experiences are like pencilled lines on flat paper. If our natural experiences vanish in the risen life, they will vanish only as pencil lines vanish from the real landscape; not as a candle flame that is put out but as a candle flame which becomes invisible because someone has pulled up the blind, thrown open the shutters, and let in the blaze of the risen sun."

I believe, Lord, that heaven will be more, not less of what I enjoy on earth. Make that fact come alive for me today.

Lent

The season of Lent can be summed up in one word: repentance. That's why my best companion during Lent is my old Book of Common Prayer. Just listen to the Collect for the beginning of Lent:

Almighty and everlasting God, who hatest nothing that thou hast made, and dost forgive the sins of all those who are penitent; Create and make in us new and contrite hearts, that we, worthily lamenting our sins, and acknowledging our wretchedness, may obtain of thee, the God of all mercy, perfect remission and forgiveness; through Jesus Christ our Lord. Amen.

If that prayer sounds a bit out of fashion, it may be we aren't reminded often enough that our sin is a stinking offence to God; that we were once poor and miserable sinners plucked out of a miry pit. As an old Puritan once advised, "Sit close to self-scrutiny." It's the best way to fully appreciate what Jesus accomplished for us on the cross.

"Even now," declared the Lord, "return to me with all your heart, with fasting and weeping and mourning." Rend your heart and not your garments. Return to the Lord your God, for He is gracious and compassionate, slow to anger and abounding in love, and He relents from sending calamity. JOEL 2:12–13

The season of Lent is a time of soul-searching preparation before the celebration of Resurrection Day. Only an honest view of our sin will give us a full appreciation of God's mercy. Only when we understand how lost mankind really is do we then grasp how great is our salvation.

Remember, Christ did not simply die for the general sins of the world, He died specifically for your specific sin.

Father of all mercy, help me to understand your message to me today from Joel 2:12–13. And if I'm dulled to the offence of my sin, help me to "worthily lament". Bless you for . . . forgiveness!

A Selfish Sacrifice

"So, what are you giving up for Lent?" That was a common question among kids as I grew up. And the answers were predictable for many of the girls: Chocolate, chocolate, and chocolate!!

If you've ever been a chocolate lover, you know what a sacrifice that can be. And that's where our understanding of Lent and sacrifice perhaps went astray. You see, while our minds focused on the *object* of sacrifice, our *purpose* of sacrifice got lost. So it is with any sacrifice, Lenten or lifelong. If we focus on the food, habit, energy, or time that we give up, we will have missed out on the gain.

"Gain?" you ask. "You're not supposed to gain anything during Lent or from any other act of sacrifice. What kind of sacrifice gains anything?" Only the sacrifice worth making, that's what kind. Because any sacrifice that is made for God must always focus on the gain: knowing Christ.

Paul was no stranger to sacrifice. In fact, he gave a list of his sacrifices in Philippians 3:1–7. He listed his heritage, his education, and his status and *"What is more,"* he adds, *"I consider everything a loss compared to the surpassing greatness of knowing Christ Jesus my Lord, for whose sake I have lost all things. I consider them rubbish, that I may gain Christ."*

PHILIPPIANS 3:8

Paul's entire life, from the moment of conversion, was a Lenten season.
"So, what are you *gaining* for Lent?"

◄ঽ

Lord, you know what I value. You know what I count as special in my life. Help me view everything — my achievements, people, things, and memories — as rubbish in order that I might gain you. Let your will be done in my life that I might know you better.

Me, a Pharisee? Never!

To some who were confident of their own righteousness and looked down on everybody else, Jesus told this parable: "Two men went up to the temple to pray, one a Pharisee and the other a tax collector. The Pharisee stood up and prayed about himself: 'God, I thank you that I am not like other men . . .' But the tax collector stood at a distance. He would not even look up to heaven, but beat his breast and said, 'God, have mercy on me, a sinner.' I tell you that this man, rather than the other, went home justified before God. For everyone who exalts himself will be humbled, and he who humbles himself will be exalted."

LUKE 18:9–14

Most of us would like to identify with the tax collector. But frankly, we may be more like the Pharisee – a good solid citizen who does things above the religious call of duty and would never consider himself capable of gross sinning.

Still convinced you are most like the repentant tax collector? Then try the test of the Lord's words from Luke 18. Are you confident of your own righteousness? Do you compare yourself with others to see if you're closer to the top? Do you, like the Pharisee, spend most of your prayer time petitioning God about yourself? If you answer yes to any of these questions, then it's time to swallow the Lord's prescription: Humble yourself.

❧

And there's nothing like an old Puritan prayer for true confession:

Merciful Lord, pardon all my sins of this day, week, year, all the sins of my life, sins of early, middle, and advanced years, of omission and commission, of morose, peevish and angry tempers, of lip, life and walk, of want of bold decision in the cause of Christ, of deficiency in outspoken zeal for his glory . . . Pardon all my sins, known and unknown, felt and unfelt, confessed and not confessed, remembered or forgotten. Good Lord, hear; and hearing, forgive.

I'm a Christian

How great is the love the Father has lavished on us, that we should be called children of God! And that is what we are! I JOHN 3:1

Recently Ken and I travelled to Maryland for an Eareckson family reunion and visited with scores of cousins, aunts and uncles. I was surprised and pleased that so many relatives remembered me by my childhood name. You see, I was named after my dad, Johnny Eareckson; he was always "Big Johnny" and I was "Little Joni".

Funny how it didn't bother me, even though my father has long since gone to heaven. And "Little Joni" didn't bother me when I was a child, either. I've always considered it a privilege to share in my dad's name because, in a way, it allowed me to share in his character and reputation, it made me a part of everything he was (and my father was very well known and respected in the community).

I once read in a Bible commentary that the word "Christian" means "Little Christs". What an honour to share Christ's name! We can be bold to call ourselves Christians and bear the stamp of His character and reputation. When people find out that you are a Christian, they should already have an idea of who you are and what you are like simply because you bear such a precious name.

If you were asked to describe yourself, what titles would be first on your list? That you are married or single, employed or unemployed? Would you then list your hair colour or height? Or would you immediately respond, "I am a Christian . . ."?

> *I'll tell the world that I'm a Christian,*
> *I'm not ashamed your name to bear.*
> *I'll tell the world that I'm a Christian,*
> *I'll take you with me anywhere.*
> *I'll tell the world how you have saved me,*
> *How you gave me a life brand-new.*
> *I'll tell the world that I'm a Christian,*
> *Eternal life I'll live with you.*

Muscles of Faith

Candy, a fellow quadriplegic, was my exercise partner in physical therapy. Every day the therapist positioned our wheelchairs in front of a wall of weights and pulleys for an hour of strenuous exercise. I remember sweating and straining all the while Candy merely played at lifting weights.

Years later when I returned to the hospital for a check-up, I ran into Candy. I was shocked. Her arms were thin and she looked weak and tired. As quadriplegics, we both had the same potential to gain strength, but because of no exercise, her muscles had atrophied and were useless.

There are many Christians who, like Candy, are playing around, believing that the Christian life will just "happen" to them without any real commitment or tough obedience. As a result, they have very little power in their lives and no stamina when the hard times hit.

For this very reason, we *must make every effort* to remain strong in the Lord. Growth in a Christian doesn't just "happen"; we grow only when we *exercise* faith.

For this very reason, make every effort to add to your faith goodness; and to goodness, knowledge; and to knowledge, self-control; and to self-control, perseverance; and to perseverance, godliness; and to godliness, brotherly kindness; and to brotherly kindness, love. For if you possess these qualities in increasing measure, they will keep you from being ineffective and unproductive in your knowledge of our Lord Jesus Christ.   II PETER 1:5–8

Are you growing stronger in Christ? You can tell if you are by measuring your life up against II Peter 1:5–8. Do you possess knowledge and self-control in an increasing measure? Has godliness and brotherly kindness made your life effective and productive?

Today may I be strong in you, Lord, and in your mighty power. Strengthen my heart with your grace so that I might add to my life goodness and knowledge, self-control and perseverance.

Lifting Barbells

Continue to work out your salvation with fear and trembling, for it is God who works in you to will and to act according to His good purpose.

PHILIPPIANS 2:12–13

Growing strong in Christ is like lifting very heavy barbells. Trouble is, no one likes to do it. We walk around those huge barbells and examine them, comparing them to other weights we've seen. We gather with other barbell lifters and discuss the proper technique involving the approach, the bend-and-grasp and the pull-and-jerk.

We enjoy listening to the testimonies of famous people who have lifted record-breaking weights, and we collect books and articles about barbell lifters of the past. We join groups of other lifters who are like-minded, and together we pray and memorize verses about barbell lifting.

We do everything but actually walk up to the barbells and lift them! Sometimes fear keeps us away. Will we succeed? What if we can't lift the heavy weights? Are we too weak? When we finally wrap our hands around the task and begin to exert force, eureka! At that point divine energy surges through us. God's power works in us at the moment we exercise faith for the task. We can do all things – even lift those barbells – through Him who strengthens us.

◆§

As you work out your salvation, God works in you, giving you the desire and power to accomplish His will. You only have the strength to say "no" to a bad habit when, in His energy, you say, "no". You only have the desire and the power to read His Word when, in His energy, you pick up the Bible and begin reading.

Lord, today I will face many challenges to my faith and I probably will feel like turning and running away. May I respond positively to each challenge, wrapping my hands around the task, and trusting you to give me divine strength as I obey.

Follow Jesus

Then He said to them all: "If anyone would come after me, he must deny himself and take up his cross daily and follow me." LUKE 9:23

"Yes, I will follow Jesus!" We'll gladly follow the Lord around the Sea of Galilee and be fed with the five thousand. We will drink wine made from water. We will applaud the blind man who can see and stand amazed at a dead man who rises from his grave. We will follow Jesus everywhere except . . . the cross.

Oh, we can handle the burdens, those everyday troubles we all must shoulder. Besides, there are always others to carry our burdens. We can accept the thorns, those inconveniences that can't be avoided. It's best to accept thorns and get on with living.

But a cross? No, it is not our inclination to take up a cross. For unlike burdens or thorns from which we can't escape, a cross is a choice. In fact, the cross was a choice for Jesus – He did not have to take it up, He could have refused it. But thankfully, He willingly took up His cross so that you and I might have power. Power to carry one another's burdens, gladly accept our thorns, and daily take up our cross and follow Jesus.

To take up your cross involves a daily choice. Perhaps your cross could be a difficult duty, a painful service, an unbelieving partner in marriage. The Lord is asking you to willingly take it on and head up the long path with Him to Calvary where pride and vanity, stubbornness and resentment are crucified.

First, I want to thank you Lord Jesus for willingly taking up your cross in obedience to the Father. You could have refused it, but you didn't! Thank you for the power released through your obedience, power which enables me to take up my cross today and follow you.

The Service You Perform

Occasionally, the blues weigh us down. And I'm no exception. The other day I was struggling all morning to breathe comfortably. I'd only been sitting in my wheelchair a few hours, and my back ached miserably. I couldn't concentrate. I just wanted to go back to bed and forget the day.

That happened to be the morning I received a note of encouragement from the eleven-year-old daughter of a friend. Her words? "I want you to know, Joni, that I appreciate your life. You've really helped me overcome a lot of things. Thanks for loving God and I hope you continue to serve Him with all your heart."

Just a simple letter with a few bright words. But God used that scrawled little note to bring sharply into focus the enormous value of serving others in His love. Only the other side of eternity will reveal to you and me the immense value our small sacrifices of service have accomplished. If you have any doubt, let today's verse bring your service into focus . . .

This service that you perform is not only supplying the needs of God's people but is also overflowing in many expressions of thanks to God. Because of the service by which you have proved yourselves, men will praise God for the obedience that accompanies your confession of the gospel of Christ, and for your generosity in sharing with them and with everyone else. And in their prayers for you their hearts will go out to you, because of the surpassing grace God has given you. Thanks be to God for His indescribable gift! II CORINTHIANS 9:12–15

Lord, help me to go out today and spend my life for you. Enable me to undertake some special task for you for this refreshes and enlivens my soul. Help me to exult in distresses of every kind, if they but promote service to you and to others.

Ups and Downs

But those who marry will face many troubles in this life.

I CORINTHIANS 7:28

The other night I fell into bed with a miserable cold. Mind you, I am not able to blow my nose because I can't use my hands, and I can't really cough because I have no chest muscles. I knew I was going to face a rough night. But not as rough as Ken.

I woke up at 3:00 a.m. and groaned, "Ken, please get up. Help me sit up so I can cough." The poor guy threw back the covers, stumbled out of bed and sat me up to pound on my back. He held a tissue to my nose as I coughed and sputtered.

An hour-and-a-half later, we repeated the routine. We were both dead tired and somewhere in between him squeezing my ribs and reaching for another tissue, he moaned, "Did our wedding vows include this stuff?"

I sniffed and reminded him, "Remember that part about 'for better or for worse'? Well, this is the worse part. And remember when we said we'd love each other through thick and thin?"

"I know, I know," Ken sighed. "This is the thin part."

Every couple agrees that marriage has its ups and downs. The up times are when love is as plain as day and fully visible. The down times are when love goes under cover and incognito. So commonplace are the ups and downs that one wonders why they aren't written into the wedding vows. But they are. When a husband and wife vow to love for better or for worse, it includes the full extent of the ups and downs.

Marriage will always ask you to prove love. To be married is not to be taken off the front lines of love, but to be plunged into the thick and thin of the ups and downs.

May my love, Lord, always cover a multitude of troubles.

A Sneak Preview?

I never used to understand Christians who longed to go to heaven. To me, it was a place where not only God would know all and see all, but my friends and family would, too. I cringed to think of their reaction to my hidden sins.

Upon my arrival in heaven, I imagined standing under a marquee of a theatre: NOW SHOWING, THE UNCENSORED VERSION OF JONI. I gasped at the next line: COME ONE, COME ALL. FREE POPCORN.

I imagined walking down the aisle passing friends and relatives, people I respected like my sixth grade teacher, my hockey coach, my Sunday school leader and the parents of all my old boyfriends. Then I spotted others like the handicapped boy in school I made fun of, all the janitors and motel maids I ignored, and rowdy-looking kids I remembered from Friday night parties.

Standing in front of the crowd, I heard a big voice boom from behind a projector, "We've been waiting for you. Before we begin, do you have any introductory remarks?" I imagined my knees shaking and stomach churning as a jumble of ugly and dirty scenes flashed before my mind. All I could do was shrink into my seat and weakly say, "Roll it."

I'm so relieved it's a figment of my imagination . . .

For as high as the heavens are above the earth, so great is His love for those who fear Him; as far as the east is from the west, so far has He removed our transgressions from us. PSALM 103:11–12

❧

God not only wipes clean the slate of your sins when you truly confess and repent, He goes one further: He credits the righteousness of Christ to you. In heaven, your life will be known for God's goodness.

Thank you, Lord, for not only paying the debt of my sin, but for crediting the righteousness of Christ to my life.

A Calf's Look at Life

On a particularly damp and windy day, hundreds of calves were huddled outside, shoulder to hindquarter, tucked between the fence and the barn. The rain had created a mess of mud and the calves looked dirty brown instead of the usual black and white. They looked miserable.

All except one calf. Although he, too, faced the same windy rain and was covered with the same mud, he chose a different shelter. The open field of muck! In the face of the wind he skipped and jumped like a child. He was oblivious to the downpour. That calf literally looked happy.

Life is quite often like the farm scene of the calves, isn't it? We huddle with others of like misery in hopes that one day our lives will be happy again. Like the calf, however, David, the psalmist, chose an unusual moment in his life to declare the joy of being a child of God. Huddled around him in the cave of Adulam were four hundred smelly, dirty renegades fleeing from Saul. But David had the audacity to declare:

Those who look to Him are radiant; their faces are never covered with shame.
                                                          PSALM 34:5

David made a choice for himself. "We may be in a mess and we may be discouraged. But my God knows I am here and knows our need. I will dance and sing."

~

David was able to do so despite his fears. He submitted them to God and was enabled to declare a calf-like joy. Are you gripped with a spirit of fear? Take each one by the horn and lead it to the face of God. Let your fears see the light of eternal day and you, too, will skip and laugh and dance and sing.

Lord, I desire to skip and dance like a calf despite the problems that face me each day. Grant me inner sunshine of your Holy Spirit.

Giving All You've Got

"I tell you the truth, this poor widow has put more into the treasury than all the others. They all gave out of their wealth; but she, out of her poverty, put in everything – all she had to live on." MARK 12:43–4

Ken and I have often enjoyed participating in the annual Wheel-a-thon to benefit our local university's centre for disabled people. We fill up sponsor forms and our friends agree to contribute for each lap we complete around the track. One year I used my portable power chair which goes faster than my old standard model.

When the race started, I zoomed ahead, passing everybody in sight. Speeding along, I noticed one quadriplegic struggling to push his wheelchair as his father walked beside him. He was pouring every ounce of effort he had into inching his chair forward. I whizzed past him every couple of minutes. I don't know if he even finished one lap in the allotted hour, but his dad was there every minute, encouraging him on.

Somewhere around my seventeenth lap, I slowed my chair to wheel beside this young man. At worst, my arm was aching a little from pushing against the "go" switch of my chair. But here was this quadriplegic, aching and straining every inch of the way. What determination to complete just one lap!

I won the prize for the most laps and I was delighted that the centre would benefit from all the pledges. But as I look back, the young man's one lap totally outclassed all of mine. Like the widow in the Bible who gave everything she had, my quadriplegic friend was the one who took first place in all our hearts.

Father, when I give, may it not be according to my power, but far beyond my power to bestow. Help me to give out of what I do not have so that you can miraculously multiply its abundance.

Wrong Expectations

They brought the donkey and the colt, placed their cloaks on them, and Jesus sat on them. A very large crowd spread their cloaks on the road, while others cut branches from the trees and spread them on the road. The crowds that went ahead of Him and those that followed shouted, "Hosanna to the Son of David!" "Blessed is He who comes in the name of the Lord!" "Hosanna in the highest!"

MATTHEW 21:7–9

No wonder those people waving palm branches were so excited. They had great expectations of Jesus. This was the one who would throw the Roman oppressors out of the Holy City. He would cast off the burden of taxes. He would feed and protect them, giving them back their national dignity.

But as the week wore on, the mood of the crowd changed. Why wasn't Jesus making His move? Sure He made a few appearances in the temple, but why did He remain aloof, retreating outside the city walls to a nearby village every night? Why wasn't He spending time with the "right" people, the political types who got things done?

The mood of the people soured by midweek. And the rest is history. I wonder : . . are we all that different from those people? When expectations are running high, when we think we've got God's plan neatly figured, when we've convinced ourselves that the Lord's job is to make our lives easier . . . don't you think our praises may sound a bit empty?

Do we sing our hosannas to the Most High when Palm Sunday turns into Blue Monday? Let's not turn on God with lack-lustre, half-hearted praises when He doesn't follow through on our expectations. Let's give Jesus praise for who He is, not what we think He ought to be.

Praise you for who are are and what you intend to do. My only expectation is that you will fulfil your glorious purpose in my life.

You Are God's Friend if . . .

"You are my friends if you do what I command."   JOHN 15:14

How do you like your friends? Do you like them to be faithful and loyal? Encouraging, thoughtful and kind? Of course you do. But how many of your friends would measure up to such standards?

Friends are people, and people are not always going to be faithful and kind. Just look at some of the people Jesus called His friends. Peter was always interrupting and telling Jesus what He should do. Then there was Mary Magdalene whose sordid past was well known. Mary, the sister of Martha, failed as a housekeeper. Indecisive Thomas never stood up for his opinions. Then there was Nicodemus, the man who came to Jesus at night, a chicken for not showing his face in the daytime.

These people had their problems. Nevertheless, Jesus valued them as friends. He didn't expect them to be perfect, He expected them to be themselves, faults and fine points together. And all He asked of them was their love. Love for Him and for each other.

❧

Perhaps you're the type who forgets appointments or birthdays. Maybe in a group, you talk too much or don't talk at all. Housecleaning doesn't top your priority list. You get intimidated easily and fail to stick up for your friends. Well, aren't you glad that none of these things disqualify you from your Lord's circle of friends?

Jesus says that you are His friend if you do two things: Love God and love others.

I must remember, Lord, that when I fail as your friend, you still remain a faithful friend to me, always caring and loving, always forgiving and encouraging. May I reflect your love back to you and share that same love with others.

Mary Listened

Then Mary took about a pint of pure nard, an expensive perfume; she poured it on Jesus' feet and wiped His feet with her hair. And the house was filled with the fragrance of the perfume. But one of His disciples, Judas Iscariot, who was later to betray Him, objected . . . "Leave her alone," Jesus replied. "It was meant that she should save this perfume for the day of my burial."

JOHN 12:3–7

For weeks, Jesus had been telling His disciples that He would soon be crucified and taken from them. Judging from their confusion after His death, it's obvious they did not listen. But one person did. One of His followers listened, really listened to the words of Jesus. It was Mary.

I'm sure the Lord was deeply touched by her demonstration of devotion, the pouring of perfume on His feet. What may have touched him more, however, was the knowledge that Mary was doing this as a preparation for His burial. Perhaps she realized that crucified criminals were not permitted to be anointed for burial; perhaps this act of devotion was her way of offering, in advance, what might not be permitted after His death.

How did Mary know all this? She sat at the feet of Jesus and drank in His every word. She pondered the things He said, weighing everything, considering it all. The disciples failed to genuinely listen and, as a result, missed the chance to minister to the Lord before He went to the cross.

We bring so much delight to the Lord when we sit at His feet and consider all the things He says. Others may miss the point or bypass the lesson. But for those who hang on His words, to them, God reveals His secret plan and purpose.

Lord, today I sit at your feet to listen. Oh, may I genuinely hear what wonderful things you have to say.

"Me Do"

The eye cannot say to the hand, "I don't need you!" And the head cannot say to the feet, "I don't need you!"　　　　　　　　　I CORINTHIANS 12:21

The first words I ever remember saying as a baby were, "Me do!" Or in adult language, "Mother, I'd rather do it myself."

My mom tells me that I wanted to be alone in the bathroom without her assistance. And as she tells it, I used the "me do" phrase for everything from holding a cup of milk to handling a baby spoon. Independence must have meant a lot to me then.

It's odd that I view differently now the independence I so valued as a child. Sure, when it comes to managing my disability I want to feed myself, arrange my own attendant care, and do as much for myself as I can. But I *need* assistance from other people. I can't always handle things solo.

It's called interdependence and it means I must rely on my husband and friends for help. But, oh, am I grateful! What's nice is that my family and friends are helped, too, as they discover the joys of serving and giving. Interdependence is a wonderful kind of working together, a depending on one another in a healthy, Christian sense.

It's the only way the body of Christ can function. "Me do" may be a proud statement for a baby, but you won't hear me say it these days.

There is no such thing as individualistic Christianity. Our personal life in Christ is not complete if we are out of touch with our brothers and sisters in the Lord. If you think you don't need the church, then please take a quick "me do" test.

Lord, I want to honour you as the head of the body by getting involved with my Christian friends. If I see a need today, help me meet it.

"You Did It for Me"

"Then the King will say . . . 'I was thirsty and you gave me something to drink . . .' Then the righteous will answer Him, 'Lord, when did we see you . . . thirsty and give you something to drink?' The King will reply, 'I tell you the truth, whatever you did for one of the least of these brothers of mine, you did for me.' "

MATTHEW 25:34–40

The year is AD 33. It's late on a stormy Friday afternoon, and I am standing on a rugged hill by a trash heap outside Jerusalem. I huddle with a group of women just a few yards from the cross. Large drops of rain begin to pelt the dust and I clutch at my head shawl, wiping away tears and rain.

I cannot take my eyes off Jesus. His body is ramrod stiff, covered with caked dirt and blood, back arched, near death, yet hands stretched and fingers splayed. Jesus' head bobs against the crossbar and He groans, "I thirst."

I step out of the group and cock my ear. Did Jesus say He was . . . thirsty? A soldier, half-drunk, cracks off a stock of hyssop, spears a sponge and, after soaking it in sour wine, laughs and thrusts it into His face.

I am horrified. *Wait. Don't give Him wine gone acid. This is the Lord who is asking for a drink. O, God, if only I had a jug of fresh spring water!* But history is written. I am helpless to do anything.

It is this year. It is late on a stormy afternoon. You drive by a nursing home, recalling a community notice mentioning the need for more dinner-time volunteers at the home.

Jesus said that when we meet the needs of our neighbours, we have ministered personally to Him. Suffering people are our neighbours. History *can* be rewritten – we can still give the Lord that drink.

Forsaken Feelings

About the ninth hour Jesus cried out in a loud voice, "Eloi, Eloi, lama sabachthani?" – which means, "My God, My God, why have you forsaken me?"
MATTHEW 27:46

I received a letter the other day from a man who described his painful feelings of separation from the Lord. He was a strong believer but because of a death in his family, he felt as though God had forsaken him. This man was ashamed and upset with his emotions, trying desperately to feel connected with the Lord. He said in his note, "Joni, I don't know if I'll ever be able to experience closeness to God again."

I put down his letter and recalled those dark times when I, too, felt like God was far away. It's frightening to feel that the Lord has turned His back on you. But if you've ever experienced that dark emptiness, you're not alone.

Jesus felt the same. There was a time when the Son of God Himself was unable to experience closeness with His Father. It happened on the cross. And when He felt separated, He cried out, "My God, why have you forsaken me?"

❧

It's hard to explain, but I draw comfort from the knowledge that even Jesus was unable – at least at one point in His life – to experience closeness with the Father. That fact alone convinces me that Jesus understands exactly how I feel; it convinces me that the Lord would not condemn me for feeling separated from Him. The lack of closeness won't last for ever. Jesus came through it and He'll give you all the hope you need to come through those feelings, too.

Lord Jesus, I can't begin to imagine your agony of feeling separated from the Father. I'm simply grateful that you understand my feelings today. With you, I am always close to God – thank you for assuring me that you will never leave or forsake me.

APRIL

Jesus' Pre-cross Crash Course

"But when He, the Spirit of truth, comes, He will guide you into all truth. He will not speak on His own; He will speak only what He hears, and He will tell you what is yet to come. He will bring glory to me by taking from what is mine and making it known to you." JOHN 16:13–14

Have you ever crammed for a "now or never" exam? On the Bible? Unless you're a seminary student, probably not. But suppose you were thrust into such a situation? You'd probably panic.

That's no doubt how the disciples felt the evening they enjoyed the Last Supper with the Lord Jesus. Up until the end, the evening had been warm and personal – there was even that touching moment when Jesus washed their feet. But the mood shifted when Jesus spoke those strange words to Judas, "What you are about to do, do quickly." Judas left and from that point on, the tone of the evening changed. It was as if the Lord realized He had pressing things to say and only a short time in which to say them.

He spoke about vines and branches, peace and persecution. So much packed in to those few hours! How would the disciples remember it all? Jesus knew their dismay. But the Lord also knew that everything would become clear. That's why He promised them the Holy Spirit. The Spirit would be teacher and guide.

❧

Are you any different from the disciples? Not really. Sometimes you feel God is pouring million-gallon truths into your one-ounce brain! But the Spirit will help you to understand. He will bring God's Word to your mind and memory, making all things clear.

Almighty God, today help me to remember that, in time, you will make known to me everything I need to understand. I welcome you, Spirit, as my teacher and guide.

God Finishes What He Starts

I cry out to God Most High, to God, who fulfils His purpose for me.
PSALM 57:2

You ought to see how many half-finished drawings and paintings I have in my art studio. They are piled everywhere. I get an idea, render a few quick sketches and then my attention gets diverted – perhaps a different art project was overdue or I was up against some other deadline. Occasionally, I get back to those sketches but, more than likely, they get thrown onto a pile in the corner.

Half-finished pastels. Almost-completed paintings. Not-quite-done watercolours. I have an idea I'll never place any of them back up on my art easel.

I am *so* relieved my Creator doesn't approach things like me. God always finishes what He begins. He completes every purpose. He fulfils every intention. God has a long way to go in my life, and I'm grateful that He hasn't finished with me yet.

That's why I cry out, asking God to fulfil His purpose for me. Yes, He is still working on me to become a better decision-maker. He's chiselling away at my thought life, hammering at my tendency to daydream. He's honing and shaping me, giving grace to praise Him in tough times rather than pout. That's why I pray, "I don't want to be a half-finished, not-quite-completed disciple, Lord; I want you to fulfil your best intentions for me."

Don't ever think God gets distracted from you in order to attend to some other child of His who might be more obedient or worthy of His attention. His attention never diverts from you for a single moment. His touch in your life is constant, unchanging, sure.

I cry out to you, God Most High, to fulfil your purpose for me. I believe that every intention you have for me is for my highest good. Thank you for finishing everything which you start!

Sow in Tears

Those who sow in tears will reap with songs of joy. He who goes out weeping, carrying seed to sow, will return with songs of joy, carrying sheaves with him.
PSALM 126:5–6

What a promise! Think of it. When you sow in tears, what a marvellous and abundant return you will enjoy on your investment. "But," you may be thinking, "when have *I* ever gone out weeping, carrying seed to sow?"

If you have ever reached through an invisible wall of pain to embrace God with willful thanks, you have sown in tears. If you've ever been rejected by a dear one and yet turned the other cheek in love, you have sown in tears. If you have patiently endured physical affliction or responded in love through a difficult marriage, then Psalm 126:5–6 could be your life verse.

Think of the pain young Elisabeth Elliot must have felt as she continued to serve as a missionary to the very South American Indians who murdered her husband! Truly, she sowed the seed of God's Word in tears, but oh, the songs of joy which ring from the millions who have been touched by her testimony.

꿍

When you hurt physically or emotionally, it's hard to muster a patient or godly response. Pain has a way of screaming for our undivided attention. But when you either offer a sacrifice of praise to God in the midst of your hurt, or respond in faith to a heartbreak or hardship, you *are* sowing in tears. Take heart, for one day God will reward you with sheaves of joy – all because you were faithful through tears.

Lord, thank you for the hope and help you offer me through my hurt. Help me to remain faithful even though my tears sometimes blind my way. May I remember that for every tear, there will be a song of eternal joy!

Getting to Know All of God

And I pray that you, being rooted and established in love, may have power, together with all the saints, to grasp how wide and long and high and deep is the love of Christ, and to know this love that surpasses knowledge – that you may be filled to the measure of all the fulness of God. EPHESIANS 3:17–19

When I think of God the Father's special gift to us, I think of His plan of salvation. The Father was the one who came up with the idea. That's why I often spend time worshipping Him in reverence and respect.

Other times in my prayers, I think about God the Son and His special gift to us of grace. Jesus is the one who followed through on the Father's plan of salvation. And my response? Gratitude that He's my Saviour and obedience to Him as Lord.

When I dwell on the Holy Spirit and His gift of strength and encouragement of heart, I remember that He's the one who gives us assurance and joy. That's why I take care not to grieve, quench or oppose Him.

Father, Son, and Holy Spirit. I am filled to the measure of all the fullness of God as I commune with each member of the Trinity. It's a glorious way to experience a full communion with the Lord and thereby discover how wide, long, high and deep is the love of Christ.

God desires to fill you to the brim with the fullness of His love. Although Ephesians 3:18–19 says that such love surpasses knowledge, we can still enjoy His love's fullness as we enter into a complete and well-rounded communion with the Father, Son and Holy Spirit.

Lord, thank you for wanting to fill me with the fullness of all of your love. Father, Son, and Holy Spirit . . . I worship you.

The Love of Christ

For I am convinced that neither death nor life, neither angels nor demons, neither the present nor the future, nor any powers, neither height nor depth nor anything else in all creation, will be able to separate us from the love of God that is in Christ Jesus our Lord.   ROMANS 8:38–9

The supreme reason why you can and should trust God through suffering is found at Calvary, for no better argument can be voiced apart from the cross. That He would endure the full fury of hell so you could escape it should tell you something as you face your own hellish circumstances.

The greatest love scene in the world happened when Christ hung and bled on the cross. It was God saying, "Look, see, this is how much I love you!" What's amazing is that He played out this love scene while we snubbed Him in cool, calloused indifference. Who would want to escape that kind of love, or ignore or deny it? And what Christian could ever dare doubt it? Christ died for you. What love!

Sometimes after I've snapped at a friend or chipped in my two cents' worth of gossip, I catch myself thinking, "Oh, God, these are the things that nailed Jesus to the cross . . . I am so sorry." Human logic tells me He should turn away from me. But nothing, absolutely nothing can separate me from His constant outpouring of love, grace, mercy and forgiveness.

❧

Often we twist God's arm for the "reasons why" before we decide to trust Him with our circumstances. We want the blueprint spread before us. But the bruised and battered apostle Paul who probably had every reason to wonder "why" never said, "I *know* why all these things are happening." Rather, he said, "I *know* in whom I have believed." The love of Christ was enough.

Love so amazing, so divine, demands my soul, my life, my all.

The Dead Shall Rise

For the Lord Himself will come down from heaven, with a loud command, with the voice of the archangel and with the trumpet call of God, and the dead in Christ will rise first.   I THESSALONIANS 4:16

What an odd Sunday afternoon I had. My mother-in-law recently purchased a family grave plot at a cemetery called Forest Lawn. However, she would not sign the papers until Ken and I looked at the lot and gave our approval. "Do I have to?" I whined at Ken. I could think of better things to do with our Sunday afternoon.

Being the submissive wife, I trekked to Forest Lawn with Ken, looked at my gravesite located in a section called "Murmuring Pines", and listened to the realtor (that's what she was actually called) remind me that what with my head "here", and my feet "there", I would have a grand view of the valley and distant mountains. That's important, I told her. I also told her I did not have plans to stay there very long. Smile.

While the realtor and my mother-in-law conferred over the papers, I looked around at the hundreds of tombstones. It suddenly struck me that I was sitting on the exact spot where my body will rise, should I die before Christ comes. Sitting on that grassy hillside did more to ignite the reality of the resurrection than hearing sermons or reading essays on the subject.

The resurrection is not something to be spiritualized away. One day actual spirits will return to actual graves and reunite to rise. Dead men, one day, shall live, hallelujah!

Lord, you are the resurrection and the life and I praise you that eternal life is your glorious gift to those who believe. One day the dead shall rise – me included!

The Call to Obey

"If you love me, you will obey what I command."　　JOHN 14:15

The husband walked through the front door at 5:50 p.m. and noticed that dinner was not on the table. After throwing his coat in the closet, he muttered to his wife who was in the kitchen, "If you love me, you will have dinner ready at six o'clock when I come home." Pressured by his intimidating tone of voice, she quickly rushed the casserole and half-cooked vegetables to the table. She glanced at her watch, relieved to be serving dinner on time.

"If you love me you will obey," *can* sound like a threat. When our motivation to obey becomes an oppressive pressure to do the right thing, to do what's expected of us as Christians, then it breeds serious problems. Obedience which is only seen as rule-keeping ruins the love relationship between us and the Lord. Why? Even though the rules may be biblically based, we will end up obeying them rather than God. Concern with the letter of the law will cause us to lose the spirit of love.

The Lord's words in John 14:15 are not a threat. His words are to be read as a promise: "If you love me, that is if you make me the centre of your thoughts and do your most ordinary duties with an eye to my glory, then you can't help but obey me for it will be your heart's desire."

When we view the Lord's call to obey as a promise, we won't so much follow His rules as we will follow His voice.

"Now that you know these things, you will be blessed if you do them."
　　JOHN 13:17

❧

Lord, may I rush to obey you not so much because it's the right thing to do, but because I long to please you with all my heart.

Faith that Blesses

So those who have faith are blessed along with Abraham, the man of faith.
GALATIANS 3:9

Over the last few months my back yard bird feeder hasn't been much to look at. No visitors except a few hardy sparrows. In fact, the other day I spent many long moments by the window, feeling a little blue, hoping to see a few birds.

Suddenly out of nowhere, the bird feeder was a-buzz with new and different friends. Finches flew out of nowhere, a mockingbird showed up, a couple of red-breasted robins hopped by to join the party, and two doves perched on a nearby fence to wait their turn for the birdseed.

I sat there wide-eyed and with the biggest smile. Without thinking, I exclaimed, "Thank you, Lord, for the birds!" It struck me that the entire back yard party was organized by the Lord Himself. Just when I needed a lift, He brought by an array of brightly coloured, happy birds. Doves and robins don't drop in by chance – if the Lord notices when a sparrow falls, then surely He directs their flight paths.

It's simply a matter of faith – faith to observe God's hand in absolutely everything that happens. Faith to believe that the flashing wings of a bluejay fluttering across the yard is a gift orchestrated personally by the Lord.

What a way to live! Those who are able to see God's sovereign hand in great or small things are full of joy. Look around you today and have faith to see His gifts. You will be blessed.

Lord, today I want to see your hand in everything that happens. Give me faith to believe that every gift is from you. Help me to recognize the wonderful ways you minister to me today. Give me eyes of faith and I shall be blessed.

A Good Soldier

Endure hardship . . . like a good soldier of Christ Jesus.

II TIMOTHY 2:3

If the Bible were filmed as an action-adventure movie, the script would read like this: The King's most trusted officer turns renegade and gathers a powerful army around him to lead a rebellion. Through treachery and deceit, the rebel leader usurps the authority of the King and sets up his own rival government, enslaving the citizens of the kingdom. In order to free the captives, the King sends His own Son into the heart of enemy territory with a battle plan more shocking than anyone could imagine.

Sound exciting? You bet. And because you, as a Christian, are written into the script, you almost feel real bullets zinging past your head. The ceaseless warfare is being waged not only for your heart and mind, but the lives of millions of others. The stakes are high. The consequences are eternal.

The story, thanks to the Author, has a great ending: The Son has won the victory. Your adversary may try to intimidate you because you live behind enemy lines while here on earth, but the whole universe knows the truth. One day the Son will be crowned the rightful King of Kings and the entire kingdom will come back under His domain.

God has given you a battle plan to invade the devil's territory and retake earth under the banner of your Lord and Captain. You can't fail. God's battle plan is perfect.

That's why you must endure hardship as a *good* soldier of Christ Jesus. Good soldiers neither question their commanding officer nor desert the conflict. You've been groomed for active duty, so be strong in the Lord and in His mighty power. The end of the war is in sight!

Lord, strengthen me to take hold of the sword of the Spirit and the shield of faith so that when the day of evil comes, I can stand my ground.

Consider it Pure Joy

Consider it pure joy, my brothers, whenever you face trials of many kinds, because you know that the testing of your faith develops perseverance.

JAMES 1:2–3

A trial is not just an assault to be withstood, it is an opportunity to be seized. And this little verse in James is intended to inspire, showing us that trials are opportunities to prove our love and enhance our faith. With this perspective, life becomes inspiring – not in spite of the trials, but because of them.

The soldier who is called to the front line is stimulated at the chance to prove his skills. The officer who is given a position of higher responsibility is roused by the rugged demands of his task. You and I are soldiers in the same way. If you are tempted to slack off from praying and instead you remain faithful, your faith develops perseverance. If you are tempted to feel sorry for yourself, you instead start thinking of the needs of others, your character becomes refined. The result? An improved you with greater faith, and a closer fellowship with the Saviour.

And *this* is where the joy comes in!

≈

It's going to happen to you scores of times today. God may test you. The devil may tempt you. And you decide the outcome. Because you can choose to either backslide or advance. You can either fudge the truth or stand firm on the facts. When it happens, consider each test and temptation an opportunity to be seized, a chance to prove your faith. Your goal? A closer friendship with God.

Lord, my lifetime on earth will be the only chance I will have to prove my faith, to show you how much I love you. When I go to heaven, the chance will be gone. Help me to consider it pure joy to face each trial as a glorious opportunity to be seized.

Compassion

Praise be to the God and Father of our Lord Jesus Christ, the Father of compassion and the God of all comfort.   II CORINTHIANS 1:3

What word best describes the way you feel when you watch a dear friend in agony? What is the word you wrap around your feelings when you see pictures on television of starving refugees in Africa or earthquake victims in Armenia? It probably is the word "compassion".

We use that word frequently yet hardly give its true meaning much thought. I looked up "compassion" in the dictionary and discovered that the first part of the word means "with", and the second part means "that which relates to the agony and suffering of Christ on the cross". Amazing what you find in some dictionaries!

When you feel compassion you experience what Christ feels. And when you say you have compassion for someone, you are standing with that person, agonizing with him, and suffering as though you were in his shoes. Just as Christ placed himself on the cross on our behalf, we are demonstrating compassion when we take on the cross that someone else is bearing.

God doesn't want you to merely feel deeply about a person in heartbreaking circumstances. Aren't you glad that Jesus did more than just "feel badly" about your sin? He went much further than pitying our sad situation. He put himself in our place and His love has given new meaning to the word "compassion".

. . . let us not love with words or tongue but with actions and in truth.

I JOHN 3:18

❧

Father of compassion, please use me today to reach out to someone in need. Help me not to just feel hurt and pain for their situation, but use me to help lighten their load. Jesus carried my cross so please grant me your compassion so I may carry the cross of another who needs your hope and encouragement.

Me Crucify God? Never!

The death He died, He died to sin once for all; but the life He lives, He lives to God. ROMANS 6:10

When I was first paralysed in the hospital, I kicked a girlfriend out of my room and screamed, "Don't come back!" I'd like to think my rage was drug-induced or related to the pain of rejuvenating nerves. That's what I'd like to think. But no, I really said those awful words. And a lot more.

When the pain began to ease, I realized I was mostly angry at God. But how could I strike out at someone who was invisible? How could I punch someone in the nose who wasn't there? Since I could not get at God directly, I settled for the next best thing: I got at Him through people. Whether the friend who preached a little too heavily by my bedside, or the clumsy nurse who banged a bedpan against the guardrail. I spat venom at God whenever I railed at them.

I discovered that the all-powerful God had an odd place of vulnerability. His people, His body. We may not be able to crucify God (really?!) but we *can* crucify a part of His body with our cutting words.

So before you strike out at a fellow believer, remember that anger against another is ultimately anger against God. Please, may it never be! You and I don't have to strike out at the Lord, because we already have. Our sin impaled Him to the cross and we would never do that to Him again. You don't need to hammer the nails into His body any more.

One crucifixion is enough.

Lord Jesus, I praise you for having died to sin once for all. One crucifixion was enough. That means your power frees me from sin and I am at liberty to love every member in your body, every sister and brother in Christ. Rather than hurting you by hurting others, help me to love you by serving others.

Will God Give Up on You?

"Can a mother forget the baby at her breast and have no compassion on the child she has borne? Though she may forget, I will not forget you! See, I have engraved you on the palms of my hands." · ISAIAH 49:15–16

I grieve to think how I treated my friends when I was in the hospital. They would sit by my bedside while I lay there in stubborn silence. They would bring magazines and I would shrug my shoulders, saying I wasn't interested. My friends would offer to wheel me outside, but I would reply, "No, I'd rather sit here in front of the television."

I'm sure I provoked a lot of exasperation in some of my friends. A few stopped coming around, and who could blame them?

We sometimes feel that way about God. Deep down we know we probably provoke Him with our sloppy prayers. We feel He must be peeved with our ho-hum approach to Bible study. We're certain He's irritated with our sins and annoyed with the constant ups and downs of our spiritual walk. God, we sadly assume, must be exasperated to the point of giving up on us.

If we are truly a part of God's family, we can be sure He will love us through the tough times. Children can be exasperating – even children of God – but the Lord will never forget us. He will never give up on us. Nothing, not death nor life, nor angels nor principalities, nor sloppy praying or half-hearted Bible study will be able to separate us from God's constant and abiding love.

In light of this, how should we then live? It should humble us to think that God will not, even cannot, walk away.

Lord, if anyone should be annoyed or provoked, it should be me with my half-hearted approach to prayer and your Word. Forgive me when I grieve you, my friend.

God Rushes to Your Aid

In my distress I called to the Lord; I cried to my God for help. From His temple He heard my voice; my cry came before Him, into His ears. The earth trembled and quaked, and the foundations of the mountains shook . . . He parted the heavens and came down . . . He mounted the cherubim and flew; He soared on the wings of the wind. PSALM 18:6–10

When you read this Psalm, you are struck by the fact that God moves heaven and earth to come to your aid when you cry to Him for help. At your heartfelt plea, your Lord thunders from heaven and scatters your enemies. Verses 16–19 then add:

He reached down from on high and took hold of me; He drew me out of deep waters. He rescued me from my powerful enemy . . . He brought me out into a spacious place; He rescued me because He delighted in me.

Don't ever think that when you pray for God's support, He remains uncaring or unfeeling about your plea. God is not off somewhere on a mountaintop at an arm's-length distance from your cry. When you pray for help, He does not lean over the wall of His ivory tower to tell you to beg louder.

God is attentive to your needs as a caring father is to his dearest son. When you send out a distress call to the Lord, He parts the heavens to come to your rescue. And if you need to be reminded, read Psalm 18 in its entirety.

No one who lets out a genuine cry of distress is thinking about manipulating God. Impossible! A heartfelt plea for help carries with it no desire to control the way the Lord deals with you. Rather, such a prayer implies that you've cast yourself on the Lord's mercy with no hint of impure motive. When you pray like that, God immediately recognizes the sincerity of your heart and rushes to your aid.

Oh Lord, how great is your compassion and love toward us!

Be a Witness

God gave my friend Jennifer a burden for waitresses. Once every two weeks, Jennifer and her Christian friends regularly meet for lunch. But before they choose a restaurant, they pray. Once it's decided where to lunch, they sit down and strike up a friendly chat with the waitress. They learn her name and ask for her suggestions from the menu.

Jennifer and her friends visit the same restaurant at least five times, asking the maitre d' that they be given the same waitress. After so many luncheons, the women become friends with the waitress and invite her to church. Jennifer and her friends have been witnessing this way for years and after visiting scores of restaurants − and as many waitresses − they have seen fifteen women come to Christ.

"But you will receive power when the Holy Spirit comes on you; and you will be my witnesses in Jerusalem, and in all Judea and Samaria, and to the ends of the earth."   ACTS 1:8

∾

Jennifer is only doing what's required of her from Acts 1:8 so we shouldn't think she's amazing. But what *is* amazing is her creativity. She and her friends not only have fun together over lunch, but they make an outreach of it. Waitresses are, in fact, their main reason for getting together.

No matter where we go or who we meet, we can have an effective outreach for Christ in our community. No, Jennifer will never organize a group called "Eating Out for Jesus" or plan a budget or print up brochures. But she will keep on doing what comes naturally: Being a witness for the Lord.

Lord Jesus, I want to be a witness for you today. I want to tell others of your love. Show me new ways to share your Gospel with others and use me to make a difference in my community.

Unlovely Traits

Hear, O Lord, and answer me, for I am poor and needy.   PSALM 86:1

My spiritual battleground is not over a pack of cigarettes or a bottle of port. It's not in a dance hall or a movie theatre. My spiritual battleground is not a back yard fence over which I gossip to my neighbour, nor is it a fast car I race past the speed limit. My paralysis prevents me from reaching for common temptations. That's why my spiritual battleground is on the field of my thoughts.

I possess a very unlovely trait: I will waste precious time in idle daydreams. I hate it because wasteful fantasies distract me from the real concerns of life, causing me to feel restless and dissatisfied with the way things are.

I draw comfort, though, knowing that my unlovely traits furnish me with my best discipline. The very fact that I am ashamed of myself drives me to God. I lie in the dust of my self-despair at His feet and find safety and acceptance. My lazy thoughts make me contrite and repentant, and I am humbled that I have to come so often to God for cleansing.

If we are to have power with the Lord, to be dear to Him, if our prayers are to prevail, and if we are to be most useful to Him, we must jerk right-side up those wrong and unlovely traits in our lives.

❧

Amy Carmichael has said, "No word can declare with what longings Divine Love waits until the heart, all weary and sick of itself, turns to its Lord and says, 'Take full possession.' "

Lord, I am poor and needy for I am so often overwhelmed by the unlovely traits in my life. May these things drive me to you, whether it's pride, half-heartedness, peevish temper, or impurity in thought, word or deed. Good Lord, hear my prayer, and in hearing, please forgive.

The Beauty of Grace

But to each one of us grace has been given as Christ apportioned it.
EPHESIANS 4:7

Grace is what beauty looks like when it moves. God's grace is what He looks like when He moves, acting out His will through us.

Those on whom God's grace rests are truly . . . gracious. They are truly beautiful. The cerebral-palsied young man who smiles despite a dreary existence in a nursing home. The elderly woman who always seems to think of others rather than her aches and pains. The mother of two toddlers who is happy to babysit the neighbour's little boy. The pastor and his wife who take in a homeless couple for a week while they look for lodgings. These people shine with a hint of glory. They shine because of God's grace.

Grace is God's energy, all bright, beautiful and full of power. And grace is most beautiful when God is moving through us to touch the lives of others who hurt.

> Grace binds you with far stronger cords
> than the cords of duty or obligation can bind you.
> Grace is free, but when once you take it,
> you are bound for ever to the Giver and bound to
> catch the spirit of the Giver. Like produces like.
> Grace makes you gracious, the Giver makes you give.
> E. STANLEY JONES

Do you desire to be gracious? Christ apportions grace. First, a small measure in accordance with your faith, which may be small. But then, like morning sun dawning, your faith grows and grace fills you with its full and excellent brightness.

God of grace, I long to be beautiful in you, I long to be gracious to others. May your beauty shine through me today as I move in your will.

Your Big and Small World

"If you do away with the yoke of oppression, with the pointing finger and malicious talk, and if you spend yourselves on behalf of the hungry and satisfy the needs of the oppressed, then your light will rise in the darkness, and your night will become like the noonday." ISAIAH 58:9–10

It's a big world out there that needs changing. It's a small world near you that needs changing, too.

You have to get the children off to school today and help evangelize the Muslim world. You have to type a letter to the gas company and feed starving hordes in East Africa. You have to buy a new car and stop abortion. The faucet in the sink needs a new washer and the Capitol in Washington needs new congressmen.

You have to get your driver's licence renewed and the Church around the world renewed. You have to go to your son's football match and go preach the Gospel to the poor in Indonesia. An insurance claim needs to be filed; a claim on lost souls must also be made. You have to go to the cleaners, drive by the bank, stop at the gas station and stop pornography.

Whether it's the big world out there or the small world just beyond your back yard fence, God has work for you to do. It's demanding, it has to be done, and many are depending on you. Whether it's your toddler, or the child you sponsor through a relief agency, your husband or the itinerant evangelist in Uganda who travels from village to village sharing Christ.

Our world is desperate for help and hope. But take heart: Your prayers and practical action make a dent. A big dent in your small world, and a small dent in the big one.

~~

Use me, Lord, in big ways and small. Help me make a difference in your world.

Praying with Scripture

"Is not my word like fire," declares the Lord, "and like a hammer that breaks a rock in pieces?"
JEREMIAH 23:29

Would you like to have greater faith in prayer? Of course you would. And it stands to reason that if faith comes by hearing, and hearing by the Word of God, then the Word alone is the source of faith especially in prayer.

The Word of God is the Christian's true prayer book. The secret to receiving answers to prayer lies in how we use God's Word during prayer time – that's why it's always a good idea to pray next to an open Bible. Do you want to tune your words of praise so they will rise like a beautiful worship song to the Lord? Then fill your praises with glorious words from the Song of Solomon or verses of adoration from the book of Psalms.

Also, bring God's Word directly into your intercessions. Pray for your loved one on the basis of Colossians chapter 1 or Psalm 20. Why is this so important? The psalmist said, "I will never forget your precepts, *for by them you have renewed my life.*" You bring God's power to bear in the lives of the people for whom you intercede when you bring God's Word into your intercessions.

Read portions of Scripture to prime your pump before you pray. Let the Spirit lead you to certain verses to use in your praise and intercessions. Then, develop personal prayers which are enriched by those same verses. God loves to hear His Word when you pray. It's like speaking His language!

Today, Lord, I praise you that your Word is like a hammer which breaks through my unbelief. Your Word is like a fire that sets my heart aflame. Teach me to use all of your Word as a powerful tool in my prayers.

Sit where Others Sit

After a recent speaking engagement, a mentally handicapped man who was wearing thick glasses and baggy trousers trotted up and gave me a big hug. We talked as he stood next to me, twisting his necktie with his finger. I asked about his church and his friends. Out of nowhere, he smiled, stuck out his chest and said, "Ezekiel 3:15 . . . that's what I like about my friends!"

It seemed a strange thing to say and so I asked him what was so special about the verse. He proudly quoted it:

I came to the exiles who lived at Tel Abib near the Kebar River. And there, where they were living, I sat among them for seven days – overwhelmed.

EZEKIEL 3:15

I gave him a strange look. He explained, "Don't you get it? 'I sat among them.' And, wow, for seven days!"

A light dawned. "O-o-o-o-h," I said. "I get it. You are pleased that your friends get down on your level, right? And they try to see things from your perspective, the way you see them." He nodded enthusiastically and went on to remind me that the captives in Ezekiel's time must have really appreciated friends who would sit down with them seven whole days. That was a long time to be feeling someone else's hurts.

As that mentally handicapped man walked away, I gained a new appreciation of how much the smallest of verses can help. Who would have dreamed that Ezekiel 3:15 would have anything to do with instructing friends on the fine art of compassion and empathy?

⇜

Lord, help me to get down on the level of those who hurt today. Help me to show a little empathy for those in need. You did it . . . Ezekiel did it . . . the friends of that handicapped man do it every day. And I can do it, too.

Lover of My Soul

Show me your face, let me hear your voice; for your voice is sweet, and your face is lovely . . . My lover is mine and I am his.

SONG OF SONGS 2:14, 16

When I approach the Lord in prayer, I relate to Him in different ways. Occasionally I talk with Him as my elder brother, which He is. If I'm under spiritual attack, I'll go to Him in prayer as the captain of my soul. He is my friend when I want to pour out my heart. I even have single friends who look up to the Lord as their husband, like it says in Isaiah 54.

Lately I've enjoyed relating to my Saviour as the lover of my soul. And when I want to tell the Lord how much I adore Him, I use the language of love in the Song of Songs. This beautiful book in the Bible is more than just a love poem; it's a picture of the love relationship between the Bridegroom and His bride.

From your heart, tell Jesus that He is the fairest of ten thousand. Praise Him for being altogether lovely. Let Him know His love is better than wine. He is the Rose of Sharon, the Lily of the Valley. And to top it off, sing to Him this beautiful hymn inspired from the Song of Songs:

> Loved with ever-lasting love, led by grace that love to know;
> Gracious Spirit from above, Thou hast taught me it is so!
> O, this full and perfect peace! O, this transport all divine!
> In a love which cannot cease, I am His, and He is mine.

Close me in your everlasting arms, Lord, and let my soul find rest and peace as I lean on your breast. May doubts and cares fly away. No one, nothing, shall ever part us. I am yours . . . praise you for being mine.

The Fellowship

I want to know Christ and the power of His resurrection and the fellowship of sharing in His sufferings.   PHILIPPIANS 3:10

The words "fellowship" and "suffering" don't look like they fit together. One communicates comfort. The other, pain. Yet God links these words, insisting that our deepest fellowship with Him can be found in the midst of suffering.

The word "fellowship" does not mean a club. It's not an inner circle of elite believers or a higher level of super-spiritual saints who have arrived. Fellowship – in the Greek, *koinonia* – means a mystical participation together with Christ. It's a marvellous mystery that Jesus feels the sting in His chest when you hurt.

When I hurt, when I'm in physical pain from my paralysis, when my heart twists in anguish, I cast myself on Jesus. In the fellowship of suffering, I know He takes my pain personally, He's close enough to catch me. As I rest in His arms, I'm amazed how often I find myself singing this hymn:

> All my life was full of sin when Jesus found me,
> All my heart was full of misery and woe;
> Jesus placed His strong and loving arms around me,
> And He led me in the way I ought to go.
> No one ever cared for me like Jesus,
> There's no other friend so kind as He;
> No one else could take the sin and darkness from me –
> O how much He cared for me!

❧

Thank you, Jesus, for the warm intimate union we enjoy together in the fellowship of your sufferings. Bless you for catching me when I fall, for holding me when I hurt.

A Call to Arms

St George was a dragon slayer. He fought all night with a bad-breathed, scaly-skinned, triple-toed dragon for the sake of the king. With one pierce of the sword, he subdued the dragon, led it before all the people with the princess's girdle, and became a legend.

Eleven hundred years later, Henry V called upon the heroic knight to inspire the troops on St George's day in the famous battle of Agincourt. At the end of that day, thousands of the enemy lay slain at Henry's feet. He was as heroic in battle as his legendary predecessor, St George.

Both St George and Henry V faced insurmountable odds. The dragon had never been beaten and the French far outnumbered Henry's forces. How could they have been victorious? Because a call to arms was made. St George to his King and Henry V to his country. The call was motive. The call was master. There was no escaping victory.

The apostle Peter also presents us with a call to arms in 1 Peter 4:1–2:

Therefore, since Christ has suffered in His body, arm yourselves also with the same attitude, because he who has suffered in His body is done with sin. As a result, he does not live the rest of his earthly life for evil human desires, but rather for the will of God.

◈

What is the call? Prepare to suffer as Christ suffered. He suffered at the hands of unrighteous accusers and he suffered temptation. Why follow the call? To do the will of God.

The battle's end? Nothing less than victory in this life and in the life to come. Expect nothing less.

Lord, arm me for battle. I am weak but you are strong. In that strength I march. Let me see your colours, your name. And then let me see the dragon of sin slain and the enemies of Christ routed, all for the sake of your kingdom.

Building on the Foundation

But each one should be careful how he builds. For no-one can lay any foundation other than the one already laid, which is Jesus Christ. If any man builds on this foundation using gold, silver, costly stones, wood, hay or straw . . . It will be revealed with fire, and the fire will test the quality of each man's work. If what he has built survives, he will receive his reward. If it is burned up, he will suffer loss . . .   I CORINTHIANS 3:10–15

Many years ago our old barn down by the creek was burned up in a roaring blaze that could be seen for miles. My father, who at that time was seventy-two years old, shuffled through the smouldering ash and rubble several days later. He overturned charred objects with a kick of his toe, searching for anything he might be able to salvage from the antique tools he had saved over the years. His only compensation was the barn's foundation. Although everything else had been consumed, the foundation had withstood the fiery test.

I think of that story every time I read I Corinthians 3:10–15. Oh, how grateful I am that the foundation of my life is the Lord Jesus. No fiery trial, not even the fire of Judgment Day, will destroy the solid rock on which I build my life.

What I build on that foundation, however, *will* be put to the test. Wood, hay and straw will be consumed in a flash, that is, the work I've done for selfish gain or out of pride. But when I build on the foundation work that is inspired by the Spirit, work done with a pure motive and with an eye to God's glory, I have confidence it will last for all eternity.

Father, help me to lay up my treasures in heaven, the kind that are made of gold, silver and costly stones.

Oleanders

For God cannot be tempted by evil, nor does He tempt anyone; but each one is tempted when, by his own evil desire, he is dragged away and enticed. Then, after desire has conceived, it gives birth to sin; and sin, when it is full-grown, gives birth to death. JAMES 1:13–15

Often the most beautiful things are the most deadly. Take, for instance, the oleander bush. These popular flowering bushes thrive in the California climate and you often see them blooming bright and colourful along the freeways.

Yes, oleanders are lovely. But they're deadly. The leaves and blossoms are highly toxic and many cat and dog lovers have uprooted oleander bushes from their back yards to protect their pets. I once entertained the idea of picking oleander flowers to use in a table centrepiece but, on second thoughts, I decided I didn't relish the idea of placing something poisonous on the dinner table.

Like oleanders, some ideas are beautiful, but, oh, so deadly. Bad thoughts never enter your mind telling you, "I want to ruin your peace of mind, I want to rob you of joy." No, harmful thoughts always disguise themselves as pleasant things to ponder. But beware. That seemingly innocent thought about a married man at church or a young co-worker at the office . . . is poisonous.

◆

So-called beautiful thoughts are like a bouquet of oleanders on your dining room table. They may be attractive to look at, but they don't belong on your table. Never learn to accept the idea of putting something poisonous in front of you.

Lord of all, I admit that often thoughts enter my head which seem acceptable, even beautiful. But in my heart of hearts, I realize they are deadly and damaging. Give me strength to say "no" to enticing ideas which not only harm me, but dishonour you. Help me to place the Lord Jesus in the front of my thinking today.

Playing Favourites

The other day as I drove into a restaurant parking lot, I was cut off by two beach boys on a brand new motorcycle. They whooped it up as they parked their bike, shaking the sand from their dirty sweatpants and sleeveless tee-shirts. They plopped on the kerb to lace up their oversized tennis shoes and rummaged through their bum bags for cigarettes. I noticed one boy wore two earrings . . . in each ear. I also noticed they parked on the white line of my handicap parking space.

Strutting into the restaurant, they proceeded to act tough while standing in line. I wheeled up behind them, deliberating whether or not I should say something. I was just ready to open my mouth when the kid with earrings turned, looked at me, and asked in a small voice, "Ma'am, excuse me, is your name Joni?"

Bother! This snotty kid was about to be nice to me and I suddenly felt like Jonah who got irritated because those rotten Ninevites started to turn soft. The boy continued, "I saw your movie when I was little and I used to go to Calvary Church up the road."

I sat there convicted as we talked about his wayward faith. I need to remember that the people God places in my path are usually those with whom He wants me to share His love – even lost and lonely beach boys in California.

My brothers, as believers in our glorious Lord Jesus Christ, don't show favouritism . . . If you show special attention to the man wearing fine clothes and say, "Here's a good seat for you," but say to the poor man, "You stand there" or "Sit on the floor by my feet," have you not discriminated among yourselves and become judges with evil thoughts?   JAMES 2:1–4

✍

Lord of even the lost, help me not to play favourites when I witness. May I share your love with all . . . and with no favouritism.

An Encouraging Word

Want a really encouraging word from God today? Try this:

A voice says, "Cry out." And I said, "What shall I cry? All men are like grass, and all their glory is like the flowers of the field. The grass withers and the flowers fall, because the breath of the Lord blows on them. Surely the people are grass."

ISAIAH 40:6–7

Isn't that wonderful?! You're nothing but grass!

Before you stop reading this seemingly discouraging word, consider this. What if the opposite of God's observation were true? What if we *did* last for ever in the flesh and never faded? I see two things:

First, you'd have to live with yourself for ever. Many people are afraid to die but I'm not so sure the opposite alternative of living for ever in our bodies is such a hot idea either. I can't imagine living in this sinful body with all of its frailties and leanings toward sin. When my deadline comes due, I'm not filing for an extension.

Second, not only would you live for ever, those who persecute you and who hate God would live for ever. Living for ever would not help us escape their influence and actions. Oh what a disaster that would be.

Now do you feel a little more encouraged about your latest medical problem, your latest fight with the boss, your latest battle with sin? Cheer up. It won't last. It's grass.

Lord, I praise you that you've allowed our sinful flesh to die. I acknowledge that you are the only one in the universe worthy to live for ever. I'm just thankful that you've given me the privilege of living for ever – after this body dies!

Fake Fruit . . . Real Fruit

But the fruit of the Spirit is love, joy, peace, patience, kindness, goodness, faithfulness, gentleness and self-control.　　　GALATIANS 5:22–3

It's impossible to manufacture the fruit of the Spirit such as love and peace, gentleness and kindness. You can paint a veneer of joy and put up a facade of self-control, but invariably you will be found out. You can only deceive yourself and others for so long with false love and plastic peace.

Fake fruit comes from self-effort. It's like growing grapes the wrong way around. First you find a cluster of white concords and fasten them to the branches of a vine. From there, you tie roots to the trunk and dig a hole, setting the entire thing into the ground. There you have it, manufactured fruit (and incidentally, fruit that will rot real fast). What you have done is put first the fruit, second the branches, third the root and fourth, the soil.

God grows genuine fruit in the opposite order. First He plants the seed of His Word in the soil of our heart. The Spirit quickens us and causes the Word to take root in our soul. Next as we grow in the Lord, the vine and branches mature until sweet and satisfying fruit clusters in abundance.

Genuine fruit comes from abiding in the Vine.

"No branch can bear fruit by itself; it must remain in the vine. Neither can you bear fruit unless you remain in me."　　　JOHN 15:4

❧

Lord, I confess that I try to bear fruit by myself, forcing self-control, reminding myself to be good and kind, often painting a smile of joy and putting on a pretence of peace. Forgive me for all this manufactured fruit in my life. May I abide in your Word and keep step with your Spirit today . . . and I look forward to the sweet and satisfying fruit you will produce in my life.

She Is Not Gone

Precious in the sight of the Lord is the death of His saints.

PSALM 116:15

Edna Hamlin was a saintly old woman. She sat humped over in a wheelchair the many years she lived in a nursing home. Edna and I were penpals those years . Her letters not only overflowed with smiles and joyful observations about nurses and friends, but her envelopes would spill over with gospel tracts, crocheted bookmarkers, and copies of poems and hymns. Edna was my inspiration.

I just received word that Edna passed away. All at once I feel sadness and joy and perhaps this poem explains why.

I am standing upon the seashore. A ship at my side spreads
her white sails to the morning breeze and starts for the blue ocean.
She is an object of beauty and strength, and I stand and watch her
until at length she hangs like a speck of white cloud just where
the sea and sky come down to mingle with each other.
Then some one at my side says: "There! She's gone."

Gone where? Gone from my sight – that is all.
She is just as large in mast and hull and spar as she was
when she left my side, and just as able to bear her load
of living freight to the place of destination. Her diminished
size is in me, not in her; and just at the moment when
some one at my side says, "There! She's gone," there are
other eyes watching her coming, and other voices ready to
take up the glad shout, "There she comes!"
And that is Dying!

AUTHOR UNKNOWN

☙

The length of our days are in your hands, O Lord. What counts, though, is not how long we live, but how we spend those days. Give us wisdom to know how short, how fleeting life really is.

A Paradox

Who can speak and have it happen if the Lord has not decreed it? Is it not from the mouth of the Most High that both calamities and good things come?
LAMENTATIONS 3:37–8

The Bible makes two things absolutely clear: On one hand, God sovereignly controls even Satan's actions. On the other hand, God is in no way a sinner nor the author of sin. When the Bible presents us with two truths like these which seem opposed to one another, how are we to handle them? How can we fit them together?

The easy way out is to deny one side or the other and, in this case, that usually means denying God's sovereignty. But that's wrong. What we should do is first be sure that both truths are really what the Bible is teaching. Once we're sure of that, we must humbly bow our reason to the authority of God's Word, accepting both truths in faith.

The best illustration of this is the doctrine of the Trinity. Scripture plainly says there is but one God, yet it also plainly teaches that the Father, Son, and Holy Spirit are each God although they are three distinct persons. No true Christian denies any of these truths even though human reason can't fit them together. Why should we treat the biblical truths about God's sinless nature and His sovereign control over Satan any differently?

"I form the light and create darkness, I bring prosperity and create diaster; I, the Lord, do all these things."
ISAIAH 45:7

How unsearchable are your judgments and your ways past finding out, O Lord. You rule over everything, you are Master over all. Nothing happens without your decreeing it, nothing occurs without your permission. And because you hold all things in your loving hand, I can trust you. I bow to you, worshipping you in awesome wonder.

MAY

Satan Schemes, God Redeems

"You intended to harm me, but God intended it for good to accomplish what is now being done, the saving of many lives."   GENESIS 50:20

God always exploits Satan's evil intentions and uses them in His own service – just one more example of God's ability to work *"out everything in conformity with the purpose of His will"* (Ephesians 1:11).
Satan intends the rain which ruins a church picnic to cause Christians to grumble against their Lord; but God uses the rain to develop their patience. Satan plans to hinder the work of an effective missionary by arranging for him to trip in the jungle and break a leg; God allows the accident so that the missionary's godly response to pain and discomfort will bring glory to Himself. Satan brews a hurricane to kill thousands in a small village in Bangladesh; God uses the storm to display His awesome power, to show people the awful consequences that sin has brought to the world, to drive some to search for Him, to harden others in their sin, and to remind us that He is free to do as He pleases – we will never figure Him out.
Satan schemed that a seventeen-year-old girl named Joni would break her neck, hoping to ruin her life; God sent the broken neck in answer to her prayer for a closer walk with Him.

As a friend once said, "God sends things, but Satan often brings them." Praise God that when Satan causes calamity, we can answer him with the words Joseph answered his brothers when they sold him into slavery, *"You meant evil against me, but God meant it for good."*

Sovereign Lord, you are all wise and powerful, able to abort devilish schemes always to serve your own ends and purposes. Suffering is a mystery, but not so much a mystery that I cannot trust you.

Hide It in Your Heart

I have hidden your word in my heart that I might not sin against you.
PSALM 119:11

As a little girl dressed in Sunday best and wearing white gloves, I would turn the beautiful gold-trimmed pages of my prayer book. But I would wince when I read, "Wherefore, fulfil now, O Lord, the desires and petitions of Thy servants as may be most expedient for them." I was a dutiful child and so I obediently memorized the liturgy even though the words sounded old and dusty.

Back then I did not realize the value of memorizing prayers for catechism class. I didn't appreciate the treasure of Psalms and verses I was storing up. And even if I had been told that "God's Word never returns void", I would have said, "Huh?"

Years later, the riches I had hidden away in my heart as a child paid a marvellous dividend. During dark lonely nights in the hospital, chunks and pieces of long-ago Psalms and prayers floated to the surface of my memory. I could almost see page fourteen of the Book of Common Prayer and the words, though old and dusty, glowed with the soft patina of timeless truth as I repeated them in a whisper:

"Almighty God, Father of all mercies, we, thine unworthy servants, do give thee most humble and hearty thanks for all thy goodness and lovingkindness to us, and to all men. We bless thee for our creation, preservation, and all the blessings of this life; but above all, for thine inestimable love in the redemption of the world by our Lord Jesus Christ; for the means of grace, and for the hope of glory. And, we beseech thee, give us that due sense of all thy mercies, that our hearts may be unfeignedly thankful."

Because your Word will never return void, help me to hide it in my heart, Lord Jesus.

His Eye Is on the Sparrow

"Are not two sparrows sold for a penny? Yet not one of them will fall to the ground apart from the will of your Father."　　　　MATTHEW 10:29

English sparrows. They're worth barely a penny, Jesus said so himself. Yet of the world's 9,000 bird species, Jesus singled out the least noticed and most insignificant of birds in order to make a point.

If God takes time to keep tabs on every sparrow – who they are, where they're going, whether or not their needs are being met – then surely He keeps special tabs on you. Intimately. Personally. And with every detail in mind.

The Bible may point to eagles to underscore courage and power, and it may talk above doves as symbols of peace and contentment. But God's Word reserves sparrows to teach a lesson about trust. Just as God tenderly cares for a tiny bird, even making note of when they are harmed, or when they fall to the ground, He gently reminds you that He is worthy of your greatest trust, your deepest confidence.

How do you approach God today? Maybe you feel like a ragamuffin house sparrow clinging to an empty bird feeder with no one to care. Stop and remember the facts behind Matthew 10:29. God does care. He notices.

Try trusting the Lord today as would a sparrow. No questions asked. No fears that He won't come through. Relax in the protection and provision of your great God.

Father, it's astounding to think that with so many things to care for, you have a heart for people the world considers small and insignificant. Forgive me for not believing that you not only notice, but intimately care for every detail of my life. Help me today to believe you for the small things. May I see every detail as an opportunity to trust you.

Gripping Hearts for Heaven

*Listen, I tell you a mystery: We will not all sleep, but we will all be changed
— in a flash, in the twinkling of an eye, at the last trumpet. For the trumpet
will sound, the dead will be raised imperishable, and we will be changed.*

I CORINTHIANS 15:51–2

Anyone who knows me, knows I love to talk about heaven. Because physical suffering and pain are a part of my daily routine, I look forward to the time when my body will be exchanged for a new, glorified version.

Suffering is God's way of helping us get our minds on the hereafter. And I don't mean the "hereafter" as a psychological crutch or an escape from reality. God wishes to instil within each of us a strong desire for the imperishable, for the incorruptible, for the inheritance that never perishes, spoils or fades.

To grip our hearts with heaven, God sometimes takes drastic measures. You and I don't appreciate His method at first, but later we're grateful for it. Scottish theologian, Samuel Rutherford, described God's dealings this way:

"If God had told me some time ago that He was about to make me as happy as I could be in this world, and then had told me that He should begin by crippling me in arm or limb and removing me from all my usual sources of enjoyment, I should have thought it a very strange mode of accomplishing His purpose. And yet, how is His wisdom manifest even in this! For if you should see a man shut up in a closed room, idolizing a set of lamps and rejoicing in their light, and you wished to make him truly happy, you would begin by blowing out all his lamps, and then throw open the shutters to let in the light of heaven."

Lord of Heaven, help me to see suffering as your path to heaven.

More of Heaven

When the perishable has been clothed with the imperishable, and the mortal with immortality, then the saying that is written will come true: "Death has been swallowed up in victory."   I CORINTHIANS 15:54

Suffering gets us ready for the resurrection.

Broken necks, broken homes, and broken hearts crush our hopes that earthly things can satisfy. Only the promise of immortality can truly move our eyes from this world. The glorious day when "death will be swallowed up in victory" becomes our passion as we realize, once and for all, that earth can never meet our deepest longings.

Suffering also prepares us to meet God when we get to heaven. Suppose you never knew pain. No stained reputation. No bruised feelings. No sore back, twisted ankle, or decayed molars. How could you appreciate the scarred hands with which Christ will greet you? What if no-one had ever offended you deeply? How could you adequately express your gratitude when you approach the Man of Sorrows who was acquainted with grief?

∿

When you meet Jesus face-to-face, your hardships will have given you a taste of what He went through to purchase the promise of your resurrection. And your loyalty to Him in your sufferings will give you something concrete to offer in return. For what other proof could you bring of your love if this life left you totally unscarred?

I praise you, Sovereign Lord, that you use suffering to prepare me for heaven. Help me to live today with the promise of the resurrection before me, giving me a reason to thank you in the midst of my pain. Keep me from complaining and grumbling. For on the day that I stand before Jesus, I want to offer Him proof of my love and faithfulness.

Rewards

"His master replied, 'Well done, good and faithful servant! You have been faithful with a few things; I will put you in charge of many things. Come and share your master's happiness!'"   MATTHEW 25:21

Pain and problems do one more thing. If in our trials we are faithful, suffering wins us rich rewards in heaven. It's not so much that the resurrection will be wonderful in spite of all our pain – it will be wonderful *because* of it.

My wheelchair, unpleasant as it may be, is what God uses to dislocate my stubborn resentment and dislodge my self-centred attitudes. My wheelchair even forces me to be more faithful to Him. The more faithful I am to Him, the more rewards are stored up in heaven. Earthly sufferings don't simply aid us today: They will serve us in eternity.

Oh, to hear my Master say on that resurrection morning, "Well done, good and faithful servant! You have been faithful in trusting through the trials . . . in obeying despite the hardship . . . in believing through the doubts. Now come and share your Master's happiness!"

❧

Join me, will you? Yield to God's method of operating, His plan in your suffering. Allow your suffering to get you ready for the hereafter, permit it to prepare you to meet God, use it to build eternal rewards . . . *then* the hope of complete spiritual, emotional, mental, and physical resurrection will throb in your heart with vibrancy.

And then, maybe after a short slice of eternity, you and I will enjoy a game of tennis on the back side of the courts of heaven.

Master, I want to hear you say to me, "Well done!" I know that's only possible if I persevere through my trials by your grace. Help me to be faithful in these few things today. Help me to look forward to greater things in eternity.

Purify Yourself

We know that when He appears, we shall be like Him, for we shall see Him as He is. Everyone who has this hope in Him purifies himself . . .

I JOHN 3:2–3

It is rare to find believers who nail their sin to the cross, desiring, like the apostle John, to lean upon the breast of Christ. It is rare to find believers who abandon themselves, like the apostle Paul, to be caught up into a third heaven; believers who wish, like Mary, to sit at the feet of the Lord. These are the ones who purify themselves that they might draw closer to the Lord and feel His heartbeat. Such people have put sin behind them.

There are precious rewards for those who sit close to self-scrutiny and cut away every sin that entangles. Such a person possesses a livelier, more buoyant expectancy of seeing the Lord face-to-face. Everyone who purifies himself has this hope, and everyone who possesses this hope, purifies himself.

As Bishop Ryle once wrote, "Heaven is a holy place. Its inhabitants are holy. Its occupations are holy. To be happy in heaven, it stands to reason we must be prepared for it. Our hearts must be somewhat in tune, somewhat ready for it."

Of all the things that will surprise us when we see Christ face-to-face, this, I believe, will surprise us most. That we did not love Christ more before we died.

Is it possible to hold onto sinful habits while at the same time hold the nail-scarred hands of Christ? We cannot consciously clutch sins we know to be offensive and at the same moment express sincere gratitude to our Saviour for bearing our sins.

Lord of heaven, I desire to be like you and so I put away sins in my life which separate us. Today, please help me get my heart in tune with heaven.

Shattered Glass

"Put your trust in the light while you have it, so that you may become sons of light."   JOHN 12:36

M y art studio is a mess of half-chewed pastel pencils, old tubes of paint and piles of illustrations overflowing my file drawers. Recently while cleaning up, I discovered some broken glass on the counter by the window. I also discovered that when sunlight struck the shattered glass, brilliant, colourful rays scattered everywhere.

Shattered glass is full of a thousand different angles, each one picking up a ray of light and shooting it off in a thousand directions. That doesn't happen with plain glass, such as a jar. The glass must be broken into many pieces.

What's true of shattered glass is true of a broken life. Shattered dreams. A heart full of fissures. Hopes that are splintered. A life in pieces that appears to be ruined. But given time and prayer, such a person's life can shine more brightly than if the brokenness never happened. When the light of the Lord Jesus falls upon a shattered life, that believer's hopes can brighten.

It's the nature of things which catch the light: The colour and dazzle of light sparkle best through things that are shattered.

ᕤᕥ

Only our great God can reach down into what otherwise would be brokenness and produce something beautiful. With Him, nothing is wasted. Every broken dream and heart that hurts can be redeemed by His loving, warm touch. Your life may be shattered by sorrow, pain or sin, but God has in mind a kaleidoscope through which His light can shine more brilliantly.

Light of the world, may you shine today in dark places all over the earth. May broken people, hurt and disappointed, respond to your loving touch. And may Christians become true sons of light as you brighten their hearts and enlighten those around them. I present to you the parts of my life that are shattered. Shine, Jesus, shine!

A Learning Experience

I'm a quadriplegic, but I can drive a van (it doesn't have a steering wheel, but that's another story). Recently I cruised into the drive-through lane of a fast-food restaurant to order hamburgers and Cokes. After I gave my order over the intercom, I explained that the boy at the window would have to help me since I was disabled. No problem.

I then drove up to the delivery window, stuck out my arm and asked the boy to take the ten dollar bill which was folded in my arm splint. That was no problem either. As another server was bagging my order, I asked him to place my change in it, as well. Both boys looked at each other, a little confused, and so I smiled and slowly repeated my instructions.

Both servers got the message and they even wrapped the change in a napkin before they dropped it into the bag with the food. They handed me my order, but I had to ask, "Could you please lean out of your window a bit more and wedge the bag right here between me and the van door?" Both boys looked at each other again. "Remember? I can't use my hands?" I smiled.

"Oh yeah," they laughed and proceeded to reach over and manhandle the package securely between my wheelchair and the door. They waved as I drove off. And I smiled back knowing those two boys would now have a new appreciation for disabled people. What could have been an awkward, embarrassing situation turned out to be fun.

The wise in heart are called discerning, and pleasant words promote instruction.
PROVERBS 16:21.

Today, take a complicated situation and with time, patience, and a smile turn it into something positive . . . for you and for others.

Lord, when I ask others to do something today, help my words to be pleasant. For your sake, may my instructions be a blessing to others.

Memorizing

"For my thoughts are not your thoughts, neither are your ways my ways," declares the Lord. "As the heavens are higher than the earth, so are my ways higher than your ways and my thoughts than your thoughts." ISAIAH 55:8–9

There's hardly a Christian who doesn't wish his thought life were more pure. After all, the first and greatest commandment is to love the Lord with all our . . . mind. Memorizing God's Word is the best way to rebuild your thoughts. Committing portions of Scripture to memory is like thinking God's thoughts after Him. When we think that way, our mind can't help but be elevated.

Also, memorizing large portions of Scripture gives us insight into understanding the very thought structures of our Lord. Through memorizing, we can appreciate the way God thinks! And that, more than anything else, will heighten your thought life to a pure level.

A story is told of a family living on the edge of a desert who were amazed to see that flowers had sprouted in the salty sand behind their home. No one could figure out how this happened since they had tried for months to grow vegetables and flowers. The mystery was solved when someone realized the mother had been throwing her dishwater out the back door every day. After many months and many dishpans of water, the salt was washed out of the sand. That's why flowers were able to grow.

As we soak our minds with Scripture, old and impure thoughts will be washed away. New thoughts – God's thoughts – will find a home in our mind.

I want to think your thoughts, Lord, and fill my mind with your ideas. Help me to elevate my thinking towards your level as you lead me deeper into your Word. And show me today what thoughts of yours you would have me to memorize.

Meditating

"If you keep your feet from breaking the Sabbath and from doing as you please on my holy day, if you call the Sabbath a delight and the Lord's holy day honourable, and if you honour it by not going your own way and not doing as you please or speaking idle words, then you will find your joy in the Lord . . ."
ISAIAH 58:13–14

Memorizing Scripture, especially paragraphs of Scripture, sounds so time-consuming. Little wonder people say, "I can't . . . where will I find the time?"

The best time to invest in memorizing Scripture is the time that already belongs to the Lord. The Lord's Day is a twenty-four hour period set aside for you to spend specifically on spiritual objectives. How does God ask you to spend your time on His holy Day? He simply asks that you do not do as you please, or go your own way, pursuing your own pleasures; He asks you to find delight in honouring Him on His special Day.

When is the best time to meditate on what you've memorized? Rehearsing God's Word is a great way to close out the evening. After all, God established that our day should begin in the evening anyway . . . *"and the evening and the morning were the first day"*. This was how the Sabbath Day was observed, and for good reasons. The last important thoughts on our minds in the evening remain on our subconscious throughout the night and unconsciously set our mental attitudes for the day.

When we go to sleep meditating on Scriptures we've memorized, we follow the advice of Psalm 63:6: *On my bed I remember you; I think of you through the watches of the night.*

~

Lord of the Sabbath, I want to look at your Day as . . . yours! Forgive me when I crowd your day with my goals. Yes, I do have time to memorize and meditate, and I will remember that, this Lord's Day.

Knowing His Name

These commandments that I give you today are to be upon your hearts. Impress them on your children. Talk about them when you sit at home and when you walk along the road, when you lie down and when you get up.

DEUTERONOMY 6:6–7

"**M**y husband and I have only been, uh . . . you know, Christians a short time. But we've been reading the . . . the Bible more and learning about, uh, the Lord." As I listened on the phone, I could tell that God was taking this woman, who had gone to church all her life, to a new spiritual dimension.

She's uncomfortable using spiritual terms right now, but all that will change as she talks more about her Saviour at home and when she goes throughout her day, when she gets up in the morning and when she retires at night. Talking about Jesus . . . makes it easier to talk about Him!

In fact, I'm looking forward to the time when she will be able to confidently say the name of her Lord. For, *"Those who know your name will trust in you, for you, Lord, have never forsaken those who seek you"* (Psalm 9:10). Until then, I'm praying that she will make a new habit of talking about the Lord Jesus freely and openly during the course of her day. It's the best way to feel at home with His name.

Some Christians have an awkward time bringing up the subject of Christ during dinner table conversations or while driving in the car. We reserve discussion about spiritual things for church or Bible study, often failing to bring Him into our everyday moments. But remember, talking about Jesus . . . *does* make it easier to talk about Him!

Make me more bold, Lord Jesus, to speak openly about you. For this will not only glorify your name, but will encourage other Christians who may be more timid than me. I love the name of Jesus!

Be Personal

"So do not fear, for I am with you; do not be dismayed, for I am your God. I will strengthen you and help you; I will uphold you with my righteous right hand."   ISAIAH 41:10

God always uses such intimate language when He relates to us. He paints warm images of sheltering us under His wings, holding us in the palm of His hand, or drawing us close to His breast. He's so personal with us, why shouldn't we be with Him?

Yet when we affirm Christ as our personal Saviour, we often talk more about Christianity than Jesus. We distance ourselves from our Lord, relating to Him in detached and objective terms. Describing Jesus becomes an exercise in discussing "the Christian experience", or "the Christian walk". We are more relaxed talking over doctrines and church traditions rather than Christ as a Person.

If we're embarrassed to talk openly about our love for Him, perhaps it's because we feel we so often fail Him. Maybe we fear total surrender to Him because of what may happen if we let go and love. Ah, but *"There is no fear in love. But perfect love drives out fear, because fear has to do with punishment."*   I JOHN 4:18

The words of I John 4:19 are so intimate: *"We love because He first loved us."* If you desire to be free of fear, memorize and meditate on portions of Scripture that describe God's love and your need. Read parts of John's gospel to hear the heartbeat of Christ just hours before the cross . . . read Psalm 51 to grasp the bitterness of sin . . . then enjoy the Song of Solomon to find warm and intimate language of love.

Oh, Jesus, thank you for being so personal with me. That you should be so intimate with me pulls at my heart. I love you, Jesus.

Yardsticks

Peter turned and saw that the disciple whom Jesus loved was following . . . When Peter saw him, he asked, "Lord, what about him?" Jesus answered, "If I want him to remain alive until I return, what is that to you? You must follow me."

JOHN 21:20-22

Christians know it's wrong to compare, yet our culture has more sociological groupings and measurements than you can shake a yardstick at. We struggle to avoid coming out on the losing end as we compare our lot in life with others. And if we have faced tragedy, we often seek a refuge where our Purple Heart medals shine more brightly.

Peter had the same problem. Jesus had just revealed that Peter would be led to a martyr's death, but not a word had been spoken about John. Obviously, when Peter sized up the situation, John appeared to be getting a better deal. "Lord, what about *him*?" he blurted out.

Jesus' answer was shocking. He allowed no room for deserved indulgence, no luxury of self-pity. In effect Jesus said, "Look, if it's my will that John lives until I come again, what is that to you? What I have planned for John is not your business. Get your eyes off him and follow me." Rather harsh words for a man facing martyrdom! But the Lord knew the greater devastation of competing and comparing.

Envy rots the bones.   PROVERBS 14:30

❧

Here's the best antidote for envy I've ever read. Romans 12:2-3 is the prescription to swallow:

Do not conform any longer to the pattern of this world, but be transformed by the renewing of your mind. Then you will be able to test and approve what God's will is – His good, pleasing and perfect will.

Lord, your will for me is good and acceptable and perfect. I have no need to compare myself with others – I have your best for me!

A Mother's Request

Then the mother of Zebedee's sons came to Jesus with her sons and, kneeling down, asked a favour of Him . . . "Grant that one of these two sons of mine may sit at your right and the other at your left in your kingdom." "You don't know what you are asking," Jesus said to them. "Can you drink the cup I am going to drink?" "We can," they answered. Jesus said to them, "You will indeed drink from my cup."   MATTHEW 20:20–23

The mother of James and John asked the Lord to bestow honour on her sons, but was told instead they would drink from the same cup as the Lord's. No-one knows if she realized that Jesus was describing His cruel death. We don't know if she understood that this meant martyrdom for her sons.

This dear mother is not all that unusual. Every parent wants to see his child promoted and honoured. But God may have a different plan for that child, perhaps one not as glamorous or full of accolades. Always, a parent's desire for a child's advancement must be held in check as the mother and father pray that God's will be done in his life.

Somehow I believe the mother of James and John ended up understanding this. When you flip over to Matthew 27 you read a startling fact about this same woman.

Many women were there (at the cross) . . . they had followed Jesus from Galilee to care for his needs. Among them were Mary Magdalene . . . and the mother of Zebedee's sons.

The mother of James and John was one of the few who remained by the cross of Jesus. She saw first-hand the terrible cup that her Lord had talked about weeks earlier. She may have realized then the hardships her sons were destined to face. Oh, the tenderness and the compassion that must have filled her heart.

I praise you, Lord, for the love of a mother.

I'll Be Back

"Men of Galilee," they said, "why do you stand here looking into the sky? This same Jesus, who has been taken from you into heaven, will come back in the same way you have seen Him go into heaven." ACTS 1:11

"It's one of the rules of church nursery," my friend with three little girls told me. "When you drop off your child, always tell them you'll come back. And then by all means, come back! It's the only way they'll accept being in nursery."

What would it be like for us if the angel on Mount Olive had said, "Jesus has gone" and nothing more? What if Jesus had said, "I'm going to prepare a place for you, but you'll have to get there on your own?" I know what I would do. I would give up hope. I'd be like a child in the nursery standing alone in the middle of toys and books, staring at the door that once framed my mother. And I'd cry. Not whimpers, but bawling screams of pain and panic. There are few things more frightening to a child than being left alone without hope that Mum or Dad will return. For the child, life has ended.

But Jesus is coming back, He told me so. I need not spend my days in tears or pain. I can enjoy the fellowship of others who are also expecting His return. And I can tell others about Jesus, friends who wonder why they came into this world in the first place.

He's gone, but He's coming back. I know. Daddy told me so. And that makes all the difference.

❧

Lord, you've promised us. You promised that you'd come back for us. It's been so long, Lord. When will it be? Please remind me often of your promise because I need to enjoy fellowship with others of like mind and I need to reach others who don't know you're coming.

The Prayers of Jesus

When Jesus went off to quiet places early in the morning to pray, what did He pray about? If you could have been close enough to cup your ear, what would you have heard Him say to His Father? What was on His heart and, for that matter, the heart of His Father?

If we could find out, don't you think it would change the way we pray? The way we live? Well, we don't have to guess what Jesus discussed in prayer. We already know. The entire 17th chapter of John's gospel reads like a secret recording, a word-for-word transcript of the Lord's prayer life. And guess what was on His mind? You and I!

Jesus devoted the major portion of His great intercessory prayer to us. He prays that we might know God in the fullest sense. That we might obey and understand and accept His word. He prays for certainty and assurance. For our protection and unity. He prays for our joy. Our sanctification. Our zeal in witnessing.

I could go on, but you can read it for yourself in John 17. Isn't it poignant that as Jesus faced a torturous death, He did not think of Himself, but of us?

"My prayer is not for them alone. I pray also for those who will believe in me through their message, that all of them may be one, Father, just as you are in me and I am in you."   JOHN 17:20–21

If the Lord had others on His mind when He spoke to the Father, shouldn't we pray the same? Jot down a list of names of people you know and then open up your Bible to John 17. Pray for these loved ones, using the same wisdom (perhaps even the same words) as the Lord. And praise God that this is the way Jesus, your great Intercessor, prays for you.

As you live to intercede, Lord, let me live to intercede, as well.

Who's the Enemy?

Be self-controlled and alert. Your enemy the devil prowls around like a roaring lion looking for someone to devour. I PETER 5:8

You've had it happen. You read a book on marriage with your spouse, set goals, make promises, and six months later the situation is the same. The same unmet expectations and hurt feelings. Your marriage could move forward if only your partner would shape up.

Or maybe it's the family. If they would just be more sensitive, more careful with the way they ask for things, you wouldn't get so down. You wouldn't feel stepped on or demoralized. If they would say "thanks" once in a while, depression would be a thing of the past.

Perhaps it's your friends. If only they would make the first move to plan a luncheon date instead of you always calling. If they would show a bit more consideration, they would be *real* friends.

But wait. Remember who your problem person really is. Because Christians have, in fact, only one enemy. The enemy is not your spouse. It isn't your children nor your friends. The devil is your only enemy. And he would love to keep your spouse spiritually retarded. Your kids, a bunch of selfish ingrates. Your friends, thoughtless and insensitive. This is exactly why you need to shower extra love and abundant prayer on these very people!

❦

Remember who your support person is. Jesus Christ is your help and shield. He is the one who has called you to love your spouse, nurture your children, and lay down your life for your friends. It's the best way to defeat the enemy in your life . . . and in the lives of those you love.

Today, Lord, I ask you to enrich the lives of those whom you've placed near to me. Where there is contention, please sow your love. Where there is disappointment, give hope. Use me to touch others with your love.

World-class Praying

"With your blood you purchased men for God from every tribe and language and people and nation." REVELATION 5:9

When I'm forced to bed for an extended time, I sometimes feel like my life doesn't go beyond the four walls of my bedroom. The perfect remedy for such shortsightedness is to expand my prayers to the remotest corners of the earth. It's a wonderful way to enlarge my vision beyond my back yard fence.

I pray for mothers of spina bifida children in Mozambique. I pray for men who become paralysed from falling out of palm trees in the jungles of the Philippines. I pray for mentally handicapped children in the closed areas of North Korea or western China.

If you desire to see God's kingdom filled with people from every tribe, language and nation, pray for the lost to ask heart questions which will direct their thinking toward God. Pray that people will ask, "Whom can I trust in life?" or "What is the meaning of life?" Pray that when they look up into the blanket of stars at night, they will ask themselves, "Where will I go when I die?"

Then ask God to reveal Himself supernaturally to these who have no access to the written Word. Pray that they will be reached through a tract or a missionary, or a Christian programme on shortwave radio. You don't have to serve on a foreign mission field to be a world-class missionary . . .

You can be a missionary through prayer!

Someone has said, "Prayer freshens our hearts, keeps us in tune with God and in sympathy with the people, lifts our ministry out of the chilly air of professionalism, makes routine fruitful, and moves every wheel with the facility and power of divine enabling."

Lord, give me a heart burden to intercede for those who need your help and hope . . . whether it's across the street, or around the world.

Hearts Fully Committed

"But your hearts must be fully committed to the Lord our God, to live by His decrees and obey His commands, as at this time."   I KINGS 8:61

Distractions have a way of getting us sidetracked spiritually and off-based emotionally. Have you ever prayed for someone only to remember, right in the middle of your intercession, that you left the laundry in the washing machine yesterday? You make a quick mental note to retrieve it after your prayer time, but as you return to your intercession . . . you can't remember for whom you were interceding! The whole incident unravels your concentration and you abandon your prayer time feeling frustrated and defeated.

For the Christian who commits his heart fully to the Lord, the devil employs a special weapon: distractions.

Thomas Kelly wrote, "The life that intends to be wholly obedient, wholly submissive, wholly listening, is astonishing in its completeness. Its joys are ravishing, its peace profound, its humility the deepest, its power world-shaking, its love enveloping, its simplicity that of a trusting child. It is the life and power of Jesus of Nazareth, who knew that 'when thine eye is single, wholly devoted, the whole body is also full of light.' "

Give me an undivided heart, that I may fear your name.   PSALM 86:11

◆◎

Full-hearted commitment is no petty duty, no piecemeal performance made up of fragments of time. Whole-hearted devotion involves the best of time for prayer, study and worship.

Lord, give me an undivided heart that is wholly devoted to you. Please unite my heart to fear your name, and may I not turn to the right or to the left, but set my face like a flint. Help me to live life straight ahead. Help me to pay attention. Arm me against devilish distractions. Let me be single-hearted and fully committed to you.

Living Sacrifices

Therefore, I urge you, brothers, in view of God's mercy, to offer your bodies as living sacrifices, holy and pleasing to God – this is your spiritual act of worship.
ROMANS 12:1

What immediately comes to mind when you hear the word "sacrifice"? Articles in *National Geographic* magazines about bloody offerings on Aztec temples? The streams running red with lamb's blood outside the temple of Jerusalem? Whatever comes to mind, it's probably not a pretty picture.

But sacrifice is what God asks of us. *Living* sacrifice. Now *that* tickles my imagination. I picture myself on an altar, and as soon as God strikes the match to light the flame of some fiery ordeal, I do what any living sacrifice would do. I crawl off the altar!

This is exactly the dilemma Christians face. First, we are to *present* our bodies, that is, give them in the Lord's service as a free will offering. And because our sacrifice is a *living* one, it involves a choice. The gift of salvation does not require us to become a living sacrifice . . . we are not forced onto the altar . . . we are not coerced to stay on that altar. It is a choice we make out of love.

❧

If presenting yourself as a living sacrifice seems downright distasteful, if you find yourself trying to devise a way of serving God that seems more agreeable to your comforts, remember this: Jesus sacrificed everything for you. Please don't argue with the Lord about how heavily He stokes the fire of your trial. Just get back up on the altar. It's your spiritual worship!

I realize, Lord, that my trust and obedience are all you ask of me through my trials. Forgive me when I sneak off the altar or try to turn down the flame of my trial. As my High Priest, you know best how to tend the altar.

No Longer a Slave to Sin

"For we know that our old self was crucified with Him so that the body of sin might be done away with, that we should no longer be slaves to sin — because anyone who has died has been freed from sin"   ROMANS 6:6–7

I love the way *The Living Bible* presents Romans 6. "Should we keep on sinning when we don't have to? For sin's power over us was broken when we became Christians and we were baptized to become a part of Jesus Christ; through His death the power of your sinful nature was shattered. Your old sin-loving nature was buried with Him; *that part of you that loves to sin was crushed and fatally wounded so that your sin-loving body is no longer under sin's control,* no longer needs to be a slave to sin."

The death of our old self is positional. That means when we became a part of Christ, it was shattered. Fatally wounded. Rendered inoperative. Our old sin nature has no real power. That's why in verse 11 we are to *"count yourselves dead to sin but alive to God in Christ Jesus. Therefore do not let sin reign in your mortal body."*

What a powerful command! Why are we told to reckon ourselves dead to sin? Because our "deadness" to sin doesn't become evident in our lives until by faith we believe it. And what happens when we fail to count ourselves dead to sin? Then sin's power over us seems real and we allow it to reign in our lives.

Lord, thank you that through your death, my old sin-loving nature was mortally wounded. I no longer have to sin! I have power to say no because I place my faith in you and consider myself alive to God!

Dead to Sin . . . Alive to God

What shall we say, then? Shall we go on sinning, so that grace may increase?
By no means! We died to sin; how can we live in it any longer?

ROMANS 6:1–2

I can hear you saying, "But that's impossible. We may be Christians, but we're still human beings and sin is a fact of life." Yes, I agree that sin is a fact of life. We are free of its power, but sin's presence is still everywhere, tempting and enticing us. But does sin have to be our master? No! Never!

Romans 6:14 is your Emancipation Proclamation:

For sin shall not be your master, because you are not under law, but under grace.

Dr Martin Lloyd-Jones shares a wonderful illustration of this in one of his commentaries. He describes the kingdom of Satan and the kingdom of God as two fields. When we become Christians, Jesus rescues us out of the devil's dry, rocky pasture and places us in His green fields. But that old master, the devil, yells at us from his side of the fence. We hear him cracking his whip and telling us to get back into his field where we belong. Fear and intimidation make us listen to his lies, and before you know it, we climb back over the fence. What's amazing is we don't have to! The devil is not our master!

You have been set free from sin and have become slaves to righteousness.

ROMANS 6:18

Close your ears to the devil's lies. Understand that fear and intimidation are a part of his strategy to force you back into his territory. You died to sin and it is no longer your master. Grace is all you need to say, "No, Satan, my master is Jesus and I wouldn't dare set a foot outside His kingdom."

Free at last, free at last! In Jesus, I am free from the power of sin over my life!

Being Clothed

For the perishable must clothe itself with the imperishable, and the mortal with immortality.   I CORINTHIANS 15:53

The apostle Paul wrote wistfully about the resurrection body, and my sentiments are his. I, too, groan over my earthly tent. Age, disease or disability have a way of making us long for a trade-in.

How we will be clothed with the imperishable, I do not know. Perhaps C. H. Spurgeon explained it best: "At present we wear our bodies on the outside and our souls on the inside. But in heaven, we shall wear our bodies on the inside, and our souls on the outside."

Oh, to wear our souls on the outside! Perhaps that's what the Bible means when it says that one day we will be clothed in righteousness. We will wear our right-standing with God on the outside as though it were a beautiful garment. Our bright-shining raiment will be all glorious, reflecting on the outside the life of Christ cultivated on the inside.

While we wait to be clothed with the imperishable for eternity, we can put on the advice of Colossians 3:12 and *"clothe yourselves . . . put on compassion, kindness, humility, gentleness and patience."*

The best way to guarantee being clothed with righteousness in heaven, is to clothe ourselves with godly attributes down here on earth.

Lord of the Resurrection, I cannot begin to comprehend what it means to, one day, be clothed with the imperishable, to put on immortality as if it were a garment. But I want to prepare for that glorious day as I demonstrate compassion, kindness, humility, gentleness and patience to all those around me. Prepare me for heaven. Fit me for eternity. Fashion me into the person you want me to be so that I will be ready for my eternal clothes of righteousness.

Sharing in God's Nature

He has given us His very great and precious promises, so that through them you may participate in the divine nature and escape the corruption in the world caused by evil desires.　　　II PETER 1:4

Just as the great and precious promise of the Old Testament was the Seed of the woman, the Messiah, so the great promise of the New Testament is the Holy Spirit. Those who receive the promises of the Gospel are renewed in the spirit of their mind, after the image of God – in knowledge, righteousness and holiness. Their hearts are set for God and His service and they have a heavenly disposition in their soul.

This is what it means to participate in the divine nature. Through the Lord Jesus we have a share in God's nature, a portion of who He is.

When I was young in the faith, I thought having "a share in God's nature" meant copying the Lord's lifestyle, mimicking His mannerisms, striving to follow Him as closely as I could. God was over there, I thought, I am here, and I must close the gap between us. Little did I realize that with the Holy Spirit residing in my heart, there was no real gap. I could actually participate in the divine nature, and be intimately one with the Lord.

❧

Who can understand or fully explain the mystery behind Colossians 3:3 where it says, *"Your life is now hidden with Christ in God."* Perhaps it's just another way of saying that we have a share within and a portion of Jesus. If the Holy Spirit is within you, you can delight in being one – actually one – with Christ.

Jesus, I confess I don't fully understand what it means to be one with you, to share in your divine nature. But thank you for the Holy Spirit who reveals what my intimate union with you really means.

The Right Way to Run a Race

We who are strong ought to bear with the failings of the weak and not to please ourselves. Each of us should please his neighbour for his good, to build him up.

ROMANS 15:1–2

My husband Ken serves as a track-and-field coordinator for Special Olympics. There is always band music, colourful banners, and flags everywhere. Scattered across the infield are teams of mentally handicapped young people.

A few years ago at the games, Ken blew his whistle to signal the contestants for the 50-yard dash. A Down's syndrome girl with thick glasses and a short, stocky boy in baggy shorts were the first to line up. There was a moment of stillness, then a "bang" from the starting gun. Off they sprinted – six contestants bobbing and weaving down the track.

Suddenly the boy in baggy shorts began running towards his friends in the infield. Ken blew his whistle to direct him back to the track, but it was no use. At that point, the Down's syndrome girl, who was just a few yards from the finish line, turned round, ran towards him and gave him a big hug. Together they got back on the track and completed the race arm-in-arm, long after the rest of the contestants had crossed the finish line.

We must run the race not to please ourselves, but to please the Lord. That often means taking time to stop and put our arms around a weaker friend who needs to get back on track.

❦

Have you watched a fellow believer get spiritually confused, and yet you've kept on going? Jesus doesn't seem as preoccupied with "winning" as we do. The important thing is how we run the race. And we are called to run it bearing with the failings of those who are weak.

Lord, may I run the race to please you . . . and to help others.

Body Building

From Him the whole body, joined and held together by every supporting ligament, grows and builds itself up in love, as each part does its work.

EPHESIANS 4:16

His name was Tom. He was a ventilator-dependent quadriplegic in a big bulky wheelchair who sat next to me in occupational therapy. I can't say I was of much help to him. I was disgruntled and despondent, angry that I had to clench a pencil between my teeth in order to learn how to write.

Tom was different. Although he was more physically limited, his attitude was anything but handicapped. His bright outlook on life and cheery disposition about mouth-writing humbled me. There was no way I could keep feeling sorry for myself, especially when I saw how skilled Tom was with that pencil.

Observing Tom was just the push I needed during those early days of adjusting to my wheelchair. If he could handle it, I decided I could, too. Looking back, I thank God for the victories Tom gained. His perseverance was the best thing he could do to help me, a fellow patient. And I have scores of mouth-painted renderings to prove it.

Although Tom died shortly after we left the hospital, he gave new meaning to words like inspiration, encouragement, edification and building up the body.

One of the best things we can do for our brothers and sisters in Christ is to gain victory in our trials. We affect one another spiritually by what we are and do individually. And because there is an intimate link between us as believers, your failures affect others, while your victories inspire and encourage them. You may not *feel* one with the Christians around you, but you *are* one.

Help me to remember that my perseverance and joy will profoundly influence the lives of others who observe me today. Help me to be a "Tom".

The Irony of God

"Not by might nor by power, but by my Spirit," says the Lord Almighty.
ZECHARIAH 4:6

The dictionary defines irony as "a combination of circumstances that is the opposite of what might be expected". God specializes in irony. I was reminded of that when I was invited to speak at Billy Graham's Mission in Moscow.

It was Sunday afternoon at the Olympic Stadium. Ken and I, along with my Russian interpreter, were seated on the front row of the Mission platform. We watched as 70,000 people tried to enter the 35,000-seat stadium to hear the Gospel. My interpreter, a young blind student named Oleg, was able to grasp it all as I leaned over and described to him the incredible scene before us. People were crammed shoulder-to-shoulder in the aisles and on the stairs. He couldn't see, but he felt the excitement.

Right before I moved to the microphone, Oleg said to me, "I can hardly believe that God has picked you, a paralysed woman, and me, a blind young man, to give His Gospel to my countrymen in this stadium. It's amazing!"

More than that, it was ironic. Oh the irony of God that He would choose to voice His message to a nation, not through the powerful or the mighty, but through the most unlikely twosome. A paralysed woman. A blind young man.

God delights in showing up His power through weak and unlikely people. He specializes in irony, always choosing a combination of circumstances opposite to what one might expect to get the job done. There are plenty of ironies in your life and each one is a reason to give God praise; for His power always is best displayed through weakness.

Mighty and powerful Lord, I praise you for the marvellous way you accomplish your purposes. You always seem to do the opposite of what people expect and you surprise us with your mysterious, awesome ways.

Getting Rid of Fear

Since the children have flesh and blood, He too shared in their humanity so that by His death He might destroy him who holds the power of death — that is, the devil — and free those who all their lives were held in slavery by their fear of death.
HEBREWS 2:14–15

Ever since the days of Eden, people have been haunted by fear of each side of the grave. Like the old song goes, "I'm tired of living, but scared of dying." On this side of the tombstone, fears are aggravated by pain and suffering. Sometimes when people peer beyond the grave, their anxieties are aggravated by the unknown. The Prince of Peace is the only one who can rid you of fear, whether it's fear of the here and now, or of the future.

Peace is the opposite of fear. A prescription for peace is found in Hebrews 2:14–15. God became a human being — that's Jesus. Jesus, through His death, broke the power of the devil and his lies. This same Jesus desires to deliver you of your fears, whether you're frightened of life as a living nightmare or fearing death as a scary unknown. To place your trust in Jesus gives you peace now and peace about the hereafter.

To place your hand in the Prince of Peace's hand does not necessarily guarantee you protection from suffering. But it does give you protection from fear, including a steadfast hand to hold onto and the certainty that a loving and all-powerful God who knows everything is standing by your side. Putting your confidence in Christ will free you from living all your life as a slave to constant dread.

Prince of Peace, forgive me for allowing fear to come between us. I have no need to fear what will happen today. I have no need to fear what will happen when I die. Free me to live every day without fear.

Memories

But Timothy has just now come to us from you and has brought good news about your faith and love. He has told us that you always have pleasant memories of us and that you long to see us, just as we also long to see you.

I THESSALONIANS 3:6

Pleasant memories are like precious snapshots in an old favourite photo album. Every once in a while you flip through them to recall warm and sunlit moments from your past.

Not long ago Ken and I were enjoying dinner in the home of a large family. Before the food was served, each child bowed his head and offered a short grace. I peeked when it came to little Mikey's turn to pray. As the youngest, he squirmed in his seat, and in between blessing the potatoes and roast beef, he prayed in a small voice, "God, help Joni help her handicapped friends."

Breathless with the tenderness of the moment, I quickly took a mental snapshot of Mikey sitting to the right of me with his eyes squeezed shut and hands folded. That brief prayer of his probably carried more impact before the throne than most of the things I ever pray.

That's one memory, sharp and clear, that I'm going to savour as I sit at my desk during a busy day. And the Lord will use it to lift my spirit. That's what pleasant memories are for.

Warm and lovely memories have a way of helping you live life better in the present. Think of the embrace of the friend who led you to Jesus. Recall the time in church when you cried as you sang a favourite hymn. Think back on a prayer meeting when the intercessions flowed so easily that you felt you could have prayed for ever. Pick out a memory . . . and savour the sweetness.

Lord, please bring to mind encouraging and uplifting memories which help me see your hand at work in my life over the years. I praise you today for thoughts that inspire and refresh.

Love God

Of friendships, Hannah Whitall Smith has said, "A certain degree of reserve and distance seems to be the suitable thing in certain friendships. But there are other relations in life where . . . the friendship becomes love. The two hearts give themselves to each other to be no longer two, but one.

"A union of soul takes place . . . separate interests and separate paths in life are no longer possible. Things that were lawful before become unlawful now because of the nearness of the tie that binds. The reserve and distance suitable to mere friendship become fatal in love . . . the wishes of one become binding obligations to the other, and the deepest desire of each heart is that it may know every secret wish or longing of the other in order that it may fly on the wings of the wind to gratify it."

If you have ever known this kind of friendship, if you have ever loved another enough to find sacrifice and service on their behalf a joy, then let it be the same toward Christ, the lover of your soul. He loves you with far more than the love of friendship. He loves you as His bride. What passion! How can we not be passionate in return?

" 'Love the Lord your God with all your heart and with all your soul and with all your strength and with all your mind'; and, 'Love your neighbour as yourself.' " LUKE 10:27

Be generous in your self-surrender and be eager to throw yourself unreservedly at His feet. Jesus is calling you to a place of intimate nearness with Him. Don't hesitate!

Lord, I don't want to go where you cannot go with me. I don't want to pursue anything in which you cannot share. I want to love you with all my heart, soul, strength and mind. I echo the words you said to our Father, "I delight to do thy will, O my God."

JUNE

Let Go and Let God?

Then the Lord said to Moses, "Why are you crying out to me? Tell the Israelites to move on."　　　　EXODUS 14:15

A phrase like "Let go and let God" sounds good, but it raises questions. Who does all the work as we grow in Christ? Do we give in to God, making certain that we put forth no energy on our part? Or do we charge full steam ahead and do our best to do what's right?

If you've wrestled with that question, you're in good company because Moses struggled with the same thing. In Exodus 14, Moses led the Israelites out of Egypt, but they screeched to a halt at the edge of the Red Sea. Pharaoh's army was in hot pursuit and the people were panicking. So in the 13th verse Moses says, *"Do not be afraid. Stand firm and you will see the deliverance the Lord will bring you today . . . the Lord will fight for you; you need only to be still."*

His was a "Let go and let God" way of looking at the problem. But that was no time to yield passively and God says so in the next verse! *"Why are you crying out to me?"* said God. *"Tell the Israelites to move on. Raise your staff and stretch out your hand over the sea to divide the water so that the Israelites can go through the sea on dry ground."*

The Lord is not about to let Moses or you sit still. If danger is about, if temptation is knocking, if a friend needs help, if the devil is gearing up for an attack, God does not want His people to stand still. "Letting go and letting God" speaks to only half the battle. The other half involves you moving forward in His power.

God of the Israelites, help me today not to sit still but courageously move onward!

Sitting . . . Carrying

Remember the story in Luke chapter 5 about the four friends who carried their paralysed companion to see Jesus? Do you recall how they couldn't squeeze through the crowds? They ripped a hole in the roof and lowered their friend down in front of the feet of the Lord. The Pharisees and teachers of the law sat there, shocked and angered that Jesus not only healed the man, but forgave his sins.

In the story, there are two groups of main characters – the Pharisees who were sitting and the men who came carrying. Compare the activities of the two. One group is sitting and listening; they are the critics and complainers. The other group is carrying a friend; they are the ones believing and taking action.

God requires us to do more than merely listen to Him. We are to do what He says. And when we stop criticizing and start taking action to carry the burdens of others, we always receive more from the Lord than we anticipate. Just consider the paralysed man and his four friends. They went to Jesus hoping for a healing, but received so much more: forgiveness of sin!

Do not merely listen to the word, and so deceive yourselves. Do what it says.
JAMES 1:22

◆

If you specialize in doing what the word says, you will always receive more than you anticipate. God will surprise you with a blessing for which you're not even seeking. Do not merely sit in the church, but carry the burdens of the church.

Jesus, my teacher and healer, I don't want to be like the Pharisees who were very good at sitting and listening; I want to be like the four friends of the paralysed man. When I see a person in need today, inspire me to believe and take action. Help me to carry his burden and, in so doing, together we will glorify you.

Crown of Splendour

Grey hair is a crown of splendour; it is attained by a righteous life.

PROVERBS 16:31

When Ken and I were in Russia, we befriended an old woman who cleaned the floors of our hotel lobby every day. Through an interpreter, we complimented her on doing an excellent job. Old and wrinkled, her round and red cheeks were framed with a tightly knotted colourful scarf. Her face sparkled with her blue eyes and golden-toothed smile. She had on layers of skirts and wore leggings and boots. With broom in hand, our elderly friend looked out of place in the hotel lobby; maybe that's why we were drawn to her.

We met many Russian "babushkas" like her. The praying grandmothers, they were called. These were the stalwart saints of whom Stalin had cruelly said, "If we can get rid of these old women, we will have the youth in our grasp."

Stalin failed. And thank God for praying grandmothers who served as a link, spanning a generation lost to atheism and connecting a new generation of young people who are asking open, honest questions about Jesus.

How grateful we can be to elderly saints who make prayer a life vocation. One day eternity shall reveal how far and wide Christ's Gospel was advanced through the faithful prayers of old and faithful Christians.

If you have even one grey hair, you could almost qualify for Proverbs 16:31. But is your life a righteous one, hallmarked by the kind of intercessory prayer so many elderly saints offer to the Lord?

Praise God for that person over the age of sixty-five whom you know, a friend who is still trusting the Lord despite arthritis, wrinkles and poor vision. These who wear a crown of splendour need our prayers, too.

Father of all ages, as grey hairs abound, may righteousness abound. May I never resent the encroaching years but view them as an opportunity to deepen my life of praise and intercession.

For God So Loved the World

"For God so loved the world that He gave His one and only Son, that whoever believes in Him shall not perish but have eternal life."   JOHN 3:16

Gloria Hawley, a friend of mine, fell into deep anguish over the bleak prognosis of her daughter's illness. Little Laura, it seemed, had already suffered enough from the degenerative nerve disease she had been born with. And now the doctors' forecast included more suffering . . . and impending death.

Gloria, like any mother, wished desperately that she could take away her daughter's pain. She vacillated from sullen times of withdrawn sorrow to furious outbursts of anger. Gloria had no problem with God's sovereignty – she knew exactly who to blame! She would leave her daughter's bedside at night and cry out in anger, "God, it's not right! You've never had to watch one of your children die!"

At that point she clasped her hand over her mouth. The truth hit her. God most certainly *did* watch His child die. His one and only child. And, like any parent, He probably wished that He could take away His Son's pain. Yet God endured the pain because God so loved the world . . .

That fact alone buoyed up Gloria's weak and demoralized spirit. She could bear the pain of her daughter's suffering and death because God bore the pain of His Son's suffering and death. That meant His strength and empathy were tailor-made for her. Gloria could rest in the comfort that God was by her side in the most amazing parent support group ever devised!

Oh Lord, there isn't a pain I endure or a disappointment I face that you haven't already overcome. Thank you that you fully and completely understand my fears and frustrations, my hurt and weakness. Thank you for loving the world so much that you would give your one and only Son . . . this is enough to calm my hurts.

The Heart of Jesus

Though He brings grief, He will show compassion, so great is His unfailing love. For He does not willingly bring affliction or grief to the children of men.

LAMENTATIONS 3:32–3

What do you think was on the Lord's heart when He healed those who were paralysed? When He opened the eyes of the blind? What was the Lord feeling when He counselled the father of the little boy who was gripped by seizures?

There are those who point to such miracles as signs of Christ's messiahship, saying, "Jesus healed those people as evidence of His authority as the Son of God. By such power, He was proving He was the Messiah." And they are right. But praise God, there is more.

Christ did not *use* helpless people to advance His own agenda. He did not enlist suffering men and women only as audio-visual aids to teach an important lesson about himself. Neither did He approach blind, deaf or paralysed people in an emotional vacuum. Scripture often tells us that He was moved with compassion when He saw the suffering masses.

When it comes to suffering, Lamentations 3:32–3 reveals the heart intent of Jesus. He does not *willingly*, or that is, *from the heart* bring affliction or grief. Suffering may be a part of God's larger and most mysterious plan, but God's intention is always to demonstrate compassion and unfailing love which touches people at their deepest point of need.

Because of the Lord's great love we are not consumed, for His compassions never fail. They are new every morning; great is your faithfulness.

LAMENTATIONS 3:22–3

❧

Lord, may I never doubt what's on your mind and heart when I suffer. You are full of love and compassion. Thank you for only permitting in my life what I am able to endure with your grace. Bless you for your unfailing love.

Get Ready

Listen, I tell you a mystery: We will not all sleep, but we will all be changed. Therefore, my dear brothers, stand firm. Let nothing move you. Always give yourselves fully to the work of the Lord, because you know that your labour in the Lord is not in vain.   I CORINTHIANS 15:51, 58

Life, as we know it, will be turned upside down when the trumpet sounds for our journey to heaven. We will have to rethink everything in light of the presence of Christ. The plans, hierarchies, principles, systems, and values that have ruled our societies for years will be thrown out. And you won't be able to distinguish bigwigs from the riffraff!

Given such a radical change, Paul admonishes us to be prepared. That's a good idea. We're not very good at handling change. Every change without preparation can create stress and division.

Paul's preparation has eternal perspective. First, *stand firm*. In the original language, the picture of that word was to literally be in place. A person seated in their faith is much less vulnerable to attack.

Second, *let nothing move you*. The phrase literally means don't move yourself from your position of faith. No one needs to point a gun at your head, Paul is saying, in order for some of you to set aside your obedience. Watch out that you don't move yourself.

Third, *always give yourselves fully to the work of the Lord*. There's nothing like godly activity in love to get you ready for Christ's return. You sense His coming more clearly and urgently when you are about His work.

Are you ready?

◆

Lord, I can spend many moments speculating what heaven will be like. But I need your prodding to keep me strong and to keep me working in your service. Fill my days of waiting for heaven with overabundant love for your appearing.

Body Parts

At a recent conference, I shared the platform with my friend Camille. Actually, she doesn't speak. Camille is an interpreter for the deaf and she often travels with me to sign my messages. As I talked, her hands were working a mile a minute just to keep up. I spoke for almost an hour, got a sore throat and had to pop a lozenge.

During break time I noticed my friend Francie sitting with Camille, giving her hands a deep massage. Camille sighed, "Joni, your throat may be sore, but my hands are sore from your talk. My tendons are tight and this handrub is as soothing as, well, that lozenge on your throat."

It never occurred to me that Camille's hands could get tired of talking, or I should say, signing. As I watched Francie give Camille back the "voice" in her hands, I thought, *what a beautiful picture of the body of Christ working together.* One part can't do the job alone. When I speak, I need someone else's hands to push my chair to the platform. My deaf friends who are present can't hear unless Camille offers her hands to interpret. And Camille can't use her hands very long unless someone else gives her wrists and fingers a massage.

When it comes to giving the Gospel, it's always a cooperative effort of love and support. The Lord takes delight when His body works that way.

Now you are the body of Christ, and each one of you is a part of it.

I Corinthians 12:27

Someone needs you today. You could be the hands or the ears or the voice of someone who needs help. We're in this together so find a part of the body that can't be complete without you.

Find a tailor-made place for me to fit in your body today, Lord. Let me be your hands to someone who needs your love.

Housebroken Sins

What sins have you housebroken? What secret, small transgressions have you tamed to make your own? A private fantasy? A daydream you've shielded against the scrutiny of the Spirit?

I had a friend in college who enjoyed gossiping with one particular classmate. She wasn't loose with her tongue with anyone else. But, oh, did that classmate get an earful! My college friend thought she had housebroken her gossip, made it domesticated and respectable.

The major problem with our minor offences is that we tend to whitewash them, thinking they are not all that offensive to God. If you are harbouring small sins in an attempt to housebreak them, tenderize your heart with this advice:

"We are too apt to forget that temptation to sin will rarely present itself in its true colours. Never when we are tempted will we hear sin say to us, 'I am your deadly enemy . . . I want to ruin your life.' That's not how it works. Sin, instead, comes to us like Judas with a kiss. It comes to us like Joab with outstretched hands and flattering words. Sin, in its beginnings, seems harmless enough – like David walking idly on his palace roof which happened to overlook the bedroom of a woman. You and I may give wickedness smooth-sounding names, but we cannot alter its nature and character in the sight of God."   J. C. RYLE

Therefore, since we are surrounded by such a great cloud of witnesses, let us throw off everything that hinders and the sin that so easily entangles, and let us run with perseverance the race marked out for us.   HEBREWS 12:1

Help me to throw off today any sin that entangles. Forgive me for trying to minimize my sin by making excuses for it. Help me to see my sins, great or small, as things which deeply offend you. For the sake of Christ, keep me from ever becoming entangled again.

Cobweb Problems

For our light and momentary troubles are achieving for us an eternal glory that far outweighs them all.   II CORINTHIANS 4:17

Growing up on a farm was one big adventure for me. My sisters and I would jump from barn rafters, build hay forts and crawl into the feed bin. I'd shinny up the ladder to the hayloft, climbing through layers of thick cobwebs which hung like candy floss strung from one post to another.

Spiders didn't bother me back then, so I thought nothing of barging through their webs. The thin threads clung to me, but I laughed – with a sweep of my hand, the cobwebs were gone.

Someone once prayed, "Lord, help us to strip off like cobwebs the troubles that we have allowed to cling to us like chains." Oh, how often we feel chained to our problems. Wouldn't it be glorious if we could consider all our trials to be as light and as momentary as cobwebs? We can! Whatever troubles are weighing you down – doubt or anxiety, insecurity or fears – are not chains. They are featherweight when compared to the glory yet to come. With a sweep of a prayer and the praise of a child's heart, God can strip away any cobweb.

Lord of all, I can hardly comprehend the eternal glory that awaits me in heaven. Help me to understand that my troubles on earth are, indeed, light and momentary. Make me to know that they achieve for me rich reward and, for your Son, glory and honour. Give me the spirit of a child and help me to brush aside like cobwebs the problems that often feel like chains.

True Service

Whatever you do, work at it with all your heart, as working for the Lord, not for men, since you know that you will receive an inheritance from the Lord as a reward. It is the Lord Christ you are serving.

COLOSSIANS 3:23–4

Sometimes I hear people say that a single man has "given his elderly parent the best years of his life". Or I hear about a mother who has sacrificed all to "devote her years to care for her handicapped child".

And sometimes I hear that this single man, mother or missionary has nearly worn out himself or herself, collapsing in bone-weary exhaustion. No wonder these people sound tired. Who do they think they're serving? Jesus must not only energize our service, He must be the focus of our service. As Colossians chapter 3 advises, *"Whatever you do, work at it with all your heart, as working for the Lord, not for men . . ."*

Yes, service to God means sacrifice and devotion. But we don't give up our lives to serve others, we give up our lives to serve the Lord. It is almost incidental that we are serving a husband or wife, an elderly parent, a handicapped child or a tribe on a mission field.

When our focus in Christian service is squarely on the Lord Jesus, our work may be tiring, but it doesn't have to be tiresome. We may get weary, but our work does not have to be wearisome if our energy comes directly from the Lord Jesus. How can service to the Lord be a tedious, boring effort?

Lord Jesus, it is you whom I love to serve. Help me to keep my focus on you today so that I will have all the energy I need to help others around me.

Hidden Sins

"For whatever is hidden is meant to be disclosed, and whatever is concealed is meant to be brought out into the open."   MARK 4:22

During the first weeks of my paralysis, I recall my mother sitting at the foot of my hospital bed with a small scrubbing brush and bar of soap. "Mother, why are you scrubbing my feet?" I asked. Her reply? "Where in the world did you walk on these feet of yours?!"

What can I say? I was a typical barefooted teenager who spent most of my time in the back yard or at the community pool. The soles of my feet were calloused and greyed from the dirt. Curiously enough, I never knew my feet had dirty calluses because I never bothered to look. Even if I did, I wouldn't have cared because that part of my body was hidden. I was more concerned about the pimples on my chin that everyone, myself included, could see.

The spiritual person should have enough sense to occasionally look, as it were, at the bottom of his feet. If we are in tune with the Lord, we are sensitive to know that everyone hides secret faults; and the wise person is the one who does not mind the Spirit scrubbing away the hidden sins – sins that, if we don't confess them, have a way of ruling over us.

Hypocrisy is a hard game to play because it is one deceiver against many observers. A hypocrite will always be found out. Secret sinning, although an easier game to play, is far more deadly. Hidden sins can be concealed and, for that reason, are far more damaging to your character.

Father, I want no sin to have dominion over me, I desire that no fault rule over me. Search me, try me, test me, and help me to face those sins in my life which I have tried to hide. Scrub me clean!

A Red Flag!

"Seek the Lord while He may be found; call on Him while He is near. Let the wicked forsake his way and the evil man his thoughts."

ISAIAH 55:6–7

This verse sounds an alarm! And there's a good reason for the red flag. It's meant to instil awesome respect and holy fear for the Lord. For God is not a jolly old saint who rebukes us with a shake of His finger. Neither is He biting His nails on our behalf or wringing His hands and hoping that we'll do the right thing. Sin still greatly offends Him as it did in the Old Testament. Sin is an insult. It is an affront.

Maybe you've been dabbling in sin. Careless flirtations. Lazy thoughts. Fudgings of the truth. If you've been sweeping them under the carpet of your conscience, if you think, "God will always be there . . . He'll forgive me sooner or later . . . so I'll choose later," then wake up! God will not always allow Himself to be found. One day you may try to call on Him, and He won't be near.

Your heart will be too hard to feel His touch. Your ears will be too dull to hear His voice. Your eyes will not be able to see the light. All because you spurned His rebuke and chose not to fear the Lord.

"They will call to me but I will not answer; they will look for me but will not find me. Since they hated knowledge and did not choose to fear the Lord, since they would not accept my advice and spurned my rebuke, they will eat the fruit of their ways and be filled with the fruit of their schemes."

PROVERBS 1:28–31

❧

Lord, I never want to lose my sensitivity to sin. I repent of my transgressions, great and small. I turn the other way and seek your face. Thank you for being near!

Pleasure

You have made known to me the path of life; you will fill me with joy in your presence, with eternal pleasures at your right hand. PSALM 16:11

Pleasurable things give delight and satisfaction to the soul. Pleasure is found lying under an oak tree on a windy day, the cool grass beneath and the rustle of leaves above. Pleasure is discovered by a cheery fire, curled up on a couch with your favourite afghan and herbal tea. Pleasure is captured in the soft smile and gentle eyes of the one you love.

Our souls are restless, raging and thirsting for fulfilment, for delight, for . . . pleasure. Someone has said, "The worth and excellency of a soul is to be measured by the object of its love." Who we are in our innermost being is revealed by those things we passionately desire. If we desire dull, sensual things our souls reflect dullness; if our desires rise to find fulfilment in the exalted, then our souls are made noble and pure.

Because God has created your need for pleasure, it stands to reason that He must be the consummation of that need. He directs our pleasure-seeking souls when He commands, "You shall love the Lord your God with all your heart." God is not only the one who gives pleasure, but *is* Himself all pleasure.

Eternal pleasures are found at God's right hand. Stop there. You don't have to look any further. God places passions within you so that you'll keep searching until you find utter delight in Him.

Don't deny your desire for delight. Gorge yourself on God and discover real and deep delight.

You are the delight of my soul, Lord, and I look to you for all fulfilment. Help me to see that the longings you've placed within me are signposts directing me always and always to you.

A Seat at the Banquet

"A certain man was preparing a great banquet and invited many guests. At the time of the banquet he sent his servant to tell those who had been invited, 'Come, for everything is now ready.' But they all alike began to make excuses . . . The servant came back and reported this to his master. Then the owner of the house became angry and ordered his servant, 'Go out quickly into the streets and alleys of the town and bring in the poor, the crippled, the blind and the lame' "

LUKE 14:16–21

The Gospel sounds like a tragedy: Die to yourself and you'll live. Salvation sounds like bad news: We are saved not because we are brave, clean and reverent, but because we are dead and our life is hid with Christ in God. In short, the good news has nothing to do with turning bad men into good men, but dead men into living men.

Little wonder the Gospel seems so distasteful, so offensive. It's mostly off-putting to people who feel they have everything, people who want to keep their winnings in this world.

That's why the Gospel is only good news to those who consider themselves losers. Whether it's crane operators or bag ladies, schoolteachers or drug addicts, the tennis pro on a world tour or the homeless drunk living in an alley. Each must consider himself a loser if he wants a seat at the king's banquet. And the price of a seat? That each dies to himself.

The price of salvation is high and, yes, you should sit down and count the cost. But when you finish counting, you have the absolute certainty that *everything you've got* turns out to be exactly the right price for a seat at the banquet. All you have to be is a certified loser and God will send His servant, Jesus, to positively drag you into His house.

I hold back nothing. I give you everything. Jesus, you win.

Grace: God's Initiative

" 'Sir,' the servant said, 'what you ordered has been done, but there is still room.' Then the master told his servant, 'Go out to the roads and country lanes and make them come in, so that my house will be full. I tell you, not one of those men who were invited will get a taste of my banquet.' "

LUKE 14:22–4

First, the master offered free food and drinks to his invited guests, but everyone RSVP'd with regrets and excuses. That made the master angry and so he decided to throw his party for the poor, the handicapped and anyone who could be found feeding off the trash cans in the streets and alleys. After the servant gathered as many social outcasts into the banquet as he could, he told his master, *"What you ordered has been done, but there is still room."*

Notice what the master does next. He orders his servant to go out to the roads and country lanes (a good distance beyond the streets and alleys) in order to find more outcasts *and make them come in.* The master's motive? He simply must have a full house and he will not settle for anything less.

In this parable, the master's grace is not lavished on the deserving, but on the undeserving. The unacceptable. Those who shouldn't be invited. And God bestows His grace on the same – not the proud, but the humble.

God's grace is not a response to what men do. God's grace is a divine initiative which is totally unconnected to a man's merit. And not only is the grace of God an initiative, but a radical one that most would consider outlandish, if not mad. But isn't it just like God to flaunt his foolishness as wiser than men's wisdom and his weakness, stronger than human strength.

Father, thank you for sending your servant Jesus to search for me, find me, and bring me to your banquet.

Trust

A furious squall came up, and the waves broke over the boat, so that it was nearly swamped. Jesus was in the stern, sleeping on a cushion. The disciples woke Him and said to Him, "Teacher, don't you care if we drown?" He got up, rebuked the wind and said to the waves, "Quiet! Be still!" Then the wind died down and it was completely calm. MARK 4:37-9

Had we been in the boat, our faith would have had an advantage over the disciples. Unlike them, we have the Bible . . . two thousand years of church history . . . the testimony of the resurrection . . . the indwelling of the Holy Spirit. The disciples had none of that.

So what would have been our response when the squall hit the boat? I like to believe I would have held onto the rigging and leaned over to whisper in Jesus' ear, "Don't wake up from your sleep, Lord. Rest easy and our Father's grace will see me through this storm. I trust you're in control no matter what you are doing." Oh, for the chance to show Jesus that, yes, I can trust Him!

Well, I have that chance every day. And so do you.

"I will not doubt, though all my ships at sea come drifting home with broken masts and sails; I shall believe the hand which never fails, from seeming evil worketh good to me. And, though I weep because those sails are battered, still will I cry, while my best hopes lie shattered, 'I trust in thee'." ELLA WHEELER WILCOX

May my trust in you be complete, O Lord. May my confidence never waver and my hope never falter. When stormy trials beset me, may I rely on you finally and fully.

All Is Well

Sometimes a good story says it all. Like this one by Robert Louis Stevenson. The scene? A raging storm at sea. The story? The passengers in the ship became alarmed when the waves began to crash over the bow. Many of them thought for certain the end had come.

Finally, one passenger – against orders – crept up on deck where the pilot was steering the churning vessel. There the pilot stood, strapped tightly to the wheel. He caught sight of the terror-stricken man and gave him a reassuring smile. At that point, the passenger backed down the steps, entered the hold of the ship and announced to the others, "I have seen the face of the pilot and he smiled at me. All is well."

This story perfectly captures what our pilot is doing when powerful waves of trials crash around us. Oh, if we would only seek the reassuring smile of God, we would be calmed. He knows the way through the waves.

My heart says of you, "Seek His face!" Your face, Lord, I will seek.
PSALM 27:8

When the Spirit of Christ whispers to your troubled heart, *"Seek His face,"* don't delay. This is what is called a prompting or a nudging of the Spirit. He is telling you what to do. Immediately say to Him in prayerful response, "Yes, Lord, I will seek you." And then, do just that: Seek Him in His Word and through prayer. The peace that passes all understanding will be yours when you hear Him whisper, in return, "All is well."

Lord, help me to listen when your Spirit reminds me to seek your face during times of trouble. Too often I've failed to listen to your promptings. I know that you are the source of calm and peace in the midst of my trials. I praise you today for your smile that reminds me, "All is well."

The Bread of Adversity

Although the Lord gives you the bread of adversity and the water of affliction, your teachers will be hidden no more; with your own eyes you will see them.

ISAIAH 30:20

God wants to refine you. Your trial is a refining. He will be true to Isaiah 48:10, *"See, I have refined you, though not as silver; I have tested you in the furnace of affliction."* Your God is a consuming fire and He sits as the Refiner purging every impurity from your life. Your response? Agree with Job that *"When he has tested me, I will come forth as gold."*

God wants to sift you. Your trial is a sifting. You are God's grain, planted by Him and to be gathered by His hand. You are coarse and rough grain and must pass through several processes of sifting. Each sieve is finer, *"However, it produces a harvest of righteousness and peace"* (Hebrews 12:11).

God wants to prune you. Your trial is a pruning. *"Every branch that does bear fruit he trims clean so that it will be even more fruitful"* (John 15:2). The pruning process hurts, but God is a careful gardener and He prunes you with great skill and love.

God wants to polish you. Your trial is a polishing. You are a living stone to be carved just as it says in Psalm 144:12, *"Our daughters will be like pillars carved to adorn a palace."* God wants to chisel away your rough edges.

Refining. Sifting. Pruning. Polishing. God gives you the bread of adversity and the water of affliction for good reasons. With God's Word as your teacher, your own eyes can see the purpose of the Lord.

Just like your Word says, no trial seems pleasant, Lord. But I thank you that your purposes are wise and wonderful.

Clean Air

God's people breathe cleaner air. And they're healthier because of it. That's what Nehemiah learned while he and a handful of Israelites rebuilt the wall of Jerusalem in fifty-two days.

Nehemiah's enemies were relentless in their hostility. They tried numerous means to destroy the work. On one occasion it says that the enemies *"plotted together to come and fight against Jerusalem and stir up trouble against it"* (Nehemiah 4:8).

It would have been a simple task but their conspiracy was their undoing. To conspire means literally to breathe together. And these enemies of God breathed each other's anger. If you've ever been in a stuffy meeting room, you know how thick the air can get. That's what happened in the spirits of the enemies. They breathed foul air and couldn't think straight.

But that's not why they failed. Notice Nehemiah's comment in contrast with the enemy's activity: *"But we prayed . . ."* (verse 9)

Praying allowed the people to have fresh insight, to make a wise decision, and let Nehemiah lead effectively. There was plenty of fresh air from above in their "vertical conspiracy". The result was to "set up a guard" as a response and thus thwart the plans of the enemy. Our daily breath dare not be amongst ourselves lest the air become stale with our own ideas and prejudices. It would only take one contemptuous soul to foul our thinking.

⁔

We must ever be praying – breathing vertically – if we are to have any wisdom from above.

Lord, teach me to breathe your words in prayer. Teach me fresh conversation with you as something to be prized above all else. Thank you for hearing me and answering me.

Who Are the Elect?

For if you possess these qualities in increasing measure, they will keep you from being ineffective and unproductive in your knowledge of our Lord Jesus Christ . . . Therefore, my brothers, be all the more eager to make your calling and election sure. For if you do these things, you will never fall, and you will receive a rich welcome into the eternal kingdom of our Lord and Saviour Jesus Christ. II PETER 1:8, 10–11

How do you know if you're saved? I've met Christians who, even after years of walking with the Lord, occasionally lack assurance of salvation. Pointing to a confirmation certificate won't do. Knowing the date you were baptized won't do it either.

True, the Spirit bears witness with our spirit, assuring us that our names are written in the Book of Life. But if the Spirit doesn't point to a confirmation certificate or a date of baptism, to what then *does* He point? He directs our attention to II Peter 1.

As the verse says, if we want to make our calling and election sure, that is, if we want to know for certain that we are among the elect, then we should look to our lives to make certain we possess in increasing measure faith, goodness, self-control, perseverance, godliness, brotherly kindness and love. A changed life is the best evidence that we are heading for heaven.

And what if your life does not reflect these godly qualities? II Peter 1:9 has the answer:

If anyone does not have them, he is short-sighted and blind, and has forgotten that he has been cleansed from his past sins.

Lord, I want to make every effort to add to my faith all the godly qualities which reflect your life. As I grow, thank you for deepening my assurance that I am safe and secure in the family of God.

The Real Thing

Whom have I in heaven but you? And earth has nothing I desire besides you. My flesh and my heart may fail, but God is the strength of my heart and my portion for ever.　　　　　　　　　　　　　　　　　　PSALM 73:25–6

In the advertising world, Coca-Cola will always be known as the "real thing". And I agree. On a hot, blistery afternoon, nothing quenches my thirst like an ice-cold bottle of Coke. Iced tea doesn't do it. I think lemonade will, but it won't. Even cold water, for me, lacks the bite I enjoy from a Coke. There are no substitutes for the real thing.

But in the world of spiritual pursuits, sometimes we don't even realize what we're thirsty for. Yearnings deep within drive us from one relationship to another looking for fulfilment. Our desires set us on edge, yet we know instinctively that once we grasp "realness", we shall be satisfied. The problem is, there are so many substitutes. If only we could find and hold onto what our souls crave.

Stop your search. Christ is the real thing. Nothing and no-one satisfies the soul like Jesus for He fills every craving. David knew that when he wrote in Psalm 63, *"O God, you are my God, earnestly I seek you; my soul thirsts for you, my body longs for you, in a dry and weary land where there is no water."*

You may think you have to actually crave God before you come to Him. No. Express your cravings to Him and expect Him to be the one who will fulfil you, and you know what? He will.

As the deer pants for streams of water, so my soul pants for you, O God. My soul thirsts for God, for the living God. When can I go and meet with God?　　　　　　　　　　　　　　　　　　PSALM 42:1–2

When can you go to meet with God? Right now. And why don't you use your own – your real – words.

Life Is Hard

We sent Timothy, who is our brother and God's fellow-worker in spreading the gospel of Christ, to strengthen and encourage you in your faith, so that no one would be unsettled by these trials. You know quite well that we were destined for them.   I THESSALONIANS 3:2–3

Sometimes life seems to be one long, unending string of trials. What words of encouragement does the apostle have for us? *"You know quite well we were destined for them."* But he doesn't stop on that morbid note. He adds: Be strengthened. Be encouraged in your faith. And don't let trials unsettle you.

We are destined for trials. In other words, life is supposed to be difficult. Yet it's amazing how many people believe that life should be easy. They bemoan the enormity of their problems, feeling as though their difficulties are a unique kind of affliction that should not be. They feel that affliction has somehow been especially visited upon them, or else upon their families, and not upon others.

Life is a series of problems to be solved. Yes, solving problems is a painful process, but it is this whole process that gives our life meaning. Benjamin Franklin said, "Those things that hurt, instruct." And the psalmist said long before him, *"It was good for me to be afflicted so that I might learn your decrees"* (Psalm 119:71).

So be strengthened and encouraged in your faith. Don't be unsettled by your trials. You know quite well you are destined for them. And for good reasons.

❧

Trials are not for our pleasure, they are for our profit. Once you accept this truth, you transcend it. Once you truly know that life is difficult, then life is difficult no longer.

Lord, you have not redeemed me to make my life happy, healthy or free of trouble. You've redeemed me to become more like Christ . . . and this is why I'm destined for trials.

Longings

Instead, they were longing for a better country – a heavenly one. Therefore God is not ashamed to be called their God, for He has prepared a city for them.

HEBREWS 11:16

Sometimes I get so homesick for heaven that the yearning swells like an ocean wave and I feel like I'm being swept away, right then and there, to a better country, a heavenly one. Spiritual growth includes an awakening of these deep longings for heaven. This awakening leads to the true contentment of asking less of this life because more is coming in the next. Such longings also heighten our loneliness here on earth.

"Godly people joyfully delight in good things and they nobly endure hard things," says my friend Larry Crabb. "They know that their existence is meaningful and that they are destined for unlimited pleasure at the deepest level. Because they keenly feel that nothing now quite meets the standards of their longing souls, the quiet but throbbing ache within them drives them not to complaint, but to anticipation."

The difference between godly and ungodly people is not that one group never hurts and the other group does. The difference lies in what people do with their hurt. Christians who long for a better country, a heavenly one, are convinced that one day something so glorious will happen in the world's finale, that it will suffice for all of their hurts.

Like tides on a crescent sea-beach, When the moon is new and thin,
Into our hearts high yearnings Come welling and surging in –
Come from the mystic ocean, Whose rim no foot has trod –
Some of us call it Longing, And others call it God.

WILLIAM HERBERT CARRUTH

꧂

Blessed Lord, my soul longs after you! Wrap my life in your divine love and keep me ever desiring you. Keep my heart from wandering away and may I never lose sight of my heavenly home.

At War with Spirits

Put on the full armour of God so that you can take your stand against the devil's schemes. For our struggle is not against flesh and blood, but against the rulers, against the authorities, against the powers of this dark world and against the spiritual forces of evil in the heavenly realms. EPHESIANS 6:11–12

The problem with superstition in our age is not its force, but its perceived folly. There are too many who laugh at the thought of evil spirits and demons in the air. Faith is meant for faith in things that are good like Jesus, heaven, the Holy Spirit and miracles. Rarely do they consider believing in the existence of Satan and his hosts as having any practical impact.

Paul did not even argue the point of existence of evil and evil spirits. His focus of attention was on what we *do* about them. What should our response be to such a reality? Since the calendar says that today is Midsummer's Eve, should we hang herbs of St John before dawn on the door?

No. That may be fine for pagans or New Agers, but Paul tells Christians to put on armour that, like the power of God and the schemes of the devil, are unseen. No dried herbs hung on the door today. No dried plants burned on the fire on June 24th or any other day. No. Paul tells us to put on armour that, like the power of God and the schemes of Satan, are unseen. Put on truth, righteousness, the Gospel of peace, faith, salvation, the Holy Spirit. This is the only way to extinguish the attacks of Satan.

Emotional fervour and tirades against the kingdom of Satan will not protect you. You would be talking to the wrong people. Talk instead with God. Listen to God. Demons scatter at such conversation.

Lord, my eyes cannot see the evil kingdom. So grant me your vision to know that evil forces are real. Equip me with your armour.

A Heart that Won't Quit

Let us not become weary in doing good, for at the proper time we will reap a harvest if we do not give up. GALATIANS 6:9

For the fourth time yesterday I needed to be lifted out of my wheelchair and laid down on the office sofa. Shallow breathing and skyrocketing blood pressure were signalling that something was pinching, bruising, or sticking my paralysed body. As my secretary shifted my body, examining my legs and hips for any telltale red spots, I stared vacantly at the ceiling, overcome by frustration. "Where do I go to resign from this stupid paralysis," I mumbled.

We couldn't find anything wrong and so I was hoisted back into my chair. Sitting there slumped, I looked at the pile of work on my desk. I felt like giving up. As my secretary left the office, I dreamed what I've dreamed of a thousand times: *The perishable shall one day put on the imperishable.* I smiled.

Don't let your heart quit. For at the proper time, we will reap!

"O Christian worker, Christian solder, Christian pilgrim, in the midst of your 'contest' and your 'running' today, or in what *seems* the midst of it, for the end may all the while be just upon you, take heart often from the thought that even so for you, if you are true to the blessed Name, it shall one day be. The last care will have been felt and cast upon the Lord, the last exhausting effort will have been made, the last witness under difficulties borne, the last sorrow faced and entered, the last word written, the last word spoken. And then the one remaining thing will be to let the Lord, 'the Man at the Gate', lift thee in, and give thee rest."

BIHOP MOULE

Lord, when my heart gets tired and my soul gets weary, strengthen me with your grace.

Language of Love

This is how we know what love is: Jesus Christ laid down His life for us. And we ought to lay down our lives for our brothers.   I JOHN 3:16

June is the month of romance, but my husband's language of love doesn't include romantic walks under the moonlight, holding hands. Ken doesn't go for mushy sentiment. Watching a baseball game together is his idea of romance. But I'm not complaining. I've learned to appreciate his language of love, and along with it, an appreciation for baseball batting averages.

I've also learned the Lord's language of love. When I tell Jesus that I love him, it has nothing to do with romance. But passion? Yes! My love for Jesus is not a syrupy sentiment, but it is definitely zealous and fervent, spirited and intense. When I praise Him, I believe He deserves adoration filled with warmth and affection. When I sing to Him, I want the melody to come right from my heart. I could never love Him in an emotional vacuum.

This is the language of love between God and His creation. We should love Him this way because this is how He loves us. Jesus could never, would never lay His life down devoid of feeling. To love to the point of death is passion with a capital P! Talk about love that is fervent and spirited!

And here's the point of today's reading: *This* is the way we are to love our brothers and sisters.

Developing an artful language of love to the Lord will cost you something. It will cost you your pride and, most valued of all, your human logic. Throw your caution to the wind and invite the Spirit of God to fill your heart with the warmth and passion of praise.

Fill my heart with your language of love, Lord, and may I love others with the same warmth and affection I reserve for you.

Vive la Différence!

The Lord God said, "It is not good for the man to be alone. I will make a helper suitable for him." GENESIS 2:18

I like men. I like ministering alongside men, whether it's my husband, the executive director of our ministry, or the pastor or elders of our local church. And there's a good reason why.

The role of men and women in ministry is complementary. True enrichment for both Christian men and women comes when these roles are being fulfilled side by side. Why? A woman's ministry is primarily maternal in flavour and style. The man's, paternal. The natural role difference between, let's say, a mother and father in a family, permeates virtually all cultures and this marvellous and rich role difference should be reflected in the *cooperative* ministry of men and women in the Church.

That's why I enjoy working in partnership with male leaders. In such partnerships, the dynamics of the "helpmeet" relationship of Genesis 2:18 comes alive. I feel fulfilled. My husband or pastor or executive director feels fulfilled – all because we are following a calling which embraces us *both*.

❦

Women are gifted for and called to service in the Church, and the Church must properly value and use women's gifts. Oh, that we would see more women *and* men giving care for the weak, ministering the Word, nurturing families and children, visiting the sick, reaching prisoners . . . ad infinitum. The Church has too much to do without squabbling about differences. Let's enjoy our different roles and get on with ministry!

Thank you, Lord, that you made me who I am. Both men and women bear your image and are equal . . . yet we are so different. Help us to complement one another and glorify you as we do.

The African Queen

"The Queen of the South will rise at the judgment with this generation and condemn it; for she came from the ends of the earth to listen to Solomon's wisdom, and now one greater than Solomon is here." MATTHEW 12:42

The queen of Sheba had serious questions about God and His ways and His will. Not content to sit on her questions, she set out on a spiritual quest which took her on a journey more than a thousand miles over land and sea. It was a lengthy and dangerous trip, especially for a woman.

But the queen's search was not a mere intellectual exercise.

When the queen of Sheba heard about the fame of Solomon and his relation to the name of the Lord, she came to test him with hard questions . . . she came and talked with him about all that she had on her mind . . . Solomon answered all her questions. I KINGS 10:1, 3

If you have serious questions about God, His ways and His will, don't sit on your curiosity. Let your thirst for God take you on a journey of questioning. It's okay to have doubts and to wrestle with spiritual issues. And like the queen of Sheba who left Israel fully satisfied, God delights in giving answers to our hardest questions.

This African queen paid a high price in time, travel and trouble. How many of us are willing to seek after God in this way?

In Matthew 12:42 Jesus commends the queen of Sheba. Out of all the seekers in the Old Testament, our Lord picked this African woman as a model of spiritual thirst and hunger.

Jesus, you are the one greater than Solomon. If the king of Israel was so willing to satisfy the queen of Sheba, how much more willing you are to fulfil my spiritual thirst and hunger. May I find all of my answers in you, dear Lord.

God Sings

"The Lord your God is with you, he is mighty to save. He will take great delight in you, he will quiet you with his love, he will rejoice over you with singing."
ZEPHANIAH 3:17

When my heart is restless and my soul is downcast, I often surround myself with the calming strains of a favourite hymn. Sometimes when I want to express sheer praise, I'll pick a happy Psalm and just put it to any old tune that comes to mind. I sing to myself. I sing to God. But I'm astonished to think that God sings to me.

God sings! Do you think He sings all four parts at once? Maybe His music, so celestial and heavenly, resounds like a great choir. No doubt He has invented chords and discords, major and minor keys that our ears have never heard. And I'm touched that He rejoices over you and me with an actual melody. What's more, He quiets us with His loving song.

I have often thought of this when a beautiful hymn keeps rolling over and over in my mind. Always, its tune lifts my spirit and carries me through the day. No, I'm not playing a broken record in my head; the song, I'm convinced, is God's melody to me direct from His heart. He is rejoicing over me with singing, hallelujah, and all I need to do is listen and be inspired.

> O Love that wilt not let me go,
> I rest my weary soul in Thee;
> I give Thee back the life I owe,
> That in Thine ocean depths its flow
> May richer, fuller be.

Put a song in my heart today, Lord, a praise song or a hymn that you wish to sing to me. May I enjoy your melody and may I remember throughout the day that it is your song. It is your singing. My, you sing beautifully!

Faith that Pleases

And without faith it is impossible to please God, because anyone who comes to Him must believe that He exists and that He rewards those who earnestly seek Him. HEBREWS 11:6

How do we speak of our faith in God? What words would we choose to describe our faith in Him? "I stand for Jesus!" many would say, or, "I am firmly committed to the Lord!" Faith, to some, is best described as an allegiance to Christ, a kind of siding with Him and His cause. This, they feel, is faith.

I don't think so. Faith has little to do with commitment or allegiance. When we place our faith in Christ, we are not so much taking a stand for Him, as we are acknowledging the stand He takes for us. Faith is self-despairing trust in the Lord. It is coming to Him in empty-handed poverty. Faith is surrendering all, even our sense of duty, allegiance or commitment.

People of great faith are not measured by their shining commitment, but by the humbling degree to which they recognize how poor, absolutely dirt poor, they are in spirit. Their faith has power because they realize no good thing dwells within them. They bring to the Lord nothing but their open hands, ready to humbly receive whatever God in His mercy will give.

Faith means being sure of Christ's commitment to you, rather than your commitment to Him. Faith is having confidence in His love for you rather than your love for Him.

So if you want to place your faith in Christ, surrender all, everything to Him. This is faith that pleases God.

O

Dear Author and Perfecter of my faith, I come to you today empty-handed with open palms. I praise you for being the source and the wellspring of my faith. Please let me be strong . . . only in you.

JULY

God with a Flannel

Recently, a friend of mine had to stay in a hospital for two weeks. When I asked him what the most difficult part was about his long hospitalization, he shook his head and gramaced, "Bed baths! I hated having those nurses give me bed baths. I wish I could have done it myself."

You can sympathize with my friend, can't you? All of us feel a deep and profound aversion to being bathed by someone else. Personal cleansing is a routine we would really rather do ourselves. To have another approach us with soap and a flannel can be humiliating and embarrassing.

But listen to what David prayed:

Cleanse me with hyssop, and I shall be clean; wash me, and I shall be whiter than snow.   PSALM 51:7

At other times, David may have felt a reluctance about being bathed by someone else. But the "someone" David was now asking, was God. There came a time in David's life when he felt so soiled, so thoroughly dirtied by sin that he cried out to God, *"Cleanse me . . . wash me!"* He knew that this sort of cleansing was something he could never do for himself, and so he humbled himself before the Lord and presented to Him all of his embarrassing sins. To pray to be washed clean from sin requires humility. After all, a "spiritual washing" is a profoundly personal thing in an individual's life.

Almighty God, thank you for desiring to make me clean. For washing me of my sins, cleansing my heart and making me pure. I humble myself before you and present all the areas of my life that need to be made right. I'm grateful that you desire to do something so powerful and personal in my life as to make me spotless and stainless — and thank you for shedding your blood on the cross, your blood which washes me white as snow.

The People You Dislike

Do nothing out of selfish ambition or vain conceit, but in humility consider others better than yourselves.　　　　　　　PHILIPPIANS 2:3

When someone read that verse to me in the hospital, I replied, "Is that so? You mean that obnoxious jerk at the medical clinic who sits by the elevator, smokes like a chimney, and taunts me because I have to use a power wheelchair and he doesn't? I'm to consider him better than me? Loving God means . . . serving him?!"

My problem with my paralysis was wrapped up in my problem with others. Especially others with disabilities. Somewhere along the line I finally had to humbly nail every snobby sentiment to the cross and become obedient to death. Dying to self would open the door to loving, really loving God. Only then would my attitude toward other disabled people change; only then would I love and serve as the Lord did. Only then would I accept my own wheelchair.

Many years have passed since that revelation. Most of them I've spent serving God by serving the very people I used to dislike. I now enjoy bantering with the militant disabled activist. My heart breaks when I sit at the bedside of a ventilator-dependent quadriplegic. I relish a hug from someone who is blind. I'm inspired by the cerebral-palsied person who hangs onto God's grace despite a dreary routine in a residential facility. I marvel at the grace of a world-class wheelchair athlete.

Passion for God will result in passion for people.

Deep and abiding devotion to Jesus will give you a new perspective on people you dislike. Affection for God that is warm and heartfelt will give boundless joy in difficult relationships. Fervent love for the Lord will give you love for needy people. Love God, and you can't help but love people.

Lord, give me passion for you!

He Delights over You

*The Lord will take delight in you . . . As a bridegroom rejoices over his bride,
so will your God rejoice over you.* ISAIAH 62:4–5

I asked my husband, Ken, on our tenth wedding anniversary, "What were you thinking on the day we married?"

His answer delighted me. He said, "I woke up so early that morning, excited that I would soon see you in your wedding gown. And even though I knew there would be hundreds of people in the church, I knew my eyes would be for you, only. In fact, I'll never forget that wonderful feeling when I saw you wheeling down the aisle in your chair, you looked so beautiful."

Hearing those words gave me so much pleasure. And just think. This is the way God feels toward us. It says so in Isaiah 62:4–5. Remember, Jesus wants us to love Him passionately and single-heartedly; but He also wants to remind us that His love for us is warm, pure and passionate.

We can only catch a glimpse of this kind of passion on this side of eternity. But one day when we, the bride of Christ, are presented to our Saviour, the Bridegroom, we will be caught up in raptures of delight. Nothing will please Jesus more than to see His bride presented to Him pure and blameless.

◄§

The Lord also says to you in Isaiah 42:1, *"Here is my servant whom I uphold, my chosen one in whom I delight."* God takes great delight in you. You give Him great joy. He finds pleasure and satisfaction in your worship and praise. And your obedience brings a smile to His face. Love Him today with all your heart. After all, every day His heart is full of love for you.

Dear Lord, I love you so much. More so, I'm glad you love me. From my heart, thank you.

Not One Ray of Light

Let him who walks in the dark, who has no light, trust in the name of the Lord and rely on his God.   ISAIAH 50:10

One summer, my family and I travelled to see a gigantic cave called Carlsbad Caverns in the southwest corner of the United States. I clasped my mother's hand as the tour guide led our little group down into the cold, dark earth. When we reached the bottom of the pit, our guide turned out the overhead lamps so we could see, just for a moment, how thick the darkness really was below the surface of the earth.

Click! I gasped as oppressive and utter blackness enveloped me. Far beyond the reaches of natural rays of light, I could not even see my hand in front of my face. Panic seized me and I thrust my hand into the darkness to reach for my mother. In an instant, her hand was around mine, washing away my fear and anxiety. "Joni," she said, "you're safe, I would never lose you."

❧

You probably have days that seem like deep, cavernous holes. Days when you can't find your way because of the darkness. You search for a single ray of light and see absolutely nothing.

Don't be alarmed. Remember your walk is not by sight, but by faith. And God, according to Isaiah 50:10, agrees with you: There are times when it's hard to see even a single ray of brightness in your circumstances. But even in the blackness, God promises you will find Him. Close. Near. He says, "You're safe, I would never lose you."

Lord of Light, thank you that you are the one who brightens any darkness. You are always close and near. Bless you for being ever-present, no matter how dark the circumstances. You, Lord, are my light!

Jesus . . . Taking a Stand

Jesus entered the temple area and drove out all who were buying and selling there. He overturned the tables of the money changers and the benches of those selling doves. "It is written," He said to them, " 'My house will be called a house of prayer,' but you are making it a 'den of robbers'."

MATTHEW 21:12–13

It's easy to picture a kindly, loving Jesus. We've had lots of help on that score from religious artists down through the centuries. The Lord sentimentally pictured with children, lambs and birds. You can almost hear the organ music.

But it's challenging to visualize an angry – violently angry – Jesus Christ. You can almost see Him overturning cash registers, grabbing the moneychangers by the scruff of their necks and heaving them out the temple door on their self-righteous backsides.

Jesus, full of fury, took a stand. No one, He asserted, was going to make His Father's house into a haven for con-men and rip-off artists. Jesus ripped the mask off hypocrisy. He exposed dark recesses of the hearts of greedy, materialistic men. Jesus squared off against sin.

We need to fully meditate on portions of Scripture such as Matthew 21 in order to get a more complete picture of the way the Lord dealt with sin. If we think that Jesus always confronted sin gently, as with the woman at the well or the one caught in adultery, remember that Matthew 21 records that He drove out *all* who were buying and selling – that includes innocent townspeople who had come to merely purchase doves for offerings.

Friend of sinners, don't be gentle with any sin that I might be safeguarding in my life. Expose the dark recesses in my heart, square off against my sin and uproot it out of my life.

Jesus . . . After the Anger

The blind and the lame came to him at the temple, and he healed them.
MATTHEW 21:14

Yesterday, we heard the Lord's angry shouts echo off the temple walls as He cleansed His Father's house. We could almost hear the grunts, the pushing and shoving, the crack of the whip. Jesus invaded and advanced, letting the people around Him feel the hot breath of His anger.

But in the heartbeat between two short verses, Matthew 21, verses 13 and 14, Jesus immediately turned His attention to the blind and the lame to heal and help them with tender compassion. He turned a face as hard as steel to religious phonies and materialistic merchants, then barely missing a beat, He smiled encouragement at those who reached to Him in simple faith.

These several verses paint a stunning picture of our Saviour. In both cases, Jesus was meeting the need of the moment. In one verse it involved squaring off against sin. The next verse, ministering to suffering people who stood nearby. Either response requires the resources of fearlessness and courage. Christ could never be accused of being one-dimensional.

The Lord could have opted for the easy way out in the temple courtyard. In front of the merchants, He could have played it safe and kept His opinions to Himself. With the blind and the lame, He could have retreated and ignored their plight.

But it takes courage and fearlessness to rattle the status quo. Sometimes it means speaking out against something, other times it means speaking up for someone.

Lord Jesus, I praise you that you always bring glory to the Father whenever you respond to the needs of people. How glorious that you always grate against my self-will, exposing my sin. And how glorious that you show tenderness and compassion when I hurt. I praise you that you are far from being one-dimensional and predictable!

What a Friend

"I no longer call you servants . . . I have called you friends, for everything that I learned from my Father I have made known to you."   JOHN 15:15

I recall times long ago in the hospital when Jesus came through as my friend. There were times when He was my one and only comfort during dark lonely nights after visiting hours. Friends or family weren't allowed in, so I soothed my pain by imagining a visit from another friend.

I pictured Jesus walking through the open doors of my hospital ward, His figure a silhouette against the light from the nurses' station down the hall. My mind's eye saw Him walking softly past the beds of my sleeping roommates. I'd comfort myself, imagining Him standing at my bedside. The sharp pang of loneliness was eased as I thought of questions He might ask, "Tell me what happened in therapy today. Was it nice to see your sister earlier in the evening? Tell me all about it."

Talking with Jesus strengthened my confidence in Him, a friend who would ultimately see me through months of suicidal depression at the prospect of permanent paralysis. He was the one who lent a sympathetic ear, His eye contact never faltering.

What a friend I have in Jesus. But I wonder . . . what kind of a friend does He have in me?

Too often we stay at an arm's length distance, pulling back from the full intensity of an intimate friendship with the Lord. We satisfy ourselves with "less" when it comes to our relationship with Him. But His love explodes our selfishness when we hear Him say, "I have called you friends." His love breaks our hearts as only an intimate friend can.

What a friend I have in you, Lord Jesus.
All my sins and griefs you bear.
What a privilege to carry everything to you, my Lord, in prayer.

Guard Your Words

Set a guard over my mouth, O Lord; keep watch over the door of my lips.

PSALM 141:3

It happens so often. You're itching to say something, and before you double-check your words against the Holy Spirit, you let the sentence slip. You drop a precisely-timed phrase that manipulates. Toss a few flirting words that entice. Aim a verbal barb that stings. Send a signal that you dare not be crossed.

Whatever the message, you've hit the target with your words. Someone's reputation has been slandered. A heart has become divided. Feelings have been crushed. A testimony is compromised. A spirit is badly bruised.

Someone once prayed, "Before I move, before I speak, perfect wisdom I will seek." That's good advice for the Christian who ignores the Spirit's prompting and proceeds to be slow to hear and swift to speak. Matthew Henry builds on that prayer when he says, "Since my lips are the door to my words, let grace keep that door, that no word may go out which in any way dishonours God or hurts others."

And in case you still think a few subtle words can't do that much harm, let the following serve as a warning:

The tongue also is a fire, a world of evil among the parts of the body. It corrupts the whole person, sets the whole course of his life on fire, and is itself set on fire by hell.

JAMES 3:6

✑

Proverbs 13:3 is another reminder: *"He who guards his lips guards his life, but he who speaks rashly will come to ruin."* Your mind, will and emotions are dangerously exposed to ruin when you say things with an impure or hurtful motive. So before you speak, ask yourself, "Will what I say hurt or help? Will it glorify God? Would I be ashamed if others heard?"

Lord, before I move, before I speak, perfect wisdom I will seek.

The School of Obedience

During the days of Jesus' life on earth, He offered up prayers and petitions with loud cries and tears to the one who could save Him from death, and He was heard because of His reverent submission. Although He was a son, He learned obedience from what He suffered and, once made perfect, He became the source of eternal salvation for all who obey Him. HEBREWS 5:7–9

Although Jesus wept and cried loudly, wrestled and struggled, He obeyed. In fact, He *learned obedience* from what He suffered. Whether or not obedience came naturally (or supernaturally) to Him is for theologians to argue; what is important to note is that our Lord submitted Himself to the school of obedience.

When we become Christians, God enrols us in the same school. Trouble is, we want to have our cake and eat it, too. Like the person who enjoys the weather of Florida that has a terrific scholarship to a university in New England, we all face the crisis of having to decide between two worlds when we would dearly love to live in both.

That's why obedience must be learned. If Jesus was schooled in obedience from what He suffered, shall the servant be greater than His Master? At times we may be like the young boy who, when disciplined by his father, complains, "He's making me suffer because he doesn't want me having any fun!" Actually, what God is doing is getting our minds off the toys and games of this world and teaching us tough obedience in preparation for the next.

Avoid all appearances of evil. Let no unwholesome word come out of your mouth. Count others better than yourself. Forgive seventy times seven. Don't let the sun set on your anger. In everything give thanks.

Lord, thank you for setting an example of obedience. Help me to see that obeying you is not following a list of do's and don'ts, but of following . . . you.

I Want to Go Home

After a week of fun-filled activities at a recent retreat, I listened as the microphone was passed from family to family, each tearfully sharing how wonderful the time had been. Some talked of meeting new friends. Others, of the games, music and hikes. A few said how they wished the week could go on and on.

Then little red-haired, freckle-faced Jeff raised his hand. He had Down's syndrome and had won the hearts of many people at the retreat. People had been captivated by his winsome smile and joyful spirit. Everyone leaned forward to hear his words. Jeff grabbed the mike and kept it short and sweet as he bellowed: "Let's go home!" He smiled, bowed, and handed back the microphone. Everyone roared with laughter.

His mother told me later that, even though Jeff thoroughly immersed himself in the week's festivities, he missed his daddy back home.

I identify with Jeff. The good things in this world are pleasant enough, but would we *really* wish for it to go on as it is? I don't think so. The good things in this life are merely omens of even greater, more glorious things yet to come. God would not have us mistake this world for a permanent dwelling. And I'm with Jeff. It's a good life, but I am looking forward to going home. I miss my Dad.

But in keeping with His promise we are looking forward to a new heaven and a new earth, the home of righteousness. II PETER 3:13

"Home is where your heart is." Never was a saying more true. For when Jesus captures your heart, you are then able to look forward to your home of righteousness.

Lord of my heart, capture my affections this day and hold me fast with your love. Turn my heart ever increasingly toward you and so I shall long for a new heaven and a new earth, the home of righteousness.

God-watching

On my bed I remember you; I think of you through the watches of the night.
PSALM 63:6

As a child, my favourite part about visiting the beach was going to the boardwalk. After a day in the ocean, we'd shower, dress and run up to the boardwalk for ice cream cones. My sisters and I would sit on a bench, lick our cones and watch all the people stroll by. Kids with candy floss. Lovers ambling arm-in-arm. Older ladies in flowered dresses with parasols. People-watching was the neatest part.

I still enjoy looking at people, thinking about where they live, wondering where they work, and if they're happy. Studying people, for me, is a habit.

Wouldn't it be great if we were as conscious about studying God as we were people. Watching Him, wondering about Him, looking closely at what makes Him who He is, and just . . . enjoying Him.

Charles Spurgeon said, "To contemplate God is a subject so vast, that our thoughts are lost in His immensity, so deep that our pride is drowned in His infinity . . . No subject of study will tend to humble the mind more than thoughts of God. But while contemplating God humbles the mind, it also expands the mind. Nothing will so enlarge your intellect or magnify your entire soul than a devout, earnest investigation of God."

As today's Scripture suggests, perhaps the best time to contemplate God is on your bed, even through the watches of the night. Without noise and distractions, and with your mind at rest, your thoughts will become lost in His immensity. Even Psalm 4:4 suggests, *"When you are on your beds, search your hearts and be silent."*

Lord, I picture you walking along the beach with your disciples . . . I see you holding children in your arms . . . I imagine you touching the eyes of the blind. You are truly lovely to watch and behold!

A Taste of Hell

"But the subjects of the kingdom will be thrown outside, into the darkness, where there will be weeping and gnashing of teeth." MATTHEW 8:12

Jesus' teaching about hell is meant to strike terror in our hearts, warning us that if heaven is better than we could dream, so hell will be worse than we can imagine. Hell warns us to seek heaven.

When I was first injured, doctors pumped me up with powerful drugs to get rid of the infection that was raging through my body. When nurses turned me face down on the Stryker frame, I could only see the floor and people's feet. Horrified, I saw the ugly cloven hooves of demons where there should have been shoes of nurses. The feet of friends were webbed with claws. I screamed at the nurses not to flip me face up, fearful that I would see ugly monsters. But when they turned me over, I was shocked to find everything normal.

What a hell. Looking back, I know my terror was drug-induced. But those frightening images remained with me even through subsequent years of backsliding and bitterness. In fact, during those years when I teetered on the brink of rejecting Christ entirely, scary cloven hooves would flash in my mind. For me, it was a warning.

We all go through hell now and then. But our hellish moments on earth can't even begin to touch the hell that awaits unbelievers. So why should we complain if God decides to give us a tiny infinitesimal taste of what actual hell *could* be like? Rather than be angry, be thankful that Jesus saves.

There's nothing you could possibly be put through on earth that can even begin to feel like the real hell. So every time you think circumstances are hellish, breathe a sigh of relief that Jesus has saved you from the real thing.

Thank you, Jesus, that you've saved me not only for heaven, but from hell.

Learning Humility

He guides the humble in what is right and teaches them his way.

PSALM 25:9

My friend Carole Danzig was a Phi Beta Kappa from Stanford University, the wife of a doctor and mother of four gifted children. Carole was also given the "thorn in the flesh" of Lou Gehrig's disease. She became a quadriplegic and endured the slow deterioration and loss of all her muscles. She typed the following words on a computer by clicking a sensor with her teeth . . .

"When I want something, frequently no one understands. When I know how to do something better, it doesn't matter. When I don't want to do something, I'm overruled. I cry and then I remember our Lord's words to Peter − that when he was old someone would lead him where he did not want to go.

"When I enter a roomful of people − Sunday services, for example − I always send up an arrow prayer: 'Please, Lord, don't let me drool.' But the answer is always the same. I drool. Finally this morning I could not stand it any more. 'Lord, people will think I have lost my mind as well as my body. They will pat me on the head and talk to me as if I'm two years old.'

"And Jesus answered, 'And how do people talk to a two-year-old? With love, with concern, with joy. Not so bad.' But I replied, 'They will talk to me in words of one or two syllables and short sentences.' Once again Jesus replied, 'You mean like "Blessed are the poor in spirit for theirs is the kingdom of heaven." '

"O Lord, thank you for the reminder. My drooling is a help to make me humble."

◆

I praise you, Lord, for the marvellous grace which sustains brothers and sisters who suffer greatly. May we learn to see our own "handicaps" as opportunities to humble ourselves so that you might lift us up.

Shortwave Praying

For the Lord takes delight in His people . . . let the saints rejoice in this honour and sing for joy on their beds. PSALM 149:4–5

This verse is "me". And my bed is where I pray best. Because my paralysis forces me to lie down early in the evening, I sometimes invite a friend over to sit on the edge of my bed and pray with me. While my husband is in the TV room tracking the latest football game, my girlfriend and I will prop ourselves up with pillows, make a prayer list, and intercede for the world.

Last week she sprang a surprise and brought a small shortwave radio. A window to the world, she called it. She flicked it on and tuned in Trans World Radio from the Caribbean. Another jiggle of the knob and we picked up someone leading a Bible study over station HCJB in Ecuador. A little more fiddling and we pulled in the BBC from Hong Kong. Together, my friend and I tuned in to the world.

Literally within the walls of my room were voices from around the globe. We covered the planet, yet didn't budge beyond my bed. That shortwave radio serves as a good lesson in prayer. In fact, the people around the world for whom we prayed that night seemed just beyond my bedroom walls. And you know what? They were.

Just as the voices of people around the world reached us through shortwave, my prayers, immediate and instant, were touching others. That very second, godly grace was being applied as I prayed and I didn't even have to leave my room.

Lord, the world is smaller than I realize and my prayers, like shortwaves, go further than I imagine. Even though my intercessions for others seem so faint, thank you for amplifying prayer with your power.

Restitution

What the locust swarm has left the great locusts have eaten; what the great locusts have left the young locusts have eaten; what the young locusts have left other locusts have eaten . . . Be glad, O people of Zion, rejoice in the Lord your God . . . "I will repay you for the years the locusts have eaten."

JOEL 1:4; 2:23, 25

I recently took inventory of my spiritual growth, beginning with that November afternoon in 1964 when I confessed Christ, all the way to the present. As I marked off the milestones, I came across chunks of years tht were spiritual wastelands.

In my early teens I memorized the words of entire Beatle albums, but memorizing Scripture was a bore. I turned down a summer missions trip because I didn't want to be away from my boyfriend. I don't need to divulge the sordid details of how we ended up spending our time. Then came my accident in 1967. More years of spiritual dryness as I sneered at nurses and generally took my anger out on my family who faithfully visited the hospital.

But even after my accident and long after I got my spiritual act together, there were more wasted years. Hidden sins that I covered up for months. A habit of prayer that I let die for almost a year. Bible reading that I ignored for ages, it seemed. Worthless years. Futile. Wasted.

At the close of my spiritual inventory, I grieved to think I would never recover, never redeem what had been lost in my life. But my grief lasted only a moment. God brought to mind the promise of Joel 2:25! The Lord promises my losses shall be repaired. He will make good on the damage I've done. And like the father who more than made up for all that his prodigal son had squandered, God vows He will restore our loss. That's what restitution is all about.

Restore my wasted years, O Lord!

Making Hay

Ever been overwhelmed with trying to get jobs done? Too much to do. Not enough time. Not enough energy. I'm sure some farmers feel that way as they approach harvest time. Imagine how a farmer feels when all of a sudden one morning he realizes that his crop is ready. He's been hoping for a dry clear day for months, fighting against diseases, cursing weeds, and now suddenly the moment arrives.

The solution? The farmer can't hope for more time, he can't cut the losses and only harvest a little and he can't destroy a part of the field. He needs help. He quickly recruits hands and machines to bring in the harvest. At the risk of projecting human emotions on God, consider how He "felt" when he looked at the harvest of souls:

"The harvest is plentiful but the workers are few. Ask the Lord of the harvest, therefore, to send out workers into his harvest field."   MATTHEW 9:37–8

I think Christ spoke those words with great emotion, excitement and pain. Because of His love for souls, you know the Lord felt pain at seeing all the work. You know there was a sense of a farmer's urgency.

What was Jesus' solution? He looked at his twelve disciples and realized they weren't enough. Haymaking of souls would require more hands and feet and voices. So He said, *"Pray for workers."* Beseech, beg, implore and ask with emotion. Pray for workers!

The disciples did. They got an answer. And you are it. You are the haymaker Christ commanded to be prayed for. Can you resist the prayers of the disciples and the scores of saints through time? Don't you dare. Make some hay today!

◄§►

Lord, grant me a measure of urgency and even panic at the thought of the harvest. There are so many people to reach. I pray for myself as a haymaker. And I pray for others to join me that the crops be brought in on time.

The Faithful God

Know therefore that the Lord your God is God; He is the faithful God, keeping His covenant of love to a thousand generations of those who love Him and keep His commands.   DEUTERONOMY 7:9

The sun is shining brightly with not a cloud in the sky. The birds are chirping. No disagreements hanging over your head. No pressures. All bills paid. Nothing but clear sailing. Little wonder you find yourself saying out loud, "Lord, this is great. You are wonderful!"

True, we get excited about God when circumstances are delightful, when the weather invigorates us, bills are paid, the medical check-up goes fine, and nobody is holding anything over our heads. When things are good, God is good. If things are bad, then God is off in Tasmania taking care of little devils, or in the Middle East setting the stage for Armageddon.

We are so prone to let our circumstances – whether good or bad – dictate our view of God. But time and again the Bible tells us God is faithful. He is not just *a* faithful God, but *the* faithful God. He is the same steadfast and good Father yesterday, today, and for ever. Scripture alone should be our frame of reference for who the Lord really is, for circumstances do not a good theology make.

❧

Remember this lesson the next time you are quick to tell God how wonderful He is on a golden morning or a peaceful fireside evening. Whether the day is grand or gloomy, *every* day is a great day to give praise to God.

Why are you downcast, oh my soul? Why so disturbed within me? Put your hope in God, for I will yet praise Him, my Sviour and my God. You are God my stronghold . . . send forth your light and your truth, let them guide me to you, my joy and my delight.

The Forgetfulness of God

Remember not the sins of my youth and my rebellious ways; according to your love remember me, for you are good, O Lord. PSALM 25:7

Poor memories are a part of the human condition. And so when God tells us he will remember our sins no more, I'm puzzled. How could God possibly forget? That's my job!

But He does. And His forgetting of my sin is a complete removal from His knowledge of every sin you and I have committed.

Then why do we feel so bad about our past sins? Because we confuse sin with its impression. Got a notepad nearby? Let me show you how this can be so. Write the word "sin" on the page. Press hard. Now tear off that sheet of paper, crumble it up, and throw it across the room. That's how God forgets your sin.

Now take your pencil and rub it on the new page at an angle, back and forth, over the same location where you wrote. And guess what. The ghost of the word "sin" appears.

That's what our flawed memories do. We go back over the deep impression left by transgressions in our life and we feel just as guilty. It's as if the sin never left. But be encouraged, the impression of sin is not the same thing as sin. And with David you can cry out, *"Remember thou me! I can't forget my scars, it seems, Lord. But you have forgotten their cause. Look upon me with loving, kind eyes."*

It's your choice. Will you continue to work over forgiven sin as with a pencil? Or will you let the Holy Spirit work His lovingkindness?

Lord, my sins are lost somewhere in an unreachable sea. You are greatly to be praised for such an act of sovereign forgetfulness. Keep Satan from bringing to mind my transgression through the impression of sin that I see in my life.

Who's Important Here?

Then they came to Jericho. As Jesus and His disciples, together with a large crowd, were leaving the city, a blind man, Bartimaeus (that is, the Son of Timaeus), was sitting by the roadside begging. When he heard that it was Jesus of Nazareth, he began to shout, "Jesus, Son of David, have mercy on me!" Many rebuked him and told him to be quiet, but he shouted all the more.

MARK 10:46–8

When it comes to the obnoxious, Bartimaeus would take the prize. He must have carried on and made quite a scene because it says *many* rebuked him. But instead of putting a lid on it, Bartimaeus yelled all the more.

The blind man's tenacity and insistence caused the Lord to stop. But at that point, Jesus did not address Bartimaeus. First, He had a thing or two to say to the people who were trying to shove the blind man aside. Jesus tells them to call to Bartimaeus and then bring him forward. Boy, did those people change their tune fast. Suddenly, the guy was given the VIP treatment. *"Cheer up!"* they said to Bartimaeus.

Once these people understood that Jesus thought this poor handicapped person was important, once they realized the Lord's priorities, their whole attitude toward the obnoxious social outcast switched from negative to positive.

Handicapped people in wheelchairs may track dirt on the church carpet. Homeless people might leave trash in the stairwell at the back of the sanctuary. Runaway teenagers who come to Sunday service in torn jeans and shaved heads may leave a bad smell in the pew. Do these people seem obnoxious? Maybe. But read Mark 10:46–8 to see how Jesus would handle the situation.

Lord, I love the fact that after Bartimaeus was healed, he followed you along the road. Help me to bring your healing touch to those the world casts aside.

Change the Things You Can

"The Spirit of the Lord will come upon you in power . . . and you will be changed into a different person."   I SAMUEL 10:6

I once visited a friend in a nursing home who was feeling depressed about conditions there. When I wheeled into her room, I noticed she *was* discouraged. I also noticed a plaque over her bed: *God grant me the serenity to accept the things I cannot change, the courage to change the things I can, and the wisdom to know the difference.*

I asked a few questions to help her open up. "You wouldn't believe the rotten care I receive," she said. "These people aren't tending to my problems and the nurses don't turn me properly at night."

After quite a while, it was my turn. I suggested ideas such as talking to the nursing supervisor together, or raising money to purchase a better mattress. I suggested we write a letter to the nurses' council or post a notice over her bed stating clearly how my friend wanted to be turned at night. We could confront her doctor with a second opinion on her health problems. We could get her family involved. Lots of things!

But with every suggestion, my friend shook her head "no". After hearing thirty minutes of excuses, I decided to talk straight. I motioned to the plaque and said, "You know, in the last six months you've been doing a good job of accepting the things you cannot change. You've laid in this bed and stuck it out without causing a ruckus. But now you need more work on the second part of that prayer. You, my friend, need courage to change the things you can."

❧

There is great honour in embracing trials, but remember God gives them to create change.

God, give me the courage to change the things I should. And give me the wisdom to accept the things you don't want changed.

Infinite Love

God is love. Whoever lives in love lives in God, and God in him. Love is made complete among us so that we will have confidence on the day of judgment, because in this world we are like Him.   I JOHN 4:16–17

More than grains of sand or stars in the sky – surely that's how many people have lived on the earth. And that God has loved and continues to love every one is astounding. How could there be enough divine love to go round? Because we're touching on such astronomical numbers, perhaps God only loves the world in a general sense.

Not so. God's love is infinite. Spurgeon defines it this way, "In maths, if you divide an infinite number by any other number, no matter how large, you still get an infinite result. Jesus' love is infinite, and even though it is divided up for every person on earth, His love is still infinitely poured out on each one of us." As today's verse says, love is made *complete* among us.

That's enough love to take away your guilt, dissipate your anger, fill up your loneliness and assure you of heaven. Love so infinite will more than meet your desires and longings. What's more, His love is for you to give away.

God's love is like trigonometry, for if you divide love, it will always multiply. Give love away, and it will always come back to you with its arms full. As someone has said, "Throw it away, empty your pockets, shake the basket, turn the glass upside down, and tomorrow you will have more love than ever."

Remember, God's love may be divided up for an infinite number of people on earth, but because His love is eternal and without end, He can still infinitely pour out His love on you. Just for you.

Oh, how He loves you, oh how He loves me. Oh, how He loves you and me.

Everything . . . or Some Things?

In Him we were also chosen, having been predestined according to the plan of Him who works out everything in conformity with the purpose of His will, in order that we, who were the first to hope in Christ, might be for the praise of His glory. EPHESIANS 1:11

Did you catch that? God works out *everything* that happens so that it perfectly conforms with His will and purpose. In fact, Ephesians 1:11 sounds very much like Romans 8:28. Whether it's "everything", or "all things", God uses triumphs and tragedies in order that we, who hope in Christ, might find our perfect fulfilment in Him.

Some people don't like that word *everything*. We reason that only some things or occasional things, or things we can explain or understand, actually conform to His purpose for us. Does God, in fact, mean everything?

Yes He does. "Everything" includes the heart-twisting pain and the accidents that turn our lives upside down. If it were only the easy-to-accept inconveniences or the problems we can saunter over, then God would not be sovereign. Our great God, however, takes delight in working all things, yes, everything so that it conforms with His will.

A verse like Ephesians 1:11 can be hard medicine to swallow for those who are genuinely facing heart-wrenching pain or an accident or illness which alters the course of life. But, in fact, believers can find ultimate comfort in knowing that their pain is *not* out of control. It is *not* beyond God's plan. You are *not* the brunt of some divine cruel joke where it concerns problems in your life. Just knowing God works out everything – not just some things – for His purpose can shore up peace and hope.

Great God, I commit to you everything that happens in my life today. May my patient response be for the praise of your glory.

Smile, God Likes You

For the Lord takes delight in His people; He crowns the humble with salvation.
PSALM 149:4

Could you imagine being invited to a party at Buckingham Palace where the invitation read:

> The pleasure of your company
> is desired because the host
> just wants to be with you

Hard to imagine, isn't it?

God would invite you to such a party because He doesn't just love you. He likes you. It's a subtle difference but it is important to know that He feels both emotions toward us. Many of my disabled friends have people who love them. Such people help with babysitting, or cleaning, or transportation. Such love is invaluable. But disabled people also need to know that they are liked. They need people to say that they want to play chess, shop, or just talk.

Perhaps you've pictured the love of God but never saw His pleasure with you. You've only pictured God going out for fish and chips with Paul or Isaiah but never with you. Or you pictured being on the perimeter of a circle while Jesus and the disciples contemplated the universe.

No! God is pleased with *you*. According to the epistles, you were called according to God's pleasure, redeemed according to God's pleasure, and you work His will for His pleasure. The smile of God is for you and it is as wide and bright as His love is deep.

Lord, I've never considered your affection and desire for my company. I've been busy assuming that your face has been in an eternal scowl since Adam sinned. But now I know you love me and are pleased with me. May I live joyfully knowing such pleasure.

Do not worry about what to wear to a party with God. He tells us that He "beautifies the afflicted with salvation".

Near the Cross

When Jesus had again crossed over by boat to the other side of the lake, a large crowd gathered round Him.   MARK 5:21

Jesus never enjoyed much elbow room during His public ministry. There was always a multitude, pushing and shoving to get close. When He taught in the temple, there was hardly space to breathe. When He taught in a home, people stood wall-to-wall, spilling out into the front yard and hanging from the roof. And when He tried to escape the crowd in a boat, He dropped anchor on the other side only to find another horde awaiting Him. No room for Jesus – His life even began that way at the crowded inn.

There was one place, however, where Jesus had more than enough room, almost too much space. It was a place where nobody was shoving to get close, no one wanted a ringside seat. There was plenty of room near the cross.

Sadly, it's true today. Many Christians are satisfied to remain at a safe distance from the cross. Yet if we are to see real and lasting change in our lives, if we are to reckon ourselves dead to sin, it requires keeping near the cross.

> Near the cross! O Lamb of God,
> Bring its scenes before me;
> Help me walk from day to day with its shadows o'er me.
> In the cross, in the cross
> Be my glory ever,
> Till my raptured soul shall find rest, beyond the river.

❧

Lord Jesus, you surrendered to hell's worst that I might attain heaven's best. You were tormented that I might be comforted, and made a shame that I might inherit glory. You entered darkness that I might have eternal light. Praise you for dying . . . that I might live for ever!

Vengeance

Do not take revenge, my friends, but leave room for God's wrath, for it is written:
"It is mine to avenge; I will repay," says the Lord.   ROMANS 12:19

God has given us many good gifts. Gifts of health, food, work, friends, and especially the gift of Himself. His gifts to us overflow in abundance, meeting our needs far more than we realize. There are two things, however, that God has not given us.

One is vengeance. God says in so many words, "Vengeance belongs to me and me alone." He is reminding us to keep hands off when it comes to backbiting or evening the score. You may say "vengeance is sweet," but God says "Vengeance is mine."

⊱

God has good reasons for warning you against getting even or retaliating against a friend. He knows that revenge can too easily infect you with anger, resentment, or a spirit of bitterness. He also wants you to know that it is not your place to judge and condemn another person. Leave judgment to God.

How wonderful to think, though, that one day on the other side of eternity, we who are saints will judge the world with the Lord Jesus (I Corinthians 6:2). Until that time, leave in God's hands what is rightfully his. Vengeance is the Lord's, not yours.

Judge of all the world, I am so grateful that you have given to me so many beautiful gifts — all things are mine and I acknowledge that I have enough. I do not want a spirit of revenge for vengeance is yours, and yours alone. Forgive me for retaliating against people around me. I leave judgment to you until that day when you will invite all the saints to judge the world in righteousness and truth.

Glory

"I am the Lord; that is my name! I will not give my glory to another or my praise to idols."   ISAIAH 42:8

Yesterday, we learned that of the many gifts God bestows, there are two things He has not given us. One is vengeance. The other is glory. Glory belongs to God alone, not to theologians or to church leaders, or even well-known saints of the past or present.

Unfortunately, we often grab glory for ourselves, proudly receiving pats on the back for a spiritual job well done.

There is, however, another way to deal with the praise of men. Corrie ten Boom, survivor of Nazi concentration camps, accepted worldwide accolades for her efforts to protect Jews during the World War II occupation of Holland. She often commented that she was able to accept each compliment as though it were a rosebud, gathering many words of blessings during the course of the day. Then in the evening, she presented God with a big bouquet of praise. Corrie knew that glory, praise and honour belonged only to the Lord.

But here's the amazing part. Although glory is God's and God's alone, He has told us in 1 Peter 5:1 that one day we will share in the glory to be revealed. How incredible of God to delight in having His glory revealed to us on that special day. Truly, He has given us all things.

God of glory, all praise and honour belong to you. You alone are worthy of adoration and worship. You give your glory and praise to no one and I am pleased today to bow before your throne and ascribe all glory and honour to you. It amazes me, God, that one day in heaven I will share in your glory — thank you for that indescribable gift. Until that day, I glory and boast in you, and you alone.

Salvation's Dirty Work

"Bring the bull to the front of the Tent of Meeting, and Aaron and his sons shall lay their hands on its head. Slaughter it in the Lord's presence at the entrance to the Tent of Meeting. Take some of the bull's blood and put it on the horns of the altar with your finger, and pour out the rest of it at the base of the altar."
EXODUS 29:10–12

Not a pretty picture, this verse. The bellowing of a bull being bound against its will. The brutal butchering with a knife. Dipping hands into the warm blood. What a gory and offensive scene. The bloody slaughter of the sacrificial animal was not even carried out behind the Tent of Meeting, hidden from view, but in the front for everyone to see.

Other ancient cultures employed animal sacrifices, but only in Israel was the blood of a sacrificial animal central in worship. Leviticus 17:11 reminds us that *"It is the blood that makes atonement for one's life."*

The shedding of blood is the "dirty work" of salvation. Just as there was nothing pretty about Old Testament sacrifices, the shedding of blood sealing the New Covenant was just as offensive. The brutal crucifixion of Christ was not hidden from the view of men, but on a hill in broad daylight for all to see.

In the Old Testament, the worshipper, who with hands placed on the head of the living animal saw it killed and its blood sprinkled, was being graphically shown that sin called for the surrender of a life. When we look at the cross, we discover a graphic picture of what remission for our sin demands – the surrender of the Lamb of God.

Lord Jesus, show me the offence of my sin when I look at the crown of thorns, your pierced hands and feet and bruised body. My guilt and sin must truly be awful to demand such a precious price as that of your blood.

Meekness

"Blessed are the meek, for they will inherit the earth."   MATTHEW 5:5

In this age of flaunting personal rights, meekness is not a valued character trait. In fact, to those who are bent on demanding what's rightfully theirs, meekness is a character flaw. Why? The meek person is the one who yields personal rights. But because of that, he is the one who lacks anger.

Anger erupts when we feel our rights are being violated. The right to be accepted. The right to express your opinions without being jumped on. The right to privacy. The right to earn and spend money. But when we dedicate our time, our holdings, even ourselves to the Lord, we transfer those rights to Him. He, then, owns our time and possessions. He owns us.

And God will always take care of His own. He will direct us on how to use His time, spend His money, or manage His possessions. Using His things will be considered a privilege, not a right! The result? Lack of anger. After all, how can you be angry over something that's not yours?

❧

Thanking God whatever the outcome is the key to determine if you have fully yielded a personal right. If you demonstrate meekness, that is lack of anger, when someone hurts you then you have successfully yielded your rights to God. Are you afraid of not owning anything, even your own life? Don't worry, one day the meek shall inherit the earth!

Someone once said, "Meekness is a willingness to allow others to say about me the same things I readily acknowledge before God. Self-protection and self-sacrifice are mutually exclusive. They cannot coexist."

Lord, you willingly yielded your rights to the Father and became the most meek and humble man who ever lived. Help me to humble myself before you as I give you my time, my possessions . . . my life.

Trials and Temptations

Blessed is the man who perseveres under trial, because when he has stood the test, he will receive the crown of life that God has promised to those who love Him. When tempted, no-one should say, "God is tempting me." For God cannot be tempted by evil, nor does He tempt anyone. JAMES 1:12–13

Trials and temptations may sound like one and the same, but they are not. A trial is a test God puts before us to prove our faith and produce perseverance. Trials are something we can face with joy.

There's nothing joyful about temptation. In fact, unlike trials, God does not even place temptations in our path. Temptations occur when we are enticed and dragged away by our own evil desire.

So how are trials and temptations related? When we fail a God-given trial, when we resist the grace He gives to persevere and obey, we miss the God-given opportunity to have our faith refined. At that point, a failed trial can turn into a temptation when we are enticed to go our own way, seek our own desires, or even grumble or complain.

"That still means God is tempting me," some would say. But James 1:16 answers, *"Don't be deceived, my dear brothers. Every good and perfect gift is from above, coming down from the Father of the heavenly lights."* God never intends for trials to turn into temptations; trials are His good and perfect gifts intended to refine our faith, develop perseverance and make us mature and complete.

We can't really know the depth of our character until we see how we react under a trial. James 1:12 encourages us:

Blessed is the man who perseveres under trial, because when he has stood the test, he will receive the crown of life that God has promised to those who love him.

Please give me the grace, Lord, to face trials with joy. And guard me from temptation!

Honesty in Heart

The heart is deceitful above all things and beyond cure. Who can understand it? "I the Lord search the heart and examine the mind, to reward a man according to his conduct, according to what his deeds deserve." JEREMIAH 17:9–10

The King James Bible says it best: *"The heart is deceitful above all things and desperately wicked."* Deceitful above *all* things? Beyond cure? Desperately wicked? What a humiliating diagnosis for our diseased hearts! But for anyone who has ever connived, finagled, schemed or plotted, the diagnosis is accurate.

Oh, for an honest heart. A heart that is set against sin and which practises regular self-search to prevent self-deceit. *"Above all else, guard your heart, for it is the wellspring of life"* (Proverbs 4:23).

Since your heart is the wellspring of your life, the devil will pull out all the stops to prevent you from being honest in heart. He does not mind your behaviour being blameless and upright in human eyes as long as your heart remains self-consumed before God. Self-conscious. Self-absorbed. Self-indulgent. Self-pitying. Self-aware. Self-centred.

"Blessed are the pure in heart, for they will see God."   Matthew 5:8

As important as the outward life of justice and neighbourly love is, far more important is the inner life of pure-heartedness. If you find yourself in constant conflict with temptations and distractions, take heart: God allows you to be assaulted so that you may be toughened, matured, and anchored in Him more deeply through the experience of fighting back in His strength.   J. I. PACKER

Father, a broken heart you will not despise. A contrite heart you will not turn away from. Break my heart with the things that hurt your heart and give me purity in my innermost being for I desire, with all my heart, to see God.

Spiritual Warfare

"He who overcomes will inherit all this, and I will be his God and he will be my son." REVELATION 21:7

Spiritual warfare against the world, the flesh and the devil is one long, continuous struggle. The battleground has front lines and rear flanks. There are soldiers of Christ and backsliders on AWOL. The enemy has a strategy and he's out to kill, maim and wound. But God's strategy is to advance His kingdom and reclaim enemy territory.

As in any battle, the troops can get demoralized. That's when you and I need to remember that when we signed up in the army of Christ, it was like having radical heart surgery. In fact, a heart transplant. In Christ we have died to the power of the enemy over us and we've been given victorious new weapons of warfare in prayer and worship. God's battle plan can't fail and the medal of honour, for those who overcome, is holiness.

If you are experiencing battle fatigue, please remember that your fight won't go on for ever. The spiritual warfare will soon be over. The end is in sight. And today's verse, if anything, should encourage you in the battle down here on earth, for eternity will be yours.

The promise in Revelation 21:7 is that we shall inherit all of heaven and earth, God shall be our God and we will live as His children if . . . we overcome. So please don't shrink from the front lines if you feel the heat of enemy artillery today. Stand strong in the Lord, the Captain of your salvation, and you *will* overcome.

Lord, my battle is rugged and demanding, as it is for any good soldier. But the rewards are precious. The front lines are a risky place to be, but the battle prize is worth it. May I, in you, overcome!

AUGUST

Changing the Subject

Imagine the scene in Luke 14:1–24. Jesus was invited to dinner at a Pharisee's home in the rich suburbs of Jerusalem. He noticed the wealthy people grabbing the best seats. At that point, Jesus launched into a story about the sorts of dinner parties people ought to give – feasts for the forgotten, the homeless and the poor. The Lord added that although these people would not be able to repay them, the hosts would, nevertheless, be repaid at the resurrection (Luke 14:14).

You can imagine what happened next. Jesus probably sat down, put His napkin on his lap, and picked up an hors d'oeuvre. Silence hung over the table as the wealthy people shot nervous glances at each other.

The party spirit was dampened, so one dinner guest cleared his throat and spoke up: *"Blessed is the man who will eat at the feast in the kingdom of God"* (Luke 14:15). What an odd thing to say! It's as if He said: "Jesus, I can't say that I follow your strange ideas about dining with cripples, but I do agree with what you say about heaven – it's so comforting to know that everything will turn out perfectly in the end."

In other words, the man was trying his best to change the spiritual subject. But just as the Lord did not allow those dinner guests to switch the subject (read Luke 14:15–24), we will find it just as difficult to divert God's attention from those issues that need to be addressed in our lives.

Almighty God, I know I've often tried to change the spiritual subject when I've sensed your conviction in my heart. When you've pricked my conscience, I've often tried to divert your attention to other areas of my life. May I listen to you today and not try to change the subject when your Word speaks loud and clear.

God Fulfils His Purpose

I cry out to God Most High, to God, who fulfils His purpose for me. He sends from heaven and saves me, rebuking those who hotly pursue me; God sends His love and His faithfulness. PSALM 57:2–3

Perhaps long ago when you first believed in Christ you may have heard those familiar words, "God loves you and has a wonderful plan for your life." That brand-new thought warmed your heart, didn't it? You excitedly embarked on your spiritual journey, pleased and comforted to know that God had a unique and special plan just for you.

But perhaps those days when you first believed are long ago and far away. You've got sidetracked, your attention diverted. If so, let me ask you: Do you still believe God has a wonderful plan for your life? If not, let Psalm 57 jar your memory. Find assurance in the first few verses.

God *will* fulfil His purpose for you. He'll do it *for* you because He keeps His promise. He'll fulfil His plan *in* you by creating in you the image of His Son. Also, God will fulfil His plan *through* you as you touch others with His love and faithfulness.

❧

Nothing ever thwarts the purpose of God. Nothing can ruin His plan. If you are trusting Him, then God's plan for you is progressing right on schedule, full speed ahead.

God Most High, I praise you that you always fulfil your purpose. You are glorified in that you always keep your promises. You never fail to send help from heaven and you are faithful in giving your love and strength. I want to get in line with your will and say "yes" to your plan for my life.

God's Plan for You

"For I know the plans I have for you," declares the Lord, "plans to prosper you and not to harm you, plans to give you hope and a future."

JEREMIAH 29:11

A woman whom I had been counselling shook her head and nervously said to me, "I could *never* live in a wheelchair totally paralysed."

"Relax," I replied with a smile, "because you'll most likely never have to."

"How can you be so sure?" she said suspiciously.

I had her flip open her Bible and read Jeremiah 29:11. After she read the verse, she frowned and said, "But what about you? Look at your wheelchair. You don't think God's plan harmed you?"

I sighed and smiled at the woman, realizing there was no way I could humanly convince her that God's plan for me has only meant spiritual prosperity and a hopeful future. But then again, I'm the only one who needs to be convinced of it. And I am!

❧

Because God is love, His plans can only be loving. Because God is good, His intentions for you are of the highest good. Because He is the Lord of hope, His purpose is to always give you hope. He can never be (or do!) less than He is.

God will only permit in your life those trials that, with His grace, you are able to handle. That includes everything from emotional pain to physical paralysis. And this is why you have the assurance that His plans only mean spiritual prosperity for you and a hopeful future.

My good and great God, I praise you today for the hope you offer your people. Thank you that I have the assurance that your plans always reflect my highest good and your most perfect glory. Whatever trials I may face, help me to trust in your promises.

Timeless Moments

Be very careful, then, how you live – not as unwise but as wise, making the most of every opportunity, because the days are evil.   EPHESIANS 5:15–16

L ast evening as I left my office, I was struck by a glorious sunset, a sassy kaleidoscope of vivid lilac and bright pink. I faced the colour, letting it wash me in its golden glow. But suddenly, just as the colour was at its peak . . . it vanished.

As I got into my van, I remembered a thought by Amy Carmichael, "We will have all of eternity to celebrate the victories and only a few hours before sunset in which to win them."

Like a sunset, life will soon be over in a flash. All the colour and glory that we now enjoy will one day suddenly vanish. Standing on the other side of eternity I wonder if we will be amazed that life went by so quickly? But I suspect at that time we literally will not have time to think about it.

That's why we must think about it at present and realize there are timeless moments to be lived right now. A smile for the gas station attendant. A pleasant "God bless you" for the woman at the market. A hug for your spouse, straight from the heart. Prayers offered in spirit and truth.

Amy Carmichael would call these victories – and there is little time to collect these, the small victories. The days are fleeting, the hours are fading. Before you know it, our chance to prove our love for Jesus will fade. The sun will have set. So hear the echo of Paul's words and make the most of every opportunity.

ᗢ

Dear Father, sometimes I live as though this life will go on for ever. I realize it will not and so help me today to live timeless moments for Jesus. Help me to win victories, no matter how small, for you.

He Satisfies

You open your hand and satisfy the desires of every living thing.
PSALM 145:16

Well of water ever springing, Bread of life so rich and free,
Untold wealth that never faileth, My Redeemer is to me.

Hallelujah! I have found Him whom my soul so long has craved!
Jesus satisfies my longings – through His blood I now am saved.

There's nothing quite like the satisfaction of a glass of cold spring water
on a hot August afternoon. A cold shower after mowing the lawn. A
dive into a stream after a long, tiring hike. A glass of lemonade fresh out
of the refrigerator. Being satisfied means you've been filled, you want
nothing more and that the thirsty longing has been quenched.

That's exactly how Jesus satisfies. To have Him means you have it all.
To trust Him means your needs are met. To know Him is to realize that
He is your dearest, most faithful companion.

*"But blessed is the man who trusts in the Lord, whose confidence is in Him.
He will be like a tree planted by the water that sends out its roots by the stream.
It does not fear when heat comes; its leaves are always green. It has no worries
in a year of drought and never fails to bear fruit."* JEREMIAH 17:7–8

The next time you pour a cold drink on a hot August afternoon, pause
and praise the Lord for the way He quenches your thirst. He, the
Wellspring of Water, overcomes, subdues, fulfils and satisfies like nothing,
like no one else.

*Lord, sometimes I feel so thirsty . . . and I'm not even sure of what I want.
I search for that which will satisfy and always come away feeling empty. Teach
me to see that you give satisfaction on the deepest and most personal level. I drink
in your love today, Lord Jesus.*

For Those Who Search

It is the glory of God to conceal a matter . . .   PROVERBS 25:2

Mysteries have a way of enticing us at the same time as they frustrate us. Take these paradoxes of Scripture: We have a free will, yet we're predestined. We're positionally perfect, but experientially imperfect. We work out our own salvation, yet it is God who works His will within us. Even Jesus was a paradox – a hundred per cent God and a hundred per cent man.

Something in us has to make enigmas understandable and puzzles comprehensible. True, many things in Scripture we will never be able to understand; we accept them by faith. But it is God's nature to hide things. He delights in concealing secret treasures so that we might be drawn to search and enjoy the discovery of finding those treasures. For *"The Lord confides in those who fear him; he makes his covenant known to them"* (Psalm 25:14).

To those who draw closest to the Lord, to those who desire His intimate company, Jesus says, *"The secret of the kingdom of God has been given to you."* (Mark 4:11) If you sit at His feet, full of awe and wonder, He will draw you into His confidence, unravelling His innermost thoughts and heartfelt hopes, voicing His desires for you and for the rest of those who search.

◆◆

The Lord Jesus is the treasure you seek, the precious gem you must mine. And Jeremiah 29:13 assures, *"You will seek me and find me, when you seek me with all your heart."* You have everything you need to equip you for the search. You have His Word, the key to heaven's hieroglyphics. You have been initiated into the fellowship of things above. You have the mind of Christ. Now you must find His heart!

I want to love you, Jesus, with all my heart, soul, mind and strength. For as I do, I believe you will reveal to me your heart!

What's Fair?

Who has understood the mind of the Lord, or instructed Him as his counsellor? Whom did the Lord consult to enlighten Him, and who taught Him the right way? Who was it that taught Him knowledge or showed Him the path of understanding?   ISAIAH 40:13–14

Have you ever walked into a room halfway through someone else's argument and been asked for your opinion? It's impossible to respond. You don't have all the facts. You don't fully appreciate both sides of the argument and, therefore, you can't give a just verdict.

Trying to discern whether or not God is fair in any given situation is much like walking into a room halfway through someone else's argument. For one thing, you don't have all the facts. And you won't have them until you get to the other side of eternity. Besides, "fairness" is impossible to grasp because you are unequipped to appreciate the hidden purposes God has in mind.

Those who don't believe in God may be presumptuous enough to play the "fairness" game, but Christians know better. The world's definition of fairness is based on the sliding scale of society's values and the changing will of the majority. But God doesn't buy that definition. That's why He will never be "fair" from society's perspective. He will, however, always maintain His justice. Justice, unlike fairness, is based on the unchanging principles of His Word.

The "fairness doctrine" is based on a person's limited value system and timetable. Remember, God is not fair, He is just. He is loving. His values are higher, far exalted above yours. His timetable is different. So bow to His justice, trust in His love and forget about fairness.

Lord, you will never seem fair from the world's perspective and that's why I praise you for being just, not fair. May your purposes prevail and may you receive glory!

Maps

Whether you turn to the right or to the left, your ears will hear a voice behind you, saying, "This is the way; walk in it."　　ISAIAH 30:21

For me, the best part of a trip is always getting there. When I was little, I would clamour to sit in the front seat of the car. I loved sitting next to my dad so I could spread out a map on my lap and help him navigate. The lines on the map would turn from thick red to thin black when the road got narrow. We'd pass farms and villages, and I would always mark off on the map each milestone.

I've always enjoyed maps. I feel good when I have a decent idea of where I'm going and how to get there. A map allows me to mark off progress, to help me see how much further I have to go.

That's why I enjoy my walk with Jesus. His Word is just like a map. Pick a verse, any verse, and you're on your way. God orders your steps. He points to the narrow road rather than the broad one. He says, "I am the way" and you certainly can't get lost when you follow the Lord. And if you're a little unsure of your directions, Isaiah 30:21 reads just like a road sign.

Look at the road ahead today as though it were a journey full of adventure. Remember that heaven is your destination. Just keep your eye on the Way. That's all the direction you need.

Lord Jesus, you are the Way and I know that no matter what lies ahead today, I am safe and secure when I keep close to you. Thank you for being my guide and my map. Your Word tells me exactly where I'm going and how to get there. I love following you!

So You're Exhausted?

When Jesus landed and saw a large crowd, He had compassion on them and healed their sick. As evening approached, the disciples came to find Him and said, "This is a remote place, and it's already getting late. Send the crowds away, so they can go to the villages and buy themselves some food." Jesus replied, "They do not need to go away. You give them something to eat."

MATTHEW 14:14–16

Here is what happened in one twenty-four hour period: After a hot, dusty afternoon of preaching to the crowds, Jesus heard the devastating news about the death of John the Baptist. Rather than take time out to grieve, He attended to the needs at hand, feeding the five thousand. Long after sunset, there was a gathering of baskets of leftovers. Then setting sail, Jesus rescued His disciples when a night storm almost wrecked their boat. By sunrise they reached shore, only to face more crowds.

And the Lord's response? *"They do not need to go away"* was always His encouragement. Although Jesus had not slept in a full day, He kept on loving people. He tenderly held the wrinkled hands of old people. He kneeled to tousle the hair of children. He lifted the face-shawl of a prostitute to give her His smile.

The love of Jesus can never be exhausted.

❧

There are days when you will know you are at the end of your rope, physically and emotionally exhausted. Jesus reminds you, *"Come to me, you who are weary and burdened . . ."*

He is able to carry your load because His shoulders were once weighed down. Even when He was on His last legs, He never lost His spiritual footing. That's why you can rest in Him and find strength to go on.

Lord Jesus, I praise you that your love is tireless, infinite, always giving, always caring. May I find rest and refreshment in you.

Studying Scripture

"You diligently study the Scriptures because you think that by them you possess eternal life. These are the Scriptures that testify about me, yet you refuse to come to me to have life." JOHN 5:39–40

Jesus was astounded that people could devote their entire lives to studying Scripture and yet fail to know the One to whom Scripture was pointing!

I have a friend who, much like those religious leaders, gets a charge out of studying doctrine. He's compiled Bible studies on the subjects of predestination and the election of the saints. He's memorized the Nicene Creed, the Apostles' Creed and the Te Deum. My friend knows by heart selections from the Book of Common Prayer and I once heard him recite the entire eighth chapter of the book of Romans.

This man diligently studies the Scriptures. But sometimes, after hearing him talk, I wonder if he realizes that creeds and doctrines, scriptures and prayer books *all* point to Jesus. He labours over the Word, but does it aid him in knowing his Saviour better? He knows *about* the Lord, but how well does he *know* Him?

I can't judge. But observing my friend has taught me something important about studying Scripture: Always ask the Spirit of God to illumine the Word to you. Otherwise, your study could end up a dry, intellectual exercise. God's Spirit is the one who makes Jesus, the Truth, come alive through the truth of the Word. Even Jesus Himself underscored this in John 16:13–14:

"But when He, the Spirit of truth, comes, He will guide you into all truth. He will not speak on His own . . . He will bring glory to me by taking from what is mine and making it known to you."

〜

Lord, as I read Scripture, help me to remember to always ask the Holy Spirit to open up my eyes and my heart to your Word. Let me see how every book, every chapter points to you.

Finding God's Will

Be joyful always; pray continually; give thanks in all circumstances, for this is God's will for you in Christ Jesus.   I THESSALONIANS 5:16–18

There's hardly a Christian who hasn't looked into the future and questioned, "What *is* God's will for my life?" Today's verse may be short and sweet, but it's all the answer you need. Be joyful. Pray continually. Give thanks. For *this* is God's will for you in Christ Jesus.

"But you don't know my circumstances," I hear you saying. "How can I be thankful for pain and heartache?" God is not asking you to *be* thankful, but to *give* thanks. There's a big difference between feeling thankful and giving thanks. One response involves emotions, the other, your will. Trusting God has absolutely nothing to do with trustful feelings.

Also, God's not asking you to give thanks *for* the tough times; only that you give thanks *in* them. Give thanks that He is sovereign . . . that He is in control . . . giving you grace and peace . . . and planning it all for your good and His glory.

Today's verse became my anchor when I was first paralysed. I gritted my teeth, pushed aside feelings of despair, and wilfully gave thanks for everything from the hospital breakfast of cold cornmeal mush to the gruelling hours of daily physical therapy. Many months later a miracle occurred. I began to *feel* thankful. My brighter attitude enabled me to give thanks for greater things. Later on, another miracle happened: I was able to rejoice in suffering.

Finding God's specific will for my life was incidental. I happened upon it as I daily made I Thessalonians 5:16–18 the anchor of my soul.

Be joyful always, pray continually, give thanks in all circumstances and God will move heaven and earth to push you forward into His will. Whatever happens, whatever you decide, you will have *every* confidence that you are completely centred in His will for your life.

Hyssop

Cleanse me with hyssop, and I shall be clean; wash me, and I shall be whiter than snow.   PSALM 51:7

In my Bible, page 717 is dogeared and dirty from years of use. That's because Psalm 51 is on that page and I often flip to this beautiful passage to wrap words around my pain and remorse over sin.

I used to think that the intense and constant pain I felt over sin was a kind of punishment from God, a display of His wrath. But not so. Remorse over personal sin is the sign of a softened conscience. A conscience which is sensitive – sometimes hypersensitive – to evil. Such pain is a prologue to God's favour.

So when I feel the sting of remorse, I rush to Psalm 51 and find comfort. Especially verse 7 where it says, *"Cleanse me with hyssop."* Why is that so comforting? Hyssop, I've heard, was used by the Hebrews during the first Passover when they dipped the branch in blood and spread it on the doorposts. But the significance of hyssop doesn't stop there. For when you flail hyssop and strike it on a hard surface, it releases a fragrant perfume.

I invite the Lord to cleanse me with hyssop for when He flails His Word against my hardened conscience, a fragrant perfume of repentance rises to His throne. To me, *that* is a comfort. A prologue to God's favour.

Sin is anything which does not express, or which is contrary to, the holy character of God. Sin then is not merely what we do, but what we are. Praise God He has dealt with our sin finally and completely on the cross – that's why nothing will soften a conscience more than a lively and buoyant love for the Saviour.

Lord, according to your great compassion, blot out my transgression and wash away all of my iniquity. Make me clean, O God!

Strength to Strength

Blessed are those whose strength is in you, who have set their hearts on pilgrimage. As they pass through the Valley of Baca, they make it a place of springs; the autumn rains also cover it with pools. They go from strength to strength till each appears before God in Zion.   PSALM 84:5–7

If you were to serve as "my hands" for a day, I'd keep you plenty busy. I would need you to sit next to me at my computer and type as I speak. Can you do a hundred words a minute? That's how fast I talk once I get rolling.

Later on you could help me organize my books, Xerox pages, file copies, brew coffee, take dictation, type letters, cook lunch, empty my leg bag, dial phone numbers, take messages, run a few errands, and if I need an adjustment with my corset or catheter, help me lie down on the office sofa. And we're only halfway through the day!

How would we accomplish so much work? Spirit-inspired energy! My secretary and I go from strength to strength. That means pausing in between projects to pray. Pulling a hymnal off the shelf to sing praise songs before lunch. Praying over the phone with someone who happens to call. Stopping for tea at four o'clock and reading a line or two of Scripture. Going from strength to strength in God's Spirit is the pause that refreshes.

It's the only way to work. It's the only way to live.

If you have set your heart on pilgrimage, you're going somewhere! But you can only get there if you move through your busy day from strength to strength.

Remind me, Lord, to take many pauses throughout the day to think about you, pray to you, share a verse of Scripture with a friend or sing a hymn even if no one's around. Carry me from strength to strength.

The Power of God

I pray also that the eyes of your heart may be enlightened in order that you may know the hope to which He has called you, the riches of His glorious inheritance in the saints, and His incomparably great power for us who believe. That power is like the working of His mighty strength, which He exerted in Christ when He raised Him from the dead. EPHESIANS 1:18–20

God has incomparably great power in store for those who believe, the same power He exerted when He raised Christ from the dead. In other words, the sky is the limit when it comes to the display of God's mighty strength in your life.

The usual word for God's power in the Greek New Testament is *dunamis* from which we get the word "dynamite". What a display of God's dynamite power it would be if, let's say, people in wheelchairs like me were raised up. Such explosive miracles would be a powerful witness of the mighty strength of God.

But wait. We also get the word "dynamo" from *dunamis*. A dynamo is just as strong as dynamite, and maybe more so. But the power of a dynamo isn't as obvious. Its power is quiet, controlled, and steady, unlike the explosive "bang" you get from sticks of dynamite. This is the kind of inward power that is displayed by God in the lives of saintly Christians who may never experience a rising up out of their suffering, believers who may never know an outward miracle.

It takes God's power to be a faithful spouse, a conscientious parent, or a responsible office worker. If you're struggling, remember that His power for you is incomparably great. If the Father could raise His Son from the dead, He can raise you above your circumstances.

Lord, by your power, I ask you to do dynamo miracles on the inside of me and, as you see fit, dynamite miracles on the outside.

Names of God

Give thanks to the Lord, call on His name . . . Glory in His holy name; let the hearts of those who seek the Lord rejoice. Look to the Lord and His strength; seek His face always.   I CHRONICLES 16:8, 10–11

When God invites us to call on His name, we should never be at a loss as to which name to use. I call the Lord my Shepherd and Friend during those times when God's tenderness melts my heart and I cry to think how rich and full His love is.

Then there are times when I'm battling pride or wasting hours in daydreams. That's when God's Word slices through my sinfulness. It stings. His hand seems heavy. That's when I call the Lord my Refiner, my Purifier.

There are times when I feel helpless and frightened, when no one, not even my husband or best friend, seems to understand. I hide under the shelter of His wings. I snuggle safely in the cleft of the Rock. These are times when I call God my Tower, my High Fortress.

When it comes to God, one name just isn't enough. And because Scripture is full of different names for Him, we can always know exactly how to relate to our Lord, whether we fall to our knees in awesome respect, or climb up in His lap to be held in His arms.

The name of the Lord is a strong tower; the righteous run to it and are safe.
                                        PROVERBS 18:10

Herman Bavnick said, "Fire does not change whether it warms or illumines or burns. In the same way, in addressing God, we use His various names because of the various effects of His unchanging Essence upon us." Dig through Scripture to find that name of God which best expresses your heart. He is your Rock. The Door. A Wall of Fire. Your Bread and Water. Your King and your Friend.

Knowing Christ

What is more, I consider everything a loss compared to the surpassing greatness of knowing Christ Jesus my Lord, for whose sake I have lost all things.

PHILIPPIANS 3:8

In the early seventies, the country music of John Denver took the States by storm and his biggest fan was . . . me. When my sister and I learned that John Denver would be appearing in a concert nearby, I sent him one of my charcoal drawings, invited him to dinner, and asked if we could meet backstage. To make a long story short, the closest I got to him was row 57, seat DD. A year later I received a letter of three sentences thanking me for the drawing.

Looking back, I'm amazed that I actually believed John Denver was my friend. It was crazy to think that he would want to see me and come to dinner at our farm after the concert. How ridiculous! For although I memorized the fact sheets about John Denver, including all the words to every one of his songs, I did not *know* him. My knowledge of him was an illusion.

Saul of Tarsus excelled all his classmates and contemporaries in learning about the God of the Bible. He was able to quote Scripture at great length and leap tall doctrines in a single bound. He was faster in a debate and more powerful than any other Pharisee. Every time he persecuted a Christian, he thought he was fighting for truth, justice and the excellent way of God. But Saul's knowledge of God was an illusion.

One day under the hot sun on the road to Damascus, the One about whom Saul had studied spoke from heaven. In that moment, the man who knew all about God from his earliest childhood began to *know* God for the first time.

Lord, I confess that I know more about you than really know you. I don't want it to be that way. Never, never do I want my knowledge of you to be an illusion. Help me to consider everything a loss compared to the surpassing greatness of knowing you.

Experiencing Christ

I consider them rubbish, that I may gain Christ and be found in Him, not having a righteousness of my own that comes from the law, but that which is through faith in Christ – the righteousness that comes from God and is by faith.

PHILIPPIANS 3:8–9

In today's reading, Paul describes what it's like to know Christ in terms of being justified, of being legally positioned on God's side. Here, Paul is saying that God has done something for us on His books. It's wonderful to have the Lord impute His righteousness to us. But many Christians think that's all there is to Christianity.

There's much more. After verse nine of Philippians, Paul discusses a different kind of knowledge of Christ. Paul no longer comments on his position, the fact that he has been *"found in him . . . through the righteousness that comes from God."* No, Paul talks about his experience of God . . .

I want to know Christ and the power of His resurrection and the fellowship of sharing in His sufferings, becoming like Him in His death, and so, somehow, to attain to the resurrection from the dead.   PHILIPPIANS 3:10–11

Positioning may have been God's responsibility, but experiencing was Paul's responsibility. To experience God means to enjoy and realize, apprehend and understand the Lord in a deep, personal union. And, like Paul, this is *your* responsibility, too.

❧

If someone were to ask, "Do you know Jesus?" what would you say? "Yes, I've been saved and I know I'm going to heaven." If that were your response, then good. You've just told everybody that you are justified and forgiven. But I hope you could also say, "Yes, Jesus and I are intimate with each other. Let me tell you about the kind of person He is and how much I love spending time with Him."

More than a head knowledge, I desire a heart knowledge of you, Lord.

The Meaning of Encouragement

Therefore encourage one another and build each other up, just as in fact you are doing. I THESSALONIANS 5:11

K en warmed my heart the other evening when he hugged me and said, "Joni, you may not be able to wash my shirts, but I just want you to know that I really feel your support."

Ken considers encouragement to be one of the best ingredients in our marriage. And it's not because I tell him he's a nice guy, a good teacher or great husband. For instance, as faculty advisor for the student government organization at his school, Ken recently had to organize an awards banquet. I decided that at the banquet I would not sit on the sidelines and just smile admiringly when he looked my way. I made a point of wheeling to each table to introduce myself to the parents of all his students. It was a special ministry to his kids, but mostly, it was an encouragement to my husband.

Later on when I congratulated him, he knew I meant it. Why? Because he saw me join him in the effort. Encouragement that builds people up is the kind that is not content to sit on the sidelines at a polite distance. Body-building encouragement will always roll its sleeves up and put words into action.

When you give encouragement to your spouse or friend, give more than pleasant words. Take the initiative. Be creative. Look for a way of supporting your loved one in his or her efforts. With up-close and personal encouragement like that, you'll be doing more than lifting spirits, you'll be helping to build another's faith.

Let me encourage those who are wounded, Lord, with your healing touch. Let me encourage those in grief with your hope. And let me find ways to put this prayer into practice as I serve others in your encouraging love.

His Yoke Is Easy

"Come to me, all you who are weary and burdened, and I will give you rest. Take my yoke upon you and learn from me, for I am gentle and humble in heart, and you will find rest for your souls. For my yoke is easy and my burden is light."

MATTHEW 11:28–30

At times we feel our yoke is just too heavy to bear. That's when Jesus says, "Here, take my yoke. It's easy. The burden is light." Oh yeah? we think. What yoke could possibly be light?

Tired Christians feel this way. They get up in the morning and are overcome by exhaustion before the wearisome routine even begins. Sometimes they feel pressured to perform up to God's expectations. Or they add to their list of religious duties as proof of their righteousness before the watchful eye of the Lord. Then when they hear that God wants to step in and relieve them of all this, it seems unbelievable.

It's sad, but some Christians prefer to hoist on their shoulders the yoke of painful self-sacrifice and religious duty. Sure, it feels burdensome and heavy, but they prefer the route of self-sacrifice. It's something they can "do", something that involves "my effort", and "my faithfulness". It's easier (although heavier) to bear burdens that are "mine" rather than cast one's self on the Lord in utter despair, weakness and helplessness. The wearisome rule-keeping exalts self, while coming to the Lord empty-handed gives self nothing to glory in.

What makes the yoke of Christ easy? What makes His burden light? Love. Daily, we move in His Spirit . . . pray unceasingly . . . look to Him for grace. These are the disciplines of love which make our daily tasks light and full of ease. If we fail to move in His love, the tasks seem tiresome.

Lord, it's not my faithfulness that counts. May I move in your love and power today and find your yoke . . . light.

Precious Moments

I read in the papers that the owner of a small original by van Gogh had put the painting on the auction block in New York hoping it would bring twelve million dollars. When the highest bid only climbed to eight million, the owner withdrew the painting. Van Gogh would probably drop dead again if he were alive to see such a thing.

Some people call a million-dollar painting, a Mercedes-Benz or a dress with a price tag of over six hundred dollars an investment. But I say if you can't pack it into your luggage when you step into the other side of eternity, please don't call it a lasting treasure.

Now I'm not poking fun at your great-grandmother's silver service which has been handed down in your family over the years. I'm just asking for a little perspective here. Because consider this: Every morning you are handed twenty-four hours free of charge. If you had all the money in the world, you could not purchase a single extra hour. So what will you do with this priceless possession? You must use it. And don't forget, once it is wasted, you can't get it back.

One day van Gogh paintings will peel and crack. The resale value on that Mercedes-Benz will only be a couple of hundred dollars. Even silver and gold will perish. So . . .

Make the most of every opportunity. COLOSSIANS 4:5

~

Build your eternal investment. Pray for an unsaved neighbour. Visit a nursing home. Ask forgiveness from someone you've offended. Such things can never be auctioned away!

"If for one whole day, quietly and determinedly, we were to give ourselves up to the ownership of Jesus and to obeying his orders, we should be amazed at its close to realize all he had packed into that one day."

OSWALD CHAMBERS

A Riddle Made Plain

"And everyone who speaks a word against the Son of Man will be forgiven, but anyone who blasphemes against the Holy Spirit will not be forgiven."
LUKE 12:10

If you weren't the wiser, this verse could sound like an ancient riddle which raises more questions than gives answers. Questions like, "Isn't speaking against Christ the same as speaking against the Spirit?" Or "The Son of Man and the Holy Spirit are one in the Trinity, so what's the difference?"

The ministry of the Son of Man is one of redemption. When it comes to redemption, a lot of people simply aren't aware that Jesus died for them. They are ignorant as to what their sin did to Christ on the cross. And as Jesus Himself said from His cross, "Father, forgive them for they know not what they do."

But the ministry of the Holy Spirit is different. The Spirit's work is one of revelation. He reveals truth to your heart, truth that convicts and convinces. Once God's truth is revealed to you, ignorance is a thing of the past. You can't play dumb. You can't say, "I didn't know," as perhaps the soldiers who crucified Christ could say. And this is precisely the point of our reading today because, if you know, you *are* accountable.

❧

When the Holy Spirit opens up your eyes and heart to salvation truth, it's dangerous to ignore it. Hebrews 6:4–6 says:

It is impossible for those who have once been enlightened, who have tasted the heavenly gift, who have shared in the Holy Spirit, who have tasted the goodness of the word of God and the powers of the coming age, if they fall away, to be brought back to repentance, because to their loss they are crucifying the Son of God all over again and subjecting him to public disgrace.

Thank you, Lord, for this awesome warning, reminding me how precious my salvation really is.

An Obi of Love

The Japanese character for love is pronounced "ai" and is pictured with the symbol for a belt found on a traditional Japanese gown known as a kimono. Called the "obi", the wide silk belt wraps around the outside of the kimono to hold it together. The obi is both functional and beautiful. No kimono is worth stunned admiration without it.

I wouldn't doubt that God, in His sovereignty, had the Japanese people reserve that character to symbolize something He would communicate to the Colossian people:

Therefore, as God's chosen people, holy and dearly loved, clothe yourselves with compassion, kindness, humility, gentleness and patience . . . And over all these virtues put on love, which binds them all together in perfect unity.

COLOSSIANS 3:12, 14

Just like a Japanese woman will put on many layers of clothing as a part of the kimono, Paul exhorts us to layer qualities of the Spirit. Each layer of a kimono has its purpose and adds to the overall effect of beauty. Such is to be our clothing of character – functional and beautiful.

Paul then exhorts us to bind the loose fitting kimono with an "obi" called love. Our qualities of the Spirit need to be held together by the relationship of the Spirit. Without that bond, we would not reflect the unity Christ obtained for us.

Not only is the obi functional, it also allows the beauty of the kimono, and the woman, to be seen. The people of God who bind themselves in love are strikingly beautiful. And the world cannot help but be attracted to it.

❧

Lay spiritual characteristics of clothing upon your life. And then wrap that "obi" of love tightly.

Lord, I desire simple beauty in my life. Work from the inside out. Make me humble and forgiving. And make me a binding spirit within your body.

The Fountain

"On that day a fountain will be opened to the house of David and the inhabitants of Jerusalem, to cleanse them from sin and impurity." ZECHARIAH 13:1

O ne hot summer day when I was a little girl, my mother took me to the park. I remember a big fountain just over the hill from the zoo and arboretum. As we strolled by the fountain, I looked longingly as neighbourhood children waded and splashed in the pool. I begged to join them and my mother did the most amazing thing – she let me.

We took off my shoes and socks and I splashed into the fountain with the other children. My shorts and shirt were soaked, but there we were, a bunch of giggling boys and girls with arms widespread and faces uplifted, squealing as the water showered on us from the fountain above. Our hearts were free. Exuberant. Uninhibited. Full of life and in high spirits.

A fountain is a place of joy. That's what I think of when I hear this hymn.

> There is a fountain filled with blood
> Drawn from Immanuel's veins;
> And sinners, plunged beneath that flood,
> Lose all their guilty stains.

❧

God has opened up a fountain to you through the Lord Jesus. He invites you to come on in and *enjoy* His love. Don't stand on the edges of His joy. He has washed away your sin and you, like a child, can be free and full of life.

Oh, to be like a child, relishing the freedom and joy of all that your love gives, Lord. Thank you for cleansing me from sin and washing away all my impurity. I lift my face and spread my hands in adoration of you.

Kneeling

I grew up in a little congregation where they read the Gospel, sang hymns from the heart and kneeled in prayer. Sunday worship was serious business and I learned as a child what it meant to bend my knee before the Lord.

Obviously, God listens whether His people pray standing, sitting or lying prone or prostrate. So what's my point about kneeling? I wish I could do it. Being paralysed, it's impossible to kneel for prayer.

Once at a convention, the speaker closed his message by asking everyone in the room to kneel on the floor for prayer. All five hundred people got on their knees. All except me. I cried, not because I felt awkward, but because I was struck with the beauty of seeing so many people bow in worship. I breathed a prayer: "Lord Jesus, I can't wait for the day when I will rise up on resurrected legs. The first thing I will then do is to drop on grateful, glorified knees."

Come let us bow down in worship, let us kneel before the Lord our Maker.

PSALM 95:6

On the day I receive my new body, I'm sure my Lord will be delighted to watch me stretch glorified muscles and dance on tiptoe. But there's something I plan to do that may please Him more. I will kneel. To *not* move will be my demonstration of heartfelt thanks for the grace He gave those many years when my legs and hands were paralysed. It will be my sacrifice of praise.

Today, do what so many who are paralysed or too lame or old *can't* do. Read Psalm 95:6 and take its advice. And when you kneel in prayer, be grateful for knees that bend to the will of God.

I bow before you, Lord, in submission to your will. And when I rise from my knees, may I serve you wholeheartedly.

Were You There . . .

"I have been crucified with Christ and I no longer live, but Christ lives in me. The life I live in the body, I live by faith in the Son of God, who loved me and gave himself for me."
GALATIANS 2:20

The cross is a place of peace and power. Just look at this man's letter:

"I spent one-and-a-half years on a kidney machine before getting a transplant. At first I did a lot of complaining, but then I stopped when I read the account of the crucifixion. Because in the kidney centre, they helped me get out of my coat; with Jesus, they stripped off his clothes. When entering the centre, the nurses always spoke a kind word; Jesus heard 'Crucify him!'

"On the machine I would develop a headache and they would bring me an ice pack and aspirin; a crown of thorns was shoved on Jesus' head. Sometimes I would get thirsty and they'd give me juice; Jesus got vinegar. I lay on a comfortable bed for five hours; Jesus hung on nails. I hardly felt the needle they inserted in my vein; spikes were driven through Jesus' hands and feet. My blood was cleansed; His blood spilled on the ground.

"Jesus turned my days of complaining into days of praising when I took time to look at the cross. A careful look into the events that took place that day on Calvary should stop all our complaining."

The cross is a place where one dies to self, enjoys no rights, and grovels in humility. How odd for our Lord to invite us to be crucified with Him; but God knows the cross is also a place of grace, and the nearer one draws to Calvary, the more abundant the peace and power.

Oh blessed cross, teach me to nail my cares to you. Crucify my complaining, mortify my grumbling, and cause me to praise!

Hard Sayings of Jesus

On hearing it, many of His disciples said, "This is a hard teaching. Who can accept it?" Aware that His disciples were grumbling about this, Jesus said to them, "Does this offend you?"　　　　　　　　　　　JOHN 6:60–61

Gentle Jesus, meek and mild, never harming, always charming. Is that so? Perhaps it's the picture occasionally painted in a child's Sunday school lesson, but it's not the historic Christ.

Jesus threw so many hard teachings at the disciples, it's little wonder they got miffed. The Lord announced: Reality is wrapped up in me. Truth can only be found in me. If you try to save your life, it'll slip through your fingers. If you give it away, you'll find it. I'll deny you before the Father if you turn back. If anything is keeping you from me, whatever it is, throw it away. If it's your eye, pull it out. Your hand, cut it off. Your sins, all of them are wiped out – I can do that! I am rebirth. I am life. Eat me. Drink me. And finally, do not be afraid for I have overcome the whole universe!　　　　　　　　　　　C. S. LEWIS

Jesus came not to bring peace, but a sword. The razor-sharp sword of His Word that divides your soul and spirit, that says, *"Does this offend you?"* He encroaches, invades and infringes on your comfort zones. He tears aside the curtains of your conscience and throws open the locked doors of your bad habits. He will brashly call your sin *sin* and He challenges you to leave it behind.

Praise God for the hard sayings of Jesus. He's not uncaring or unfeeling about your life. He's not uninvolved. God has a way of offending – and thank His holy Name He does.

Thank you, Lord, for caring enough to offend me. Don't let me ever get comfortable in my sin. Press me up against your hard teachings until I see the offence as . . . a blessing.

The Measure of Love

May our Lord Jesus Christ himself and God our Father, who loved us and by His grace gave us eternal encouragement and good hope, encourage your hearts and strengthen you in every good deed and word.

II THESSALONIANS 2:16–17

If love could be measured, it would be measured by how much it gives. Would you like to know the extent to which you love your children, your spouse, your roommate or your co-workers? Then ask yourself: How much do I give? To be honest, love that gives without limits doesn't even ask that question. Love like that doesn't even care to measure itself. It just joyfully gives without taking any notice of how much has been sacrificed.

That's how God loves. And the measure of the love of God is in what, or I should say, who, He gave. He gave His Son. His life. His only begotten. He gave everything, nothing held back, every last ounce, all in all. He squandered His love extravagantly and unashamedly on vile sinners.

That's why God should be so easy to trust. With you He never uses words of despair or defeat, hopelessness or frustration. His encouraging love never mentions fear or failure. Those aren't words of love. Not His love. When God encourages your heart, He speaks words of hope and victory, rest and peace, joy and triumph.

Read today's verse again and you'll discover God's eternal encouragement. It's the measure of His love. If your heart needs to be strengthened today, let Him speak to you His loving words of hope and comfort.

Because your love is in my heart, Lord, I have something to give. I know your love cannot be idle in my soul; it must grow in me and I, in turn, must give without measure. Encourage me today with your extravagant love and help me to see that you are absolutely worthy of all my trust.

A Breathtaking View of Grace

There are times in my life when I am breathless. It may come when someone gives me a gift I never expected. At other times it comes from seeing an incredible painting or from reading a beautiful story. And, of course, there is always that moment when I see a "breathtaking view" of nature.

I can feel that way spiritually at times. Consider the grace of God in John 1:16:

From the fulness of His grace we have all received one blessing after another.

Now that's breathtaking!

I've grown to see grace on its own as part and parcel of our incredible Lord. His grace saved me. His grace sustains my life. His grace showers rain and sun on the good and the evil. His grace withholds judgment on nations. Inexplicable, His grace. But I accept it and live on.

But grace *upon* grace?! I'm floored. What can I say? His grace upon grace not only lets me live, His grace lets me serve, it lets me worship, it lets me take His name as my own, it calls me by name, it grants me *fulness* of life as John says.

His grace upon grace is too much for me. Sometimes I cry out for God to remove it because there is no way I deserve such grace. At that very moment His Spirit says, "I'm glad you see your complete dependence on me. Now, loosen your limbs. Clear your throat. I've got more work for you to do. And more grace."

My breath restored, I live and move again until another day when He takes away my breath again.

❧

Lord, you are too good to me. I don't deserve even the simple pleasures of life let alone your bountiful grace. It's too much. But teach me how to move according to that grace. For by it you will be glorified and I shall rejoice.

Conditional Promises

"If you remain in me and my words remain in you, ask whatever you wish, and it will be given you."   JOHN 15:7

Certain promises have strings attached. Like this one from John 15:7. True, we may ask whatever we wish, but Jesus qualifies our prayers with two important conditions: We must be living in close fellowship with Him and our requests must be in line with His will.

Some Christians think that prayer is like a blank cheque. Just fill in the amount whenever you like, no matter what your spiritual condition, and God will cash it for you. Not so. When Jesus says, *"Remain in me,"* He's talking about a consistent life style of closeness to Him, not a sporadic spirituality.

And as far as the other condition, *"If my words remain in you,"* Jesus doesn't mean you have to have a seminary degree or a Bible school diploma. You can know tons of theology without ever letting it grip your soul. Jesus was referring to running Scripture through your mind over and over again in order to find new ways to please Him and bring Him praise. Whatever we ask will be given us if we walk closely with the Lord and remain consistently in His Word.

One more thing. For years I applied this prescription to my own prayer request for divine healing. I have sought to remain in the Lord and have His words remain in me. But after twenty-five years, I'm still paralysed. The lesson? Sometimes God says . . . no. Or at least, not yet.

I John 5:14–15 says:

If we ask anything according to His will, He hears us. And if we know that He hears us – whatever we ask – we know that we have what we asked of Him.

Lord, I'm asking only that your will be done in my life. I have the assurance you will always say "yes" to that prayer!

To Love or Not to Love

He who pursues righteousness and love finds life, prosperity and honour.
PROVERBS 21:21

I wheeled into the house the other day and had a very biblical experience – I felt like Jonah entering the mouth of the whale. The house stank of fish. My fisherman husband had caught twenty-two tuna. I glanced into the kitchen and saw my dishes pushed aside to make room for mounds of tuna fillets. My heart sank when I noticed tuna blood dripping between the sink and the stove where no sponge can reach.

I knew what this meant. Tuna noodle casseroles. Fried tuna. Grilled, baked and barbecued tuna. Souffléd and steamed. Poached and pancaked. And the rest Ken would freeze for later on. My anger began to well.

That evening Ken barbecued his tuna, fixed his special sauce, cut lemons and parsley, and set my place before me with a big smile. Even though I hate tuna and was still mad over the mess in the kitchen, I decided then and there that love was stronger than the smell of fish. As I forced it down, I realized it was far better to please my husband than to please my tastebuds.

Love is lived out that way. Last-minute choices that decide for someone else. Quick decisions to lay aside differences and cheer someone on. Skin-of-the-teeth, under-the-wire bits of love that say, "You mean a lot to me." Always, love is a choice.

∾

You come up against scores of opportunities every day to love or not to love. You encounter hundreds of small chances to please your friends, delight your Lord and encourage your family. That's why love and obedience are intimately linked – you can't have one without the other.

I choose to love, Lord. I choose to obey. May the small things I do today tell others, "Jesus loves you."

Habakkuk

Though the fig-tree does not bud and there are no grapes on the vines, though the olive crop fails and the fields produce no food, though there are no sheep in the pen and no cattle in the stalls, yet I will rejoice in the Lord, I will be joyful in God my Saviour.　　　　　HABAKKUK 3:17-18

This guy had it bad! Can you imagine being a farmer and waking up one morning to see your fig trees and vines bare, the olive orchard dead, the fields barren, and all the sheep and cattle gone? If I were the farmer surveying the scene of devastation, I might have a difficult time rejoicing in the Lord.

But not Habakkuk. He knew that the time to trust God in triple measure was during those days when "everything bad happens at once!"

Ever had a day when everything that could go wrong does go wrong? The alarm doesn't ring, the shower runs cold, a button pops, the sink plugs up, a light bulb blows out, the dog escapes the yard, and the telephone goes dead (someone forgot to pay the bill!) You could handle the irksome problems individually, if they were spaced apart a bit. But your sanity unravels when irritations and inconveniences pile on at once.

Habakkuk had such a day. What's worth noting is that he not only trusted God in the midst of topsy-turvy disappointments, but he determined also to put a smile on his face. So the question is not can you trust Him, but . . . will you?

God my Saviour, you tell me time and again to rejoice in you despite the daily headaches and heartaches. Sometimes it's so hard. But if today happens to see everything unravel at once, empower me not to give in to defeat. Help me to do what Habakkuk did. May I trust you . . . with a smile.

SEPTEMBER

Exaggeration

The Lord detests lying lips, but He delights in men who are truthful.
PROVERBS 12:22

"I can't believe my pastor preached for a whole hour-and-a-half last Sunday." Translation: The pastor preached ten minutes longer than usual which cut into my lunch time.

"Our junior high group *never* does anything interesting and our youth leader is *really* boring." Translation: The junior high group doesn't plan activities in which I enjoy participating.

"It rained all day and I got soaking wet." Translation: It sprinkled lightly and my hair and sweater got slightly damp.

Sometimes we exaggerate to puff ourselves up in the eyes of friends, playing a competitive game of topping each other's stories. Other times we feel insecure and slant the facts to grab people's attention. Sometimes we play the actor and exaggerate just to add colour, drama, or to gain sympathy. Whatever the reason, if we never tell a story the way it happened, we end up hurting ourselves — people will never have a chance to get to know the real person behind the exaggerated stories.

The Bible tells us to *"let your 'Yes' be yes, and your 'No', no"* but Christians, perhaps more than most, are guilty of embellishing the truth. We play into the hands of Satan, the father of lies, when we distort the facts.

❧

If you'd like to break the habit of exaggeration, begin by listening carefully to what you say. Shading the truth may seem like one of those grey areas of behaviour, but always strive for the ideal: tell the truth.

Father, show me when I am not living out or speaking forth the truth. Stop me if I begin to shade the facts of stories or events, and help me to see that these are lies. May Jesus, the truth, speak through me today.

What's at Stake

Now I want you to know, brothers, that what has happened to me has really served to advance the gospel.   PHILIPPIANS 1:12

Some things are facts of life. Tyres blow out and computers bomb. Teeth decay and inflation skyrockets. Ants invade picnics and people get promoted ahead of us. Some things can't be avoided.

Few of us have actual control over these facts of life. But before you totally absolve yourself from any responsibility, there's one more fact to consider. You are responsible for the way you respond to these everyday, unavoidable inconveniences. You can either give up in dismay, or you can look to your sovereign Lord who has everything under control.

The apostle Paul assumed responsibility for his attitude towards trials. When he wrote Philippians 1:12, he knew that his response played a part in advancing the Gospel – that's why he took seriously his attitude when he stumbled upon unavoidable problems. Why? Because much more was at stake. Other lives could be influenced. God was taking notice.

You may not be in prison like Paul. However, today you may find yourself in a set of circumstances over which you have no control. The weather has ruined your outdoor plans. The traffic forces you to be late for an appointment. The electricity went out this morning in your home. You may not be able to claim responsibility for the situation, but you *can* be accountable for a godly response. Just remember what's at stake.

Dear Lord Jesus, I realize I have an oppoprtunity today to advance your Gospel by my patient response to problems. I pray that as others look on – whether my family, neighbours or co-workers – they will see you give me power and strength to smile through the circumstances. I know others will be influenced by my attitude. And because you are watching, assist me to honour you today in all that I do.

Assurance

Let us draw near to God with a sincere heart in full assurance of faith, having our hearts sprinkled to cleanse us from a guilty conscience and having our bodies washed with pure water.   HEBREWS 10:22

Ah, to have full assurance of faith! Faith, full grown and come of age. Faith that gives spiritual sight into spiritual realities, helping us be far more certain of things we do not see.

The Puritans believed that full assurance of faith comes to believers who have endured through some great trial or time of testing. Having endured, the Spirit gives us assurance and our faith receives a new degree, a new release of energy at every point in our life. The eye of the soul is strengthened and spiritual understanding is quickened.

If I've gained anything from my life in a wheelchair, I've gained fuller assurance of faith. My times of trial have made me certain of rich and deep spiritual realities. The Spirit has given me conviction that all things are, indeed, working together for good. I have assurance that I am never alone and that heaven is real. I know full well that the smallest of good deeds done in Christ's name will result in a powerful display of glory. Such is the life of full assurance of faith.

❧

Your times of trial and testing can be God's way of applying Hebrews 10:22 in your life. Through hardships, you can draw nearer to God. Your heart can be made more sincere. Your faith will rise to full assurance of wondrous spiritual realities. Remember, faith is the assurance of things hoped for!

Father, I am grateful that you have given me assurance of my salvation, but there are so many more spiritual realities of which I long to be certain. As I trust you in my trials, thank you for brightening the eye of my soul and quickening my spiritual understanding.

Be Joyful in Hope

Be joyful in hope, patient in affliction, faithful in prayer.

ROMANS 12:12

Forced bed rest is no fun. But I know a secret that helps me face it in faith. I choose a theme verse to help me keep focused. During a recent four-week stint in bed, I chose Romans 12:12.

While meditating on that verse, I wondered why God asks us to be joyful in hope. I can understand why He reminds us to be faithful in prayer – so many times in hardships we slack off in prayer. I can also understand why God asks us to be patient in affliction – patience is hard to muster when you're suffering.

But why does God say to be joyful in hope? Obviously, there must be many times when we lack joy in hope. Think about it. The focus of our hope is yet to be fulfilled; we don't yet possess that for which we hope. And you'll agree that it's hard to be joyful about something we don't yet have!

Lying in bed, it hit home that God wants me to be *joyful* about future things. Just as we have the command to be faithful in prayer and patient in affliction, we have a command to be joyful in hope. How can God command joy? It's easy once we realize what's over the heavenly horizon.

Does the idea of heavenly glories above put a smile on your face? Do you get a charge when you talk about the return of the Lord? Words like "pleasure", "happiness", and "delight" should come to mind when you hope in the Lord. Heaven will seem more near and real to you as you stir up your joy over that for which you hope. And remember, it's a command for your own good.

You give me so much hope, Lord, that I can't help but be joyful. You are the focus of my hope and the source of my delight. Whatever I face today, may I face it with the attitude of Romans 12:12.

Limitations

But He said to me, "My grace is sufficient for you, for my power is made perfect in weakness." Therefore I will boast all the more gladly about my weaknesses, so that Christ's power may rest on me. That is why, for Christ's sake, I delight in weaknesses, in insults, in hardships, in persecutions, in difficulties. For when I am weak, then I am strong. II CORINTHIANS 12:9–10

Sitting on my dad's knee and watching him swirl oils on his canvas . . . those are my earliest memories of painting. It wasn't long before I had my crayons out, working at his side. Art, for me, was a wild and fun-filled adventure of fingerpaints, colouring books and doodling on the backs of restaurant placemats.

My diving injury changed that. Art was no longer a wonderful exploration of limitless creativity. Paralysed from the shoulders down, I was suddenly confined with something I had never faced as an artist: limits.

All I could see were obstacles. My teeth grasped the pencils and paintbrushes. My eyes were only inches from the canvas. My weak neck muscles tired easily. My hands were unable to hold an eraser. If anything, my interest in art should have plummeted downhill.

But my limits had a purpose. I was forced to plan more carefully my compositions. And because I couldn't erase, I had to sit and think more – probably the most important discipline of any artist. Now I delight in my weaknesses and hardships because my paintings are far more beautiful. Praise God for limitations!

Suffering has always been intimately linked with creativity. Limitations force us to yield, to abandon ourselves to our Creator, God. And when we do, His creativity flows!

God, you have an amazing way of always doing more with less. We give you our limitations and your Spirit is set free to accomplish far more through us than we ever imagined. I bless you for my weaknesses.

Gifts

We have different gifts, according to the grace given us. If a man's gift is prophesying, let him use it in proportion to his faith. If it is serving, let him serve; if it is teaching, let him teach.   ROMANS 12:6–7

Fresh out of the hospital, my first few weeks at home in a wheelchair were terribly depressing. I knew that the Bible probably contained answers to my problems, but I had no idea where to look.

Now you'd think God would have brought my way a smartly dressed church youth director. He would have grabbed my attention. But no. God brought to my house a boy in the neighbourhood, a sixteen-year-old named Steve. We made a deal: I would supply plenty of cola if he would come every Friday evening to open the Bible and help me piece together the puzzle of my suffering.

My heart is still vibrating from what I learned under Steve's instruction. That young man had the gift of teaching, and it's interesting to note that Steve, at that point, never studied in Bible college or graduated with a seminary degree. He wasn't a pastor skilled in counselling or a youth director trained in methods of discipleship. Steve simply loved God, realized he had the gift of teaching, and opened himself to the Lord's direction. Thank God He pointed Steve to my house.

When it comes to spiritual gifts, the Lord gets a charge out of picking the most unlikely, ill-equipped people for a job. You don't need a diploma in domestic engineering to exercise the gift of service and the gift of giving does not require you to be wealthy. Giftedness works best in people whom the world would never choose to accomplish a task.

❧

Giver of every gift, thank you for the spiritual gift with which you've blessed me. May I use it to bless the lives of others and to bring you glory.

Heart Knowledge

I want to know Christ and the power of His resurrection and the fellowship of sharing in His sufferings, becoming like Him in His death, and so, somehow, to attain to the resurrection from the dead.   PHILIPPIANS 3:10

Greek scholars tell us that when the apostle Paul wrote about knowledge of Christ, he often described a head knowledge or an intellectual comprehension. But in Philippians 3:10 when Paul wrote, "I want to know Christ," he used a different word for "know". He meant a knowledge of the heart, an experiential fellowship of intimacy.

When Paul wrote Philippians 3:10, he used the word "know" in the Old Testament sense of the word, such as when Adam "knew" Eve or Abraham "knew" Sarah. As intimately as a couple would know one another physically, Paul wanted to know his Lord spiritually. His was a desire to fellowship with the Lord through direct experience, not through mere head knowledge.

The apostle Peter echoes this desire in II Peter 1:4 where believers are told that we *"participate in the divine nature"*. In other words, believers have a share within and a portion of the Lord Jesus.

This is how up-close and personal your spiritual fellowship with the Lord is meant to be. Not a head knowledge . . . but a heart knowledge.

Take time to participate in Jesus. Taste the Bread of Heaven. Drink deeply of the Living Water. Be the branch that relaxes in Him, the Vine. Get to know Him through direct experience, not merely through intellectual comprehension.

Lord of my life, you have shed your blood for me, dying on the cross so that we might have intimate fellowship. Forgive me when I only demonstrate a desire to know about you, rather than truly know you. I echo the apostle Paul when I say today that I desire to enjoy a close and personal union with you.

Not Getting What We Want

Going a little farther, He fell with His face to the ground and prayed, "My Father, if it is possible, may this cup be taken from me. Yet not as I will, but as you will." MATTHEW 26:39

For years I pleaded with God to give me hands and feet that would work. I never got what I wanted. Looking back, I can see God's wisdom in not granting my wish. I've come away from those torrid times of pleading all the better for not having received my greatest desire. My faith is stronger. My love for Jesus is brighter. It wouldn't be the same had my wish been granted.

Great things can happen when God does not give us what we want. Even the Father did not abide by the pleadings of His Son. In the Garden of Gethsemane, Jesus longed to bypass the cross. He hoped it might be possible for His Father to take Him in another direction. But at the close of His prayer, Jesus knew His pleading was over. He was heading for Calvary.

But, oh, the glorious things that happened as a result of the Father denying the Son His request. For one thing, the salvation of the world hinged on Christ's obedience to the Father's will. Thank heaven the cross happened.

A lot may hinge on God saying "no" to your wants and wishes. A lot of good may result in His taking you in another direction.

So, what is it that you want? Popularity or a clean reputation? An agreeable husband, an understanding wife? A bank loan? A thin body? If God does not grant you your wish, please know that He wants to strengthen you as you accept what comes from His hand. Ultimately, that may be the very thing your heart desires most.

Lord, not my will, but your will be done today!

Dry Wastelands

At noon Elijah began to taunt them. "Shout louder!" he said. "Surely he is a god! Perhaps he is deep in thought, or busy, or travelling. Maybe he is sleeping and must be awakened."   I KINGS 18:27

Elijah may have been describing Baal here, but I confess I've occasionally felt the same about God. I go through dry and weary times in prayer when I would swear God wasn't listening, that He was deep in thought over some global crisis or busy caring for refugees in Thailand.

Meditations are sometimes barren and they seem to yield no fruit. Dryness of soul provides a dangerous climate for sprouting seeds of doubt. We begin to wonder if it's all an illusion. But even Saint Teresa acknowledged that in every fifteen minutes of prayer, there are fourteen minutes of distraction.

During such times, please remember that God is not busy or off travelling or taking a snooze. His love is changeless and constant. His purpose for you is still on course. True, there may be times when He leads you through a stretch of dry wasteland, when His joys aren't as evident, but remember that even the Israelites who wandered in the desert for forty years were, the whole time, actually only a few days journey from the Promised Land.

Take the advice of Luke 21:28 and *"When these things begin to take place, stand up and lift up your heads, because your redemption is drawing near."* Take heart. Be of good courage. And lift before your Lord Psalm 63:1:

O God, you are my God, earnestly I seek you . . . in a dry and weary land where there is no water.

∾

Lord, may the dry times in my soul serve as a reminder for me to keep seeking you and keep loving you. Help me to remember that during barren times, you still seek and love me.

Fences

"The ox knows his master, the donkey his owner's manger, but Israel does not know, my people do not understand."   ISAIAH 1:3

Growing up on a farm in the hills of Maryland, God used horses to teach me a few of life's lessons. Like my sister's two horses, Shotgun, and his best buddy, Reds. The goal in life for Reds was to weasel his way through the pasture fence, while Shotgun was content to remain behind.

Reds would find a way, almost every night, to escape through the fence. After a late-night phone call from over the hill, my sister would have to climb out of bed and hunt down her horse with a flashlight – usually finding Reds standing placidly on the yellow line of our country road, munching weeds and being target practice for oncoming cars. She'd lead him back, always finding Shotgun in the pasture, whinnying and waiting for his buddy to come home.

I've been like Reds. For the longest time I was restless, looking for life's loopholes to crawl through. But for what? Greener pastures? No, life's weeds. Shotgun knew his place behind the barriers. Unfortunately, Reds was relieved of his pasture privileges to spend his nights in the barn. If I wanted to be safe, I knew I had better learn a lesson from those horses!

Despite having an owner and master, the fact remains that we are not always content with God's control or satisfied with His provisions. We sneak beyond the limits He has set for us. God has given us boundaries in our marriage, our friendships, and in our knowledge of evil. There are even borders for your desires and lines for your emotions. Stay within the boundaries God has placed around you.

Father, forgive me when I search all along the fence line of my thoughts for an escape. I want to stay behind your fence of protection!

Hate . . . but Cling to What Is Good

Love must be sincere. Hate what is evil; cling to what is good.

ROMANS 12:9

Christians have a lot to fight against these days. Pornography. Corruption in government. Abortion. Homosexual rights. Euthanasia. Humanism and secularism in schools.

But our campaigns simply can't be aimed at what is wrong in our society. We can't rebuke evil, expose the works of darkness, and simply stop there.

Rather, God calls us to lay down our lives for the *people* behind the issues we fight. Heroism is an extraordinary feat of the flesh and campaigns are occasionally won that way. But not people. Holiness is the only power which not only defeats darkness, but changes our lives, including the lives of those behind the things we fight.

That means praying for the pimp who exploits wayward teenagers on the street. It means interceding for the homosexuals who march against city hall for sexual civil rights. It means campaigning in prayer for the pornography mongers. It could mean connecting with the director of a nearby abortion clinic or contacting a government leader who's on the "take" and letting them know you care about their spiritual needs. It could mean taking a right-to-die advocate out to lunch to discuss life worth living.

Fighting and winning a campaign may bring one personal glory, but fighting for souls in prayer and winning them to Christ brings glory to God.

Approach problems in our society with a Romans 12:9 frame of mind. Hate what is evil. But, in prayer, love the individuals behind those hateful issues. As Jesus said somewhere, bless those who persecute you and love your enemy.

Oh Lord, I confess I am so critical of so many wrongs in society, but I don't pray for the people who perpetuate the wrongdoing. May my love be sincere and may you use my prayers to win these people to you.

Losing

At that time the disciples came to Jesus and asked, "Who is the greatest in the kingdom of heaven?" He called a little child and had him stand among them. And He said, "I tell you the truth, unless you change and become like little children, you will never enter the kingdom of heaven. Therefore, whoever humbles himself like this child is the greatest in the kingdom of heaven."

MATTHEW 18:1–4

Who is great in God's eyes? Jesus sets up a little child as His answer. Mind you, childhood back in those days was a condition not to be desired by any adult, and Jesus points to the child not as a winsome example of how charming and simple we're supposed to be, but rather how lowly.

When it came to the social ladder, children were losers. In the disciples' eyes, they didn't even qualify for the first rung. Yet if we want to follow Jesus, we must be like children – lacking rights, needing instruction, and enjoying little to no respect.

Throughout Scripture, Jesus exalts losers. Whether highlighting children or hobnobbing with prostitutes and tax collectors, Jesus rubs the salt of lostness into the sensibilities of those who are preoccupied with the sweetness of their successes.

Jesus lifts up the last. The least. The lost. The little. And even the dead. He drives home that He will not reward the rewardable or improve the improvable. His grace is reserved for those who, like a little child, see themselves as . . . little. Who is great in God's eyes? Whoever humbles himself like such a child, is greatest in the kingdom of heaven.

ঙ্গ

Malcolm Muggeridge said, "Jesus is not a prophet to the winners, but to losers, proclaiming that the last shall be first, the weak, strong, and the fools, wise. It is the lowly, not the proud, who shall inherit the kingdom of heaven."

When I see a child today, Lord, help me to see who you want me to be.

We Are Most Like Jesus when . . .

For if you live according to the sinful nature, you will die; but if by the Spirit you put to death the misdeeds of the body, you will live, because those who are led by the Spirit of God are sons of God.   ROMANS 8:13–14

If you were to list on a chalkboard ways we become more like Jesus, what would you write? The following might top your list: We become patient. Loving. Sympathetic. Wise. More pure. More sensitive. More discerning.

But in fact, because Christ was sinless, we become most like Him when we sin less. That's why a "hatred of sin" should top the list of qualities which make us most like Christ.

Jesus' primary purpose in coming was to deal with sin and its effects. He sternly confronted the Pharisees. He scolded the crowd about to stone an adulteress. He pointedly reminded the rich young ruler to relinquish his wealth. He even confronted sinful attitudes and actions in those who were dearest to His heart. He admonished His mother. He corrected Martha and then later on, her sister, Mary. He chided doubting Thomas and harshly rebuked Peter.

Jesus squared off against sin because He knew it was the ruin of those He loved. We feel His love most when He makes us most conscious of our rebellion. If you desire to become more like Jesus, if you want to get closer and know Him better, then be prepared to have Him uproot sin out of your life.

☙

Little wonder Jesus despised sin. John Bunyan gives insight: "Sin is the dare of God's justice, the rape of his mercy, the jeer of his patience, the slight of his power, and the contempt of his love."

Father, help me to understand that I am most like you when I am truly sensitive to evil — whether around me or inside me. I forsake my sin and cling to you!

Number Your Days

Teach us to number our days aright, that we may gain a heart of wisdom.
PSALM 90:12

I have this habit of numbering my days. When I wake up in the morning, I make a point of thinking, "Lord, this day is worth a thousand years of eternity and that means that the people I meet, the letters I write, the conversations I have . . . these all have value in your sight. Teach me to measure each moment."

I haven't cultivated this habit overnight. Because of all the things to be counted, this is the hardest – to number our days. We number everything else so easily. We know how much money we have in our purse and how many dollars in the bank. Farmers number their sheep and cattle. Restaurants number meals served in a week. Teachers check off attendance records. Gardeners can tell you how many tomato plants are in the back yard.

Yet we find it hard to number something so precious as our days. Perhaps that's because we see our days stretching on and on. They seem infinite and so there is no need, we think, to number them. Things we fail to account for, we waste. That's why it is wise to ask God to teach us to consider each day separate from the next, distinct in its purpose, unique in the way it is to be lived.

James 4:14 says, *"What is your life? You are a mist that appears for a little while and then vanishes."* And if we need another reminder, Isaiah 40:6–7 says, *"All men are like grass . . . The grass withers and the flowers fall, because the breath of the Lord blows on them. Surely the people are grass."* When we finally arrive in heaven, we will be surprised by many things, but nothing will amaze us more than how short life on earth really was.

You have written this day in your book, Lord, so teach me to spend it wisely for your glory.

Salt

Last night, I telephoned the family farm back in Maryland to see how my sister Jay was doing. She was up to her elbows in pickles! Cucumbers are ripe off the vine from Jay's garden so she's spending her evenings boiling and blanching, straining and sealing. I love my sister's pickles and I think her secret is . . . salt. She adds a lot of salt and tells me it's the best way to preserve a pickle at its crunchiest, tastiest best.

Those words go well together – salt and preserve. As Christians, we act as a salty preservative in this world, infusing godly values into life around us. We have the work of restraining evil and advancing good. And just as salt brings out flavour in food, we can "season to taste" our words when the world asks us for the reason for the hope that is within us.

Let your conversation be always full of grace, seasoned with salt, so that you may know how to answer everyone. COLOSSIANS 4:6

"You are the salt of the earth. But if the salt loses its saltiness, how can it be made salty again? It is no longer good for anything, except to be thrown out and trampled by men." MATTHEW 5:13

Preserving good in the world. Flavouring your words with the Gospel. These are big responsibilities. And remember that God did not say that you *should* be the salt of the earth, but that you *are*. So don't lose your saltiness, whatever you do today.

Lord of the Harvest, you have chosen me for a special task in this world. Thank you for the privilege of being salt in order to make people around me thirsty for you. Show me today how I can preserve all that is good around me and how I can flavour my conversation to make people long and look for you.

God's Anger

God made Him who had no sin to be sin for us, so that in Him we might become the righteousness of God.　　　　II CORINTHIANS 5:21

All of the Father's white-hot wrath against your sin was hurled at Christ as He hung on the cross. All of the Father's anger and indignation was heaped on the shoulders of His Son, as if saying, "Jesus, how could you have lied and murdered? I'm furious at you for stealing and raping! I'm punishing you for dealing drugs, for cheating on your wife, for abusing those children!"

"Why that's blasphemy to say Jesus did those things," some would say. True, Jesus never committed one of those sins. But you and I did. And God made Jesus to be sin for us. "Not to that extent," some would add. "Those are terrible crimes committed by wicked people. My sin isn't in that category."

Ah, but . . . *"You, therefore, have no excuse, you who pass judgment on someone else, for at whatever point you judge the other, you are condemning yourself . . . do you think you will escape God's judgment? Or do you show contempt for the riches of his kindness, tolerance and patience, not realizing that God's kindness leads you toward repentance?"*　　　　ROMANS 2:1, 3–4

All of our sin caused all of the Father's fury. And all of God's wrath against you for your rebellion was poured out on Jesus. That means God has no more anger left for you. Only kindness, tolerance and patience.

❧

Jesus bore the crushing pain of having His Father forsake Him. That's why your Saviour can now say to you, "I will never leave you or forsake you."

Lord Jesus, before your cross I kneel and see my sin that caused you to be made a curse. I am deeply humbled, Lord. Thank you for becoming sin for me that I might become the righteousness of God.

Obligated to Be Like Us

J esus Christ was obligated to be like us.

That was cruel, don't you think? The Son of God was obligated to step into cumbersome time from endless eternity. Obligated to put on finite flesh and disrobe deathless radiance. Obligated to endure the playground of Satan when He had the throne of God.

What could have obligated Him to such a thing? God always has a reason. Hebrews 2:17–18 tell us why:

For this reason He had to be made like His brothers in every way, in order that He might become a merciful and faithful high priest in service to God, and that He might make atonement for the sins of the people. Because He himself suffered when He was tempted, He is able to help those who are being tempted.

Why was He obligated? So that He could be merciful and faithful and so that He could come to the aid of those who are tempted.

Christ fulfilled his obligation because it is incumbent upon every High Priest to know why he is doing what he is doing. Reverently speaking, had Christ not been tempted in every way, I doubt the Garden of Gethsemane would have had much of a chance of seeing Christ stick around. Why die for something when you don't know the nature of that for which you are dying? The first-hand knowledge of the depth of our temptations kept Christ's face toward God so that He could utter, *"Not my will but thine."*

Lord, my flesh is weak and you know it well. I thank you that you know what it is like to live in such flesh. And I thank you that this knowledge channels your mercy toward me, a sinner saved by grace.

Crazy Moments

Your eyes will see the king in His beauty and view a land that stretches afar.
In your thoughts you will ponder the former terror . . .   ISAIAH 33:17–18

It's easy to lose sight of God. You get home late, you put on a casserole, but the phone rings and you forget about turning off the oven. Exasperated, you dump the casserole in the garbage. So you whip up something quick only to have three out of five around the dinner table turn it down. And for dessert? How about refereeing a fight over who gets the last of the chocolate chip ice cream?

God barely gets noticed during times like that. If we're thinking, we may quickly fire off a prayer for help. But we need more than that. We need to be driven to our knees by the overwhelming conviction that we have absolutely nowhere else to turn.   LINCOLN

It takes crazy moments, times when you almost border on mental collapse, to force you to your knees to seek Jesus. Maybe you sing a hymn as tears splatter on the hymnal pages. Maybe you pray the Twenty-third Psalm over and over until your nerves quit jangling. Then, oh, the delicious calm that sweeps over you when all you see is the king in his beauty and an uncluttered landscape of peace. When your focus is fixed so on the Lord, those crazy moments fade into the background, just as today's reading assures.

Ah, but what about that late dinner and the failed casserole and the fight which spilled over into the evening? It hasn't changed. But your focus has. Be driven to your knees by the overwhelming conviction that you have absolutely nowhere else to go.

You are the Lord of my crazy moments and I thank you, God, for allowing those nerve-wracking times. When they happen, it's your way of reminding me to look to you, my king.

Talking with God

Moses said to the Lord, "O Lord, I have never been eloquent, neither in the past nor since you have spoken to your servant. I am slow of speech and tongue."

EXODUS 4:10

Talking to God could be intimidating. Talking *with* God could strike even greater fear in your heart. Little wonder that Moses, when approaching God, became a nervous wreck. He stammered. He stuttered. He excused himself as ineloquent, unable to put two sentences together without stumbling.

Some Christians find it easier to talk to God than with Him. But prayer is cultivating a relationship with the Lord of the universe. Prayer is holding a conversation with Him, sharing *your* hopes, dreams and affections, as well as listening to *His* hopes and affections. That we can talk *with* God is truly astounding.

If you have a desire to talk with God, you are already halfway there. Because if you pay attention to those desires, your prayer life *will* be a conversation with your Saviour and Lord. Talking with God is not first and foremost petitioning or finding answers or getting things . . . talking with Him is a new level of listening to the voice of your Lord.

When you talk with someone, you share your thoughts and ideas and then listen. You listen to what your friend has to say. The same is true when we talk with God. Pause during your praise and intercession for long moments just to . . . listen. Wait on the Lord to hear what Scriptures He places on your mind. Focus the ears of your heart on Him, keeping distractions at bay and your wandering mind in check. This is listening. This is talking *with* the Lord.

How I praise you, Lord, that you desire a two-way communication with me. Forgive me when I talk at you . . . and fail to speak to you and then listen. May my prayer life grow in this way.

The Messiah Manifesto

The air in the synagogue was hot and tight. The attendant handed Jesus the scroll of Isaiah. He quietly unrolled it, found the verse he was looking for, and began to speak with the voice of uncommon authority:

"The Spirit of the Lord is on me, because He has anointed me to preach good news to the poor. He has sent me to proclaim freedom for the prisoners and recovery of sight for the blind, to release the oppressed, to proclaim the year of the Lord's favour."   LUKE 4:18–19

For some reason, He stopped. Just like that, Jesus stopped mid-sentence and sat down. The eyes of everyone were fastened on Him. Little wonder. They had never heard Isaiah 61 read in such a way, as if the words were His own. Finally Jesus broke the silence, concluding, *"Today this scripture is fulfilled in your hearing."*

The rest was a blur. The crowd demanded, *"Do here in your hometown what we have heard that you did in Capernaum!"* A scuffle broke out and then a riot. The story abruptly ends there, with Jesus escaping and going on His way to do what He had been sent to do.

And that's what made the crowd so angry. Jesus failed to say what the people were hoping He would say, that He had come to institute *"the day of vengeance of our God"*. Vengeance against the Roman occupiers. Vengeance against the political oppressors. When Jesus quoted Isaiah 61, He left off the most terrifying part of the second verse, the part about God's vengeance. He did so to make it clear that He had not come to condemn or destroy, but to seek and save the lost.

❧

Lord, I'm so grateful that when you came to earth, you came not to destroy, but to save. You came not to condemn wicked people, but to seek them out in order to give them your love.

Great and Terrible Day of the Lord

The Lord is not slow in keeping His promise, as some understand slowness. He is patient with you, not wanting anyone to perish, but everyone to come to repentance. II PETER 3:9

Jesus did not come to execute the wrath of God – He made that clear when He announced His Messiah manifesto from Isaiah 61. Jesus had come to proclaim the year of the Lord's favour, and not the day of vengeance of our God.

Rather than administer judgment, Jesus bore judgment. Rather than carrying out the wrath of God, He bore in His body the wrath of God.

For almost the last two thousand years, God has been proclaiming the year of the Lord's favour. He has been patient with wicked men, not wanting anyone to perish, but everyone to come to repentance.

But one day Jesus is coming back. And He is coming to finish that terrifying part of the second verse in Isaiah 61. He is coming to judge the living and the dead, to crush the wicked, punish evildoers and overthrow rulers of nations. Just picturing the scene tempers my pleas for Jesus to return soon – I know of too many people, even family members, who may end up getting trampled in the grapes of God's wrath!

Often I pray, "Come quickly, Lord Jesus." On the other hand, I sometimes ask the Lord to hold off a bit longer that great and terrible day of His return, the day of vengeance of our God. We only have a short time left until the Day of Christ, so let's get out and proclaim the year of the Lord's favour!

Thank you, Lord, that nearly two thousand years has passed since you announced your Messiah manifesto. Bless you for being patient, for not instituting God's wrath. So many people have come into your kingdom as a result of your patience.

Humility

Clothe yourselves with humility toward one another, because, "God opposes the proud but gives grace to the humble." Humble yourselves, therefore, under God's mighty hand, that He may lift you up in due time.

I PETER 5:5–6

When you think of the apostle Peter, you don't often think of humility. Brazen, outspoken Peter often talked out of turn and acted on impulse. This rough, tough fisherman spoke without thinking and often ended up embarrassing himself along with the rest of the disciples. What did he know of humility?

When Peter penned these verses about humility in his first epistle, I believe he drew his words from a vivid, clear memory of his Lord. He probably recalled the picture of Jesus in the upper room the night he was betrayed. Peter no doubt remembered the Lord wrapping the towel around his waist, stooping beside a wash basin, and gently wiping the feet of each disciple. Peter was the one who protested, but the Lord was demonstrating a lesson in humble service. A lesson that Peter, more than most, needed to learn.

Greek scholars tell me that the phrase "clothe yourself with humility" means to wrap humility around you as you would a towel or a servant's apron. That's a fitting picture for all of us who follow the example of our servant Lord.

✧

Christian leaders best demonstrate their leadership when they wrap around them the apron of a servant. To lead others means to wash their feet in humility, looking out for their interests before your own. If you are placed in a position of leadership today – leading your children, co-workers or friends – let your first act toward them be one of service. Service in humility.

Servant Lord, my heart kneels before you in praise and adoration. I bow before you in reverence and place myself under your authority. I lower myself beneath your hand of discipline and give you thanks.

Searching for Sinners

"Suppose one of you has a hundred sheep and loses one of them. Does he not leave the ninety-nine in the open country and go after the lost sheep until he finds it? And when he finds it, he joyfully puts it on his shoulders and goes home. Then he calls his friends and neighbours together and says, 'Rejoice with me; I have found my lost sheep.' I tell you that in the same way there is more rejoicing in heaven over one sinner who repents than over ninety-nine righteous persons who do not need to repent." LUKE 15:3–7

What a bad lesson on successful sheep ranching – leaving an entire flock to search for one lost sheep is a sure way to lose ninety-nine more. But who cares?! The shepherd certainly didn't! Yes, he loved the ninety-nine, but his heart was with the lost one. After searching high and low, he finally found the sheep and carried it home. He called his friends so they could rejoice with him. The lost had been found!

Most people can understand a God who forgives sinners who crawl to Him and beg for mercy. People can relate to a gruff God who makes sinners grovel in the dirt and plead for forgiveness. A God like that, we can understand.

But a God who actually runs to search for sinners in order to forgive them? A God who seeks out rebels in order to save them? A God who would lay down His life for His enemies? Little wonder we stand amazed at the love of Jesus!

❧

That our Good Shepherd leaves His large flock so He will not lose one sinner, shows the abundance of His care. And that He would carry the lost one on His shoulders, once he was found, shows the abundance of His tenderness.

Oh Lord, this parable shows me how much you care for the lost ones I love. Thank you, Shepherd!

Suffering According to God's Will

All suffering is within God's sovereign will. There is not a sparrow that falls without His knowledge or a soul lost for eternity without His tearful purpose being accomplished. In the midst of the expanse of the sovereign will of God is one kind of suffering initiated by us which God not only allows, but rewards.

So then, those who suffer according to God's will should commit themselves to their faithful Creator and continue to do good. I PETER 4:19

There are many ways to suffer in this world, where things happen to us. But the kind of suffering referred to by Peter is suffering we experience by choice, through obedience. Such obedience may result in mockery, beatings, discrimination, trials, and temptations. It's the price one pays for having our bodies in the world and our spirits in the kingdom. Like being on a rack, we can't escape the torture.

My wheelchair is a suffering that came from the sovereign purpose of the glory of God. And since that time twenty-five years ago, I've also suffered things that have come upon my spirit as a result of being in the kingdom. I have chosen to flee temptation to drag my body from church to hospital, to endure the scorn of those who don't know God. And I have suffered as a result. Such is the will of God for my life.

The common suffering He comforts. The godly suffering He rewards. Exchange neither for anything. We can "entrust our souls to a faithful Creator".

Lord, grant me strength to endure the common sufferings of life and the willful sufferings of your kingdom. In all these, may your presence sustain me and your glory made known.

God Gets Emotional

"Here is my servant, whom I uphold, my chosen one in whom I delight."
ISAIAH 42:1

Have you ever taken delight in someone? Maybe you've burst into laughter over an infant's first smile. Perhaps you've beamed with pride as a dear one graduates from college with honours. Or you've felt the delicious warmth of a loved one's gaze.

To take delight in someone close means to relish in his achievements. To be jubilant in his triumphs. To be captivated with his beauty and to find pleasure in the adoration and love given in return. And praise God, this is the way He feels about you!

When you obey, for instance, God doesn't merely observe from a distance and nod approvingly. He is not dispassionate or inexcitable about your obedience. Rather, when you grit your teeth and decide to obey, when you stem the tide of temptation and heroically follow Christ, the Lord is thrilled. He is delighted.

Oh, how it must give Jesus joy when we choose to obey. How it must delight Him when He sees our face and hears our voice in praise. And just in case you still think God isn't emotional toward you, consider Isaiah 62:5, *"As a bridegroom rejoices over his bride, so will your God rejoice over you."*

Near the end of Jesus' public ministry, the fog began to lift from the disciples' thinking. At the end of John chapter 16, the light dawns and they rise to a new level of trust and understanding. In John 16:31, Jesus exclaimed, *"You believe at last!"* Now *that's* getting emotional!

Lord, you are the one in whom I delight. You are the one whose love I relish. I am captivated with your beauty and I find pleasure in adoring you and worshipping you. May my praise be lovely in your sight!

God's Friends

"The Lord has sought out a man after His own heart and appointed him leader of His people . . ."   I SAMUEL 13:14

"You have not been like my servant David, who kept my commands and followed me with all his heart, doing only what was right in my eyes."
                                                      I KINGS 14:8

A woman named Mary Lance once asked the Lord if He would please introduce her to His best friends. She desired to meet believers on whom rested God's favour, people whose hearts were bent on pleasing the Lord. From these Christians, Mary Lance knew she would gain insight and wisdom. She also knew these "best friends" of God's were His joy and crown, so she expected a lot of joy in these relationships.

Mary Lance hasn't been disappointed. She relishes several unique and extraordinary friendships with exceptional people whose devotion to God is just as exceptional. Who are these Christians?

They are believers whose lives have intensity and depth. Their joy is fervent, but not feverish. They are energetic people, but not excitable. They are speedy in doing things, but not hasty. Prudent, but not timid or selfish. They are resolute and fearless, but not rash. They seem silent and yet make people around them feel their influence. Such believers are full of joy and peace, yet without parade and noise.

One more thing. Mary Lance has told me that many of these people have suffered, and suffered greatly. They are the ones who tenaciously cling to the foot of the cross in the stormiest of trials, saying with Job, *"Though He slay me yet will I hope in him."*   JOB 13:15

◯℧

God shows no favouritism. The Gospel is open to all. But I believe God reserves special affection for certain people – David was one, a man who sought after God's heart.

I would love to know your best friends, Lord. Would you introduce me to them?

The Poor Shall Be Rich

Listen, my dear brothers: Has not God chosen those who are poor in the eyes of the world to be rich in faith and to inherit the kingdom He promised those who love Him?
JAMES 2:5

George is an evangelist in Malawi who uses an old badly battered wheelchair. Not long ago he wrote to ask me to send him my husband's used shirts – his were wearing out and he wanted to dress his best as an ambassador for Christ.

George wheels himself from village to village over bumpy, rutted dirt roads that connect the small towns in Malawi. He longs for a power wheelchair during such exhausting journeys, but realizes such a luxury is beyond his grasp. Despite sore muscles and callouses on his hands, he keeps going. His deepest desire is to share Christ with others who are handicapped, to tell them that, despite their poverty, God is in control for their good and His glory.

George is dirt poor. The people to whom he ministers are even more poor. But there is none so rich in faith as George.

Remember, Christ willed to be born poor and He chose disciples who were living, for the most part, in poverty. Christ made Himself a servant of poor people. And He reminds us that whatever we do to help the least of the brethren – those most poor – we are personally ministering to Him.

All they asked was that we should continue to remember the poor, the very thing I was eager to do.
GALATIANS 2:10

❧

Lord, let me see those who are poor through your eyes. And when I see them, may I not turn my back on their need . . . for if I do, I would be turning my back on you.

Prophesy!

At this I fell at his feet to worship him. But he said to me, "Do not do it! I am a fellow-servant with you and with your brothers who hold to the testimony of Jesus. Worship God! For the testimony of Jesus is the spirit of prophecy.

REVELATION 19:10

I'm no prophet, but I'm intrigued by Peter's words in Acts, " *'In the last days,' God says, 'I will pour out my Spirit on all people. Your sons and daughters will prophesy . . . even on my servants, both men and women, I will pour out my Spirit in those days and they will prophesy.' "*

There aren't many Old Testament prophet types around these days. No bearded Jeremiahs wagging their finger at wicked men. No Elijahs rising to heaven in chariots of fire. But their legacy lives on. For we are their fellow servants. Today, the average homemaker with three children and thirty-three chores might prophesy, because whoever shares Jesus with a neighbour or friend is a prophet. *"For the testimony of Jesus is the Spirit of prophecy."*

These are the last days. We are God's sons and daughters. And whether you give the Gospel to a bunch of cerebral-palsied residents at a care facility or witness alongside Billy Graham at a gigantic crusade, the Spirit of God rests upon you as you testify of Jesus.

On second thoughts, maybe I *am* a prophet of Acts. And you could be, too. So get out there and prophesy!

The pouring out of God's Spirit on His sons and daughters has been happening ever since the last days kicked off with the book of Acts. But something is now shifting in God's timetable . . . His Spirit is being poured out abundantly and in a special sense . . . now is the time to hold to the testimony of Jesus, the spirit of prophecy.

Give me, O God, a sense of urgency to hold to the testimony of Jesus in these last days.

A Vision for Prayer

But the Lord said to me, "Do not say, 'I am only a child.' You must go to everyone I send you to and say whatever I command you. Do not be afraid of them, for I am with you and will rescue you," declares the Lord. Then the Lord reached out His hand and touched my mouth and said to me, "Now, I have put my words in your mouth. See, today I appoint you over nations and kingdoms to uproot and tear down, to destroy and overthrow, to build and to plant."

JEREMIAH 1:7–10

What a grand scale vision is today's reading! Uprooting nations and kingdoms? Destroying and overturning realms? Building and planting in remote corners of the earth? Little wonder we quiver and whine, "That's not for me, I am only a child."

But God is with you as you grab hold of this magnificent vision. That's right, God has appointed you over nations and kingdoms. He has appointed you to uproot and tear down . . . through prayer! God will touch your mouth and give you the words to intercede for the nations of the world. If you can't actually serve on the foreign mission field, you can travel there through prayer.

The world is starving for your prayers. And the devil is terrified of them. So don't let Satan shrivel and shrink your vision down to a size which he finds more manageable. If your heart needs to get pumped up, read Jeremiah 1:7–10 one more time and rejoice over God's vision for you to reach the world through prayer!

Dig out an old *National Geographic* map and thumbtack it opposite your desk to remind you of God's grand scale vision to reach the world with His love. Ask Him to fill your mouth with intercessions and then start building and planting through your prayers.

Enlarge my heart, Lord, to pray the way you would have me to pray for the world!

When All Else Fails

Grace and peace to you from God our Father and the Lord Jesus Christ.
PHILIPPIANS 1:2

With our quarrel still hanging heavily in the air, Ken and I sat in stubborn silence. Finally he spoke, "So we don't measure up to each other's expectations . . . maybe the only thing to do is pray." I knew he was right but at that moment I didn't feel like praying for him.

I listened as Ken mechanically prayed things about God, asking for His grace and peace. By the end of his prayer, I thought I heard his heart begin to soften through his words. After a long moment, I started praying, too, sounding just as hollow. But then my heart also began to melt. Feeling broken, I asked for mercy for me, a sinner, and for Ken, who is just trying to do his best. Ken prayed one more time and I wondered at the way he exposed his naked and bleeding heart. Tears began to well and I had an overwhelming desire to embrace him. Grace and peace hung heavily in the air.

As a married couple, our problems are not all that extraordinary, and most likely our problems won't go away. But prayer, heartfelt and honest, opens up the floodgates of God's grace and peace.

Are you caught in a vice of crushing circumstances, thinking that you have nowhere to turn? Sometimes we are driven to prayer by the overwhelming conviction that it is the only place of refuge, the only place to turn. At that point, prayer becomes an anguished cry, a laying bare of the heart, and it is the key to accessing God's most abundant grace. John Bunyan said, "In prayer it is better to have a heart without words, than words without a heart."

I praise you, Lord Jesus, that grace and peace are your abundant gifts to us. My heart kneels before you today as I receive these precious gifts.

OCTOBER

"Spiritual" Activities

The Lord said to Moses, "Speak to the entire assembly of Israel and say to them: 'Be holy because I, the Lord your God, am holy.' "   LEVITICUS 19:1-2

Have you noticed how some activities seem more spiritual, more sacred than others? Singing hymns, teaching church school or preparing a care basket for a sick friend – all of these seem exalted.

But what about when you drive to the petrol station for a fill up? Or when you count up coupons to the shop assistant at the supermarket? Or while you're waiting for the salesperson to wrap what you've bought?

We do it all the time – separate "religious" activities into one group and "regular" into another. But Leviticus 19 addresses that problem. In one verse Moses says, *"Do not steal,"* yet the verse next to it states, *"Do not go over your vineyard a second time or pick up the grapes that have fallen"* (Leviticus 19:10, 11). Again He says in one verse, *"Do not mate different kinds of animals"* (Leviticus 19:18-19).

Why didn't Moses group together all the spiritual activities and leave those nonessential things for another chapter? It's no mistake that God spoke these commands in one breath, mingling "spiritual" and "nonspiritual". In God's eyes, all of life's activities are sacred.

God wants you to understand that all life is spiritual; all of life's activities come under His domain. How you "tend your vineyard" and how you talk to the shop assistant. How you "mate animals" and how you treat your neighbour. Everything you do can be a way of worshipping the Lord. Remember that the next time you wash dishes.

Dear God, I want to view everything I do as a way of worshipping you. Remind me that every activity is spiritual in your eyes, no matter how small or insignificant it seems.

Stop and Listen

A man of knowledge uses words with restraint, and a man of understanding is
even-tempered.   PROVERBS 17:27

It happens all the time. You get together with a friend, or someone
you haven't seen in a while, and before you know it, you've filled the
air with a lot of talk about . . . you. You realize in embarrassment that
you're rambling on about yourself and have nearly forgotten to include
your friend or even God in the conversation. Oh, to be able to use words
with restraint.

That's why I love travelling with my husband or my best friends. We
are able to relax and be silent in each other's presence. No forced
conversations. No filling the air with empty words. What a blessing it
is to be able to sit with someone you love, smile at each other occasionally,
and enjoy the quiet together. Friendships, whether with others or with
God, are deepened in silence.

When you stop talking long enough to listen, you learn something –
only in silence can what you hear filter from your head into your heart.
Only in silence can you hear the heartbeat of God and His still, small
voice. In quiet, you realize spiritual insights that reach far beyond words.

If you meet with a friend today, make a concerted effort to talk less
and listen more. It may do wonders for your friendship. And this evening
when you retire, say less in your prayer time and devote more moments
simply listening to God.

Father, I desire to be a person of knowledge and understanding. That means I
must use words with restraint. Forgive me when I fail to even think about what
I say to you, and to others, as well. I don't want to fill my prayers with petitions
so much as wordless worship today. Thank you for what you will teach me in silence.

Cisterns and Springs

"My people have committed two sins: They have forsaken me, the spring of living water, and have dug their own cisterns, broken cisterns that cannot hold water."

JEREMIAH 2:13

Jesus said that rivers of living water would flow out of the lives of those who believe in Him. His living water would brim over from the wellspring of the Spirit within us, quenching our thirst and touching the parched lives of those around us. The life of the Lord Jesus is a constantly flowing stream, a river even, keeping us fresh, filled and satisfied.

We stop the flow, however, when we try to reservoir God's spring of living water in our lives. We become cisterns – holding tanks for past victories or other people's ideas. At that point, we have forsaken the spring of living water. We have tried to store that which cannot be saved, we have tried to keep that which must keep flowing. The result? Our lives lack freshness and freedom, and we become stagnant pools reflecting old experiences and tired testimonies.

God says that these cisterns of our own making will break. What we try to save, we will lose. The warning is clear: Throw out the broken cisterns and get in the flow of God's spring of living water.

If you know anything about springs and cisterns, this warning in Jeremiah 2:13 should be easy to grasp. A spring is a flow of water from the ground, often a source of a stream. A cistern is a large receptacle for storing water. Don't rely on yesterday's experiences or last month's victories. God wants to give you fresh, thirst-quenching life each new day. So start with this prayer . . .

Jesus, the Living Water, I thirst after you. May your life in me not be a trickle or even a small stream, but a river. I confess my sin, clearing away any obstruction which might hinder your flow in my life.

Freedom

Now the Lord is the Spirit, and where the Spirit of the Lord is, there is freedom.
II CORINTHIANS 3:17

Jesus never said to His disciples, "Obey my rules." Instead, He told His followers to "Obey me." And because the Lord did not leave us with a long list of "Thou shalt not's," we have freedom.

Jesus stripped the fear and intimidation away from obedience when He wrapped His life around His Word. What liberty! The Lord made obedience something that you would *desire* to do because He gave His life that you might be free. What a brilliant motivation for us to trust and obey!

Sometimes I wish God would give me less freedom and force me to do the right thing, making me obey. It would be easier that way. This "freedom stuff" carries with it a heavy weight of responsibility. I am required to discern between white and black, light and dark, good and evil. I am required to make choices. I am required to be free.

But that's the beauty of the freedom of the Lord. And it is His love which makes me *want* to obey.

❧

This is why Jesus said His commandments were not burdensome. Obeying God was never meant to be a chore or a duty, but a joyous response to His love.

Lord of Liberty, thank you for setting me free from the bondage of sin, death and the law. Yours is the law of liberty, the law of love. May I never abuse this precious freedom or use it as an excuse to sin. And may I obey you with a joyful spirit, knowing that your love is all the motivation I need.

A Long Obedience

When Ken and I drive north from Los Angeles to visit his relatives in Stockton, we take the interstate highway, a long, straight road through the central valley of California. Once when we were driving through Illinois, we took another long highway straight through miles and miles of cornfields. And once when I drove across Texas, I squinted to see the horizon many miles far down another long, flat road across the Texas plains.

When I think of the word boring, I think of those highways. One straight stretch in the same direction. No matter if it's a road, someone's two-hour lecture, or waiting in a line that stretches for blocks, it's hard not to become weary. It's hard just keeping your mind awake, your senses sharp, and your eyes focused on what's ahead.

We balk at developing a long obedience in the same direction. A marriage that is forever struggling, a church that seems to produce little results, or housekeeping routines that never vary from week to week. Caring for an elderly parent or a handicapped child can be a long obedience in the same direction.

Let us not become weary in doing good, for at the proper time we will reap a harvest if we do not give up.   GALATIANS 6:9

⤟

If I've described you, then you need to pay attention to the grace of God, finding daily renewal from his storehouse of fresh strength and hope. So be alert and be on guard. If you're tempted to feel that your life is like a long, boring stretch of highway, don't you dare fall asleep at the wheel. Don't be weary in doing good because your heavenly destination will be worth the long obedience.

Please, Lord, give me your grace today. Help me not to become weary at what needs to be done. Help me to obey!

Heaven in the Here and Now

But you have come to Mount Zion, to the heavenly Jerusalem, the city of the living God. You have come to thousands upon thousands of angels in joyful assembly, to the church of the firstborn, whose names are written in heaven.

HEBREWS 12:22–3

D o you notice anything odd about that verse? It's the verb tense. The writer of Hebrews says we "have already come" to heaven. Resurrection promises are never written for the far and distant future, but rather for the here and now.

God wants us to have a present-tense excitement, a right-around-the-corner anticipation of heaven. He wants us to believe that we have already come to the heavenly Jerusalem. He wants us to realize that we are already seated with Christ in heavenly places, "having our conversation in heaven". As far as God is concerned, the coming of the Lord is at hand, ready to explode on the world's stage at any moment.

The resurrection throbs with present-tense excitement when we learn to invest our days in eternity. When we sit close to self-scrutiny, when we examine our motives, words and actions to make certain we are building for eternal glory, then heaven will seem as close as a heartbeat. The future, the distant, and the vague, will appear as the present, the near, and the real. The kingdom of God is within you, Jesus said, and it whets our appetite for kingdom fulfilment at any day, any moment.

A lively hope of heaven will bring forward the things which most believers call invisible and distant. Such a hope will disclose to you the heavenly mansions, the happy courts, the adoring multitudes. It opens your ears to hear heavenly melodies, to catch the very words of angels' anthems.

Lord, help me to see heaven so I might live today for eternal glory.

No One Cares Like Jesus

O Lord, what is man that you care for him, the son of man that you think of
him?   PSALM 144:3

N o one ever cared for me like Jesus,
There's no other friend so kind as He;
No one else could take the sin and darkness from me –
O how much He cared for me!

Whether you are weak or strong, saintly or struggling, Jesus cares for you.
I realize you may be thinking, "Sure, Jesus cares for me in the general
sense, as for the whole world, but when it comes to specifics, surely there
must be others He is more interested in. After all, I can't pray out loud
. . . I have a hard time understanding the Bible . . . I can't seem to shake
bad habits. Yes, I know He cares but not as much as He does for more
obedient types."

Not so. The Lord's care for you does not hinge on your hang-ups. His
care for you has nothing to do with your baggage of personal problems.
You could be a wimp when it comes to standing for the Lord, always
getting distracted by everyday pressures. It doesn't matter. As a child of
God, *you* matter. For you, dear believer, have the full force and undivided
attention of eternal love. Love which cares with no strings attached.

The Living Bible translates I Peter 5:7 as, *"Let him have all your worries*
and cares, for he is always thinking about you and watching everything that
concerns you."

What other friend is there who thinks about you every moment, every
second of the day and night? What other friend is so jealous for your love
and affection? What other friend forgives seventy times seven, and then
some? Truly, no one ever cared for you like Jesus!

You are always thinking of me and watching everything that concerns me. I love
you, Jesus!

The Thought Patrol

We demolish arguments and every pretension that sets itself up against the knowledge of God, and we take captive every thought to make it obedient to Christ.
II CORINTHIANS 10:5

When I catch myself, I'm aghast at how many lazy, anxious or lustful imaginations wheedle their way into my head. When they do, the "thought patrol" goes on alert and I ask myself, "What are you doing in my mind, you silly thought? You have no business thinking those things in my head, so in Jesus' name, scram!"

I'm sure you identify. Perhaps for you, it's a problem with daydreaming. Keeping track of another's wrongs. Stewing over worries. Whatever, God expects you to take responsibility for the ponderings that creep into your brain. He requires you to take charge of those ideas that finagle their way into your head. You are accountable.

❧

If your head is a nesting place for harmful imaginations, then it's time to set up a thought patrol – just another name for the Holy Spirit. Let Him set up watch, keep guard, and prevent harmful thoughts. The only way you can exercise power over your thought life is to do so in the power of God's Spirit. II Corinthians 10:4 says, *"The weapons we fight with are not weapons of the world. On the contrary, they have divine power to demolish strongholds."*

Double-check what goes on in your mind today because II Corinthians 10:5 says it is possible for every thought to be made obedient, to become captive to Christ.

Lord of all, please set up watch over my thoughts. Quickly interrupt any idea today that is not glorifying to you or beneficial to me and stop me from labouring on thoughts that only lead to sinful indulgence. I want to take responsibility for what goes on in my mind . . . rule my imagination this day, Lord.

Lust

"If your right eye causes you to sin, gouge it out and throw it away. It is better for you to lose one part of your body than for your whole body to be thrown into hell. And if your right hand causes you to sin, cut it off and throw it away. It is better for you to lose one part of your body than for your whole body to go into hell." MATTHEW 5:29–30

When it comes to lust, God prescribes a severe operation. That's because if we don't deal severely with lust, then a glance becomes a gaze. Something we would dare not touch before, becomes something we brazenly handle. The result? A seared conscience which mistakes evil for good and good for evil.

Putting away lustful thoughts is so painful. Pulling your eyes away from sensual images is incredibly difficult. Slamming the door on an unhealthy relationship seems impossible to do. In fact, doing away with such sin is so excruciating that when you do it, it feels as though you are losing a part of yourself. The pain is so severe that it feels like you are gouging out your eye or cutting off your hand. But it must be done.

And, oh, the peace and joy that results. We would take giant steps forward in our fellowship with the Lord if we would but take our eyes and hands off what is not permitted, and place our eyes on Jesus and our hands on His Word.

❧

It could be a magazine. The wife of a friend at church. The husband of a neighbour. It could be a certain section in the video rental shop. A television show. Or, maybe it's the world of your daydreams. Keep a constant watch over your heart . . . suppress the first rising of temptation . . . avoid the occasions of sin . . . decline the company of those who are a snare . . . keep out of harm's way.

Father, even when it comes to things that are lawful in my life, help me to limit them if I find them to be a temptation. May I walk in the Spirit so as to not fulfil the lusts of the flesh.

Acorns

The other day, I watched a stiff autumn breeze roll around some acorns. I knew most would blow away. Others would become cracked and dried on top of the hard dirt. A few would take root under the soil – these were the acorns destined to become trees.

If you were to tell that tiny acorn that one day he would be as tall as a building, with heavy branches and thick, green leaves, that nut would say you were crazy. A gigantic oak tree bears absolutely no resemblance to an acorn. The two, although one and the same, seem as different as night and day.

Little wonder heaven is mind-boggling. Trying to understand what our bodies will be like in heaven is much like asking an acorn to understand his destiny as a tree.

When you sow, you do not plant the body that will be, but just a seed . . . the splendour of the heavenly bodies is one kind, and the splendour of the earthly bodies is another . . . So will it be with the resurrection of the dead.

I Corinthians 15:37–42

⧠

Your glorified body will be so grand, so glorious, that you can only catch a fleeting glimpse of the wonder to come. You – and one day what you will be – are one and the same, yet so very different. In order to understand what that means, go find an acorn on the ground, look up into the billowy skirts of the tree from which it fell, and then praise your Lord that *"So will it be with the resurrection of the dead."*

Lord of the Resurrection, I kneel before you today because you are the resurrection and the life. Because of you, I will one day enjoy the splendour of a heavenly body. Thank you that although I am now an acorn, I am one day destined to be a tree.

Peculiar People

Jesus Christ, who gave himself for us to redeem us from all wickedness and to purify for himself a people that are His very own, eager to do what is good.
TITUS 2:13–14

Down against the southern edge of Pennsylvania sits the little hamlet of Honey Brook. It's Amish country. Schoolboys in black hats walk along the roadside. Girls in starched hats and aprons sit on milk cans at the end of a farm lane.

My Christian friends, Amos and Hannah Stoltzfus, and their many children, had invited a group of us to their home for dinner. We drove to their farm, following the country road that wound through rows of corn. We passed a white dairy barn, a buggy shed, and then stopped at the back door of their farmhouse. Amos and Hannah welcomed us in out of the cool, fall night into their cosy kitchen.

After a delicious Pennsylvania Dutch dinner, the family pushed back the table and brought out benches for a hymn-sing. Sitting straight-backed, hands on knees, and facing each other, the Amish folks and a few of their Mennonite friends launched into a rich and rigid harmony on a couple of old German hymns. What a glorious night of fellowship!

As we left their farm that night, I realized that we had everything in common with our Amish friends. How people dress, the way they talk, or the fact that they drive a horse and buggy instead of a car, doesn't matter. What counts among friends is the heartfelt hospitality, the smiles, the singing of a hymn that warms the spirit, and the dear embrace from a brother in Jesus who really means it. The Amish are called the "peculiar people" from the King James version of Titus 2:14 – oh, if only the rest of us were so peculiar!

❧

Help me, Lord, to be eager to do what is good today.

Can Jesus Count on You?

"We are going up to Jerusalem, and the Son of Man will be betrayed to the chief priests and the teachers of the law. They will condemn Him to death and will turn Him over to the Gentiles to be mocked and flogged and crucified."
MATTHEW 20:18–19

The dirt road to Jerusalem was bustling. Jesus and His disciples had to step into a ditch while a camel caravan shuffled past. A group of boys herded their goats. Women chattered and carried baskets of figs and olives.

Jesus and the disciples continued their trek up the road, yet no one noticed the Lord's strange, heavy tread. Finally, when they rounded the top of a hill and caught sight of the gleaming temple of Jerusalem, Jesus stopped. Peter, John and the rest strolled a few yards ahead. Then they turned round. Something was wrong.

Jesus began to pour out His heart, telling them exactly what was about to happen to Him when He passed through the city gates. The disciples wondered what in the world He was talking about. But that's not all. They not only ignored the Lord's troubled words, they began arguing and jockeying for positions in the coming kingdom – two of them even dragged their mother into the dispute.

Perhaps the Lord had hoped to lean on His friends at such a time. Instead, He found a bunch of squabbling men who only half listened. He found no friendly words, no sympathetic ears.

Think of all the things friends share – heart-to-heart talks, the sacrifice of time, joys and sorrows. Jesus covers His side of friendship, but what about our side? What sort of friend does He have in you?

Oh Lord, it's easy for me to criticize the behaviour of the disciples, but I am no better. Forgive me when I fail you, but thank you for being such a faithful friend to me.

The Written Code

For when we were controlled by the sinful nature, the sinful passions aroused by the law were at work in our bodies, so that we bore fruit for death. But now, by dying to what once bound us, we have been released from the law so that we serve in the new way of the Spirit, and not in the old way of the written code.

ROMANS 7:5–6

Put off falsehood. Avoid all appearances of evil. Forgive seventy times seven. Flee from sexual immorality. Let no unwholesome word come out of your mouth. Get rid of bitterness.

The longer the written code, the more oppressive the pressure to obey. A list like that seems tiring. Obtrusive. Burdensome. And the more you concentrate on the do's and the don'ts, the more tempted you are to break the law. Like the mother who tells her child, "Don't go in that room," you can then be sure her child will, sooner or later, head for that room. As the verse says, sinful passions are aroused by the law.

Thank God, we have been released to serve the Lord in the new way of the Spirit and not in the old way of the written code. We serve Jesus; we don't serve a list of rules. This is exactly why we should stop using words like "victory" and "defeat" to describe our obedience. We are never defeated by this or that sin. Rather, we are obedient or disobedient to the Lord.

If you see obedience as merely a duty, it will quickly become a burden. The letter of the law has no saving or sanctifying power, and human will, no matter how strenuous, cannot give that power. So look to *Jesus* and obey *Him* with glad, reckless joy.

Lord, although you don't give me rules, you give me your love – may I return that love and obey you out of sheer joy.

When He Is Easily Lord

"Return, faithless people; I will cure you of backsliding." "Yes, we will come to you, for you are the Lord our God."   JEREMIAH 3:22

Who is the truly obedient Christian? Is it the one whose life exhibits blue ribbon behaviour? Is it the believer who demonstrates the Lord's commands in their highest possible measure?

When we heed the call to begin afresh a life of obedience, we may think that by more Bible study and self-scrutiny we will grow into it. Then, we assume, obedience will gradually come. That's a mistake. Jeremiah learned this lesson when the Lord said to him, *"Return . . . I will cure you."* God pointed to Himself as the cure. In the Lord's eyes, the truly obedient person is the one who truly longs to know Him.

God doesn't want our achievements, He wants us. God doesn't want our rule keeping, He desires us. But remember, Jesus will never force you or coerce you into obeying. He will never insist on being your Master. Instead, He insists on loving you.

❧

"In certain moods we wish God would make us do the right thing, but He will not; and in other moods we wish He would leave us alone altogether, but He will not. If we do not keep His commandments, He does not come and tell us we are wrong," says Oswald Chambers.

When you make Jesus the centre of your thoughts and the desire of your heart, when you live in adoration of Him . . . He is easily Lord.

Father, I know now that the life of continual obedience is impossible without continual fellowship with you. Help me to see that obeying you is perfect liberty and that in turning to you, I shall be happy, safe and free. Have sway over my heart that I might turn to you and obey.

You Are an Eagle

Once there was an eagle who didn't act at all like the great, proud bird he was born to be. This was an eagle who lived among chickens in a hen house and covered coop. He could be seen every morning scratching the dirt for bits of grain and pecking at the cobs of corn the farmer threw to him and the rest of the chickens. The eagle's eyes were as dull as his feathers. He was one sad bird.

One day, a passer-by who felt sorry for the eagle entered the cage, grasped the bird with both hands, and carried him to the top of a nearby mountain. A sweeping spectacle of rugged peaks, turquoise lakes and pine forests stretched before them. The heart of the great eagle began to pound in the man's grasp.

The eagle's eyes focused on the glacier-scarred mountains and deep cliffs. He lifted his head, breathing in the icy air and cool, fresh scent of alpine flowers. Feeling the bird struggling, the man lifted the eagle up and . . . let him go! The bird stretched his wings and soared across the valley until he was a tiny speck against the distant mountains.

The eagle had realized his destiny.

But you are a chosen people, a royal priesthood, a holy nation, a people belonging to God, that you may declare the praises of Him who called you out of darkness into His wonderful light. Once you were not a people, but now you are the people of God; once you had not received mercy, but now you have received mercy.

I PETER 2:9–10

I have to confess, Lord, that sometimes I act like an eagle in a chicken coop. But I am a child of God! May I realize my destiny as I focus on the immense wonder of eternity and breathe in celestial air.

The Day of Evil

Therefore put on the full armour of God, so that when the day of evil comes, you may be able to stand your ground, and after you have done everything, to stand. Stand firm then, with the belt of truth buckled round your waist, with the breastplate of righteousness in place, and with your feet fitted with the readiness that comes from the gospel of peace. In addition to all this, take up the shield of faith, with which you can extinguish all the flaming arrows of the evil one. Take the helmet of salvation and the sword of the Spirit, which is the word of God.   EPHESIANS 6:13–17

When exactly *is* the day of evil talked about in this verse? Is it some great and terrible day of the Lord yet to break on the horizon? Is it the day when the Antichrist is revealed, ushering in a great tribulation?

No. The day of evil is when you feel like dropping the shield of faith, unbuckling your breastplate of righteousness, kicking off the shoes of the Gospel of peace and throwing down the sword of the Spirit. *This* is the evil day.

You don't need a great tribulation to feel you're under attack. For you, the evil day may come when your reputation gets dragged through the mud or when the dog tracks dog-doo all over the kitchen floor and carpet in the hall. The evil day may happen when your pot roast turns to charcoal in the oven while you referee a fight between a few members of your family.

What are we to do on the evil day? Read again our verses for the day and you'll discover tht in the span of a few sentences, the word "stand" occurs at least three times. Stand firm in the Lord!

Finally, be strong in the Lord and in His mighty power. Put on the full armour of God so that you can take your stand against the devil's schemes.

EPHESIANS 6:10–11

Know Your Transgressions

For I know my transgressions, and my sin is always before me. Against you, you only, have I sinned and done what is evil in your sight, so that you are proved right when you speak and justified when you judge. PSALM 51:3-4

Some of my friends tell me I'm too hard on myself. They say I berate myself too much. But I know the truth. I know when I'm vying for attention or when I'm shading the truth or hiding the facts. I know when I'm deliberately ignoring the Spirit's direction. I know the times when I switch the subject to avoid my husband's scrutiny or when I turn my back in anger to punish him or make him feel guilty.

As the psalmist says, I *know* my transgressions. Sensitivity to one's sin is not a curse, but a blessing. It's maturity to know the evil you are capable of, to realize the depths of your depravity. And to a sensitive conscience, pain on account of sin ought not to be an occasional thing, but intense and permanent. Praise God if, like the psalmist, you are able to say, *"My sin is always before me."*

Mercy is defined as kindness in excess of what might be expected. And for the multitude of your sins, God has a multitude of mercies. Tender mercies they are, compassionate kindness far in excess of what you deserve. Where sin abounds, grace abounds. To know your transgressions provides an opportunity to confess and receive abundant mercy, compassionate grace.

How sensitive are you to the sin in your life? Does your Spirit-sharpened conscience warn you when you shade the truth? Do red flags wave when you backbite with gossip? Know your transgressions, for when you do, His tender mercies are there to forgive.

Father, make me aware of every sin, hidden and exposed. And thank you for your tender mercy that forgives.

I'd Never Do That!

So, if you think you are standing firm, be careful that you don't fall!
I CORINTHIANS 10:12

"Nope, not me, you'd never catch me doing *that!*" Oh yeah? Upright and obedient Noah stood alone against a carousing, lustful world that drank itself silly. Who would have thought Noah would end up drunk? Abraham was ready to push obedience to the point of sacrificing his only son. Who would imagine he would lie straight-faced?

Look at Lot standing against the filthiness of Sodom. Hardly does he get delivered from the city's destruction than he falls into incest with his own daughters. Who would have guessed? Bold and courageous David was brave enough to go up against Goliath, the warrior giant of the Philistines; later on he made believe he was a madman for fear of his enemies.

And consider Elijah. We take him to be a rather brave man, wielding the sword of God's vengeance against tens of thousands. But the threat of one woman then sends him into suicidal despair. Peter, as part of the inner circle, followed the footsteps of Jesus closer than anyone. He ended up cursing and denying the Lord.

These things happened to them as examples and were written down as warnings for us, on whom the fulfilment of the ages has come. I CORINTHIANS 10:11

◄§

Just when you think you know yourself, you do or say something that seems so out of character. But it's not. The character of our body of sin and death is to sin. Don't be surprised. Just be careful that you, too, don't fall.

Lord, please subdue my corruptions and grant me the grace to live above them. Make me realize that I could easily fall at any time. May I lean on your grace to deliver me from the evil in my life of which I'm not even aware.

Lip Surgery

"Woe to me!" I cried. "I am ruined! For I am a man of unclean lips . . ."
Then one of the seraphs flew to me with a live coal in his hand, which he had
taken with tongs from the altar. With it he touched my mouth and said, "See,
this has touched your lips; your guilt is taken away and your sin atoned for."
ISAIAH 6:5–7

And I know of no greater sin of mine than my lips. My unholy
thoughts, though many, are my private sins that affect only me. My
unholy deeds, though heinous, are few and far between.

But my words are many and their damage is public. In a few short
sentences, I can cut a baggage handler at the airport down to size for
dropping my wheelchair. In a string of vexings and hammerings, I can
skewer my husband's plans for the weekend. In a twisted maze of
flatterings, I can manipulate any unsuspecting soul.

Oh what a burden. To possess such an instrument is more than I can
bear at times. But while the reality of my sinful lips depresses me, God
corrects me with one important observation: *"See, this has touched your
lips."*

For Isaiah, it was the burning coal used by God to drive home His point
that outside intervention needed to be done. Through the painful imagery
of cauterized lips, Isaiah learned an important lesson. His lips were impure,
but God touched them and declared them clean.

But that is not the end of it. God desired to use those lips. When asked,
"Whom shall I send?" Isaiah had the righteous audacity to say, *"Here I
am. Send me."*

❧

*Lord, purify my words by Thy presence in my life. Remove the dross of selfishness
and pride from these lips. Make them sing and speak of you all my days.*

Crowns

For we must all appear before the judgment seat of Christ, that each one may receive what is due him for the things done while in the body, whether good or bad.   II CORINTHIANS 5:10

Adults pooh-pooh the idea of rewards in heaven, but children don't. Like a student before his teacher, a child squirms in delight at the anticipation of a reward, much less a jewelled crown of his very own. Maybe that's why Jesus said that children were best fitted for the kingdom of heaven.

The kid in me would love, just love, a crown in heaven. What's the big deal about crowns? The Bible celebrates the crowning day in II Corinthians 5:10 and goes on to mention specific crowns.

The crown of life mentioned in James 1:12 is reserved for those who persevere under trials and withstand God's tests. The crown of rejoicing in I Thessalonians 2:19 is a reward for believers who introduce others to Christ. The incorruptible crown in I Corinthians 9:25 is for those who are found to be pure and blameless on the judgment day. And in I Peter 5:2–4 there's a special crown reserved for Christian leaders who have guided others – it even says the chief shepherd Himself will present that crown.

But the child in me jumps up and down to think that I might be rewarded by the crown talked about in II Timothy 4:8: *"Now there is in store for me the crown of righteousness, which the Lord, the righteous Judge, will award to me on that day – and not only to me, but also to all who have longed for his appearing."*

Heavenly crowns are not just rewards for a job well done on earth; crowns are a glorious consummation of the job itself.

❧

How I long to hear you say, Lord, "Well done, good and faithful servant." What a reward that will be.

Oaks of Righteousness

He is like a tree planted by streams of water, which yields its fruit in season and whose leaf does not wither. Whatever he does prospers.　　PSALM 1:3

The leaves on almost all the trees have fallen now. Just a few hardy types are still dangling on the branches, but even these are withering fast. That's why this time of year Psalm 1 comes alive as we are reminded that, as Christians, *our* leaf does *not* wither.

God had a great idea when He chose a tree as a symbol for growing Christians. Just consider it. It's a fact that the branches of growing trees not only reach higher, but their roots grow deeper. It's impossible for a strong tree to have high branches without deep roots. It would become top heavy and topple over in the wind. The same is true with Christians. It's impossible to grow in the Lord without entwining our roots around His Word and deepening our life in His commands.

Other parallels? A growing tree will always provide shade and comfort for others. A growing tree takes in light and processes it for food. Such a tree is always able to reproduce itself. And sometimes, the best trees give their life for others as branches are lopped off for firewood or lumber.

They will be called oaks of righteousness, a planting of the Lord for the display of His splendour.　　ISAIAH 61:3

God employs symbols to point us to truth about Himself and about us. People of faith in Scripture are symbolized as sheep, buildings, fishermen, grain, children and trees. Study each of these symbols and learn God's lessons.

May my roots grow deep in your Word, Lord, and may my branches grow high. When winds of adversity come, I then will remain strong.

When I Awake

*And I – in righteousness I shall see your face; when I awake, I shall be satisfied
with seeing your likeness.*   PSALM 17:15

I have to confess. I have often wished that I could just die. To close
my eyes and wake to the sight of my Lord and the sound of angels
has consumed my thinking on numerous occasions. Especially when I
get fatigued or forced to bed with pressure sores.

David, the psalmist, was no stranger to the desire to die. But his words,
unlike those who promote euthanasia, are guarded. They are carefully
crafted to delete all thoughts of death for the sake of escape: *"And I –
in righteousness I will see your face . . ."* There is no way I'm going to end
my life sinfully just so I can behold God. Such a thing is contradictory.
I must be righteous in my death as I am in my life.

"I will be satisfied with seeing your likeness." I have to realize that no matter
how much peace or contentment I feel on this earth, I will not be satisfied
until it is my time to die. Our earthly life in Christ is *meant* to be one
of discontentment. Such was Paul's confession when he debated the pros
and cons of life. His conclusion, and that of David's, was to choose life
at all costs in order that Christ and the face of God would be gained:

For to me, to live is Christ and to die is gain.   PHILIPPIANS 1:21

❧

*Lord, I want to be with you. Now. I confess it. And I confess my reasons are
not always righteous. Too often they are because life here is hard. Make my desire
for heaven conform to the face of your will. Whether in person or in faith, let
your face be my stay, my life's choice.*

Patience

"Surely, O God, you have worn me out; you have devastated my entire household. You have bound me – and it has become a witness; my gauntness rises up and testifies against me . . . All was well with me, but he shattered me; he seized me by the neck and crushed me." JOB 16:7–8, 12

You've heard of the patience of Job? To me that never made sense. Because the book of Job is one long list of complaints. Not one to take suffering meekly, Job cried out in protest against God. Even his friends were shocked at his impudent anger. Goodness, most of us would bite our nails in fearful trembling if we ever talked to God that way.

God, however, does not get offended. He doesn't get insulted or intimidated. In fact, in a supreme touch of irony, in the end God orders Job's pious comforters to seek repentance from the man himself, Job, the very source of so many heated complaints.

I love that about God. Where it concerned Job, the guy was only human. And, yes, his patience was gloriously played out in that he refused to curse God and die. But it was the Lord who demonstrated the very best of what it means to be patient. God, as it says elsewhere in Scripture, refused to break the bruised reed or snuff out the smouldering wick. God even defended Job! YANCEY

The patience of Job? I would think it should be the patience of God. The God of Job – your God – defends the hurting, uplifts the oppressed, and listens to the complaints of the suffering. He may not respond to your questions with neat, pat answers, but He will always, always answer your questions with His own patience.

Oh patient and long-suffering God, thank you for being so tolerant with me, with all your children who tend to complain. Patiently lead us through our trials until praise is on our lips.

Hold Lightly Your Blessings

Cast your bread upon the waters, for after many days you will find it again.
ECCLESIASTES 11:1

My friend, Peter Sumner, directs the Christian Blind Mission in New Zealand. Peter himself was blinded at an early age and has spent decades in darkness. A miracle happened in Peter's life several years ago when an eye specialist performed a corneal graft on Peter's eyes. Suddenly, after years without sight, he was able to see. Peter relished brilliant sunsets and smiles on the faces of friends. He told me that he never imagined yellow to be so . . . yellow!

Peter told me in a recent letter that he has suffered a setback. The corneal graft has developed an ulceration. "This reduced my vision significantly and was rather worrying," he wrote. "Sight, I have found, is quite addictive and the thought of losing it all, once again, was very difficult to bear. I'm pleased to say that my condition has stabilized and, at present, I can read letters with the help of a strong light and a magnifying glass."

At that point, Peter inserted a line from a poem by William Blake, "He who binds to himself to a joy, does the wingèd life destroy; but he who kisses the joy as it flies lives in eternity's sunrise."

Peter then added, "Joni, I have had to learn not to bind to myself the joy of sight, but to kiss this winged blessing as it flies through my life. At times, the urge to grab and hold onto it is overwhelming, but in my heart of hearts, I realize one has to develop a certain detachment to joys of all kinds in order to escape the insidious poisons of bitterness and despair."

Great Giver of all gifts, thank you for the blessings of this life. Help me to hold loosely, very lightly the gifts you bestow. Help me to hold fast to you.

Tears

"For the Lamb at the centre of the throne will be their shepherd; He will lead them to springs of living water. And God will wipe away every tear from their eyes."   REVELATION 7:17

Years ago when I was in the hospital, I noticed something peculiar. Even though there was so much pain in the lives of my roommates, even though I *knew* they were hurting, no one cried. Sometimes I would lie awake in the middle of the night, wanting so much to cry, but afraid to. I was afraid I would wake up my roommates and maybe, just maybe, they would make fun of me the next day at physical therapy. So I kept my tears to myself.

After I got out of the hospital, I learned about David, the warrior-king who cried. The pages of the Psalms are salted with this man's tears. I learned about big, burly Peter who wept bitterly when he recognized his sin. I read about Jesus who offered prayers and petitions *"with loud cries and tears"*.

Learning about these people in Scripture gave me courage to cry. No longer were tears an embarrassment, a mark of weakness or shame. And I have the confidence that one day God will wipe away all my tears. How ironic that in heaven, where I will be able to once again wipe my own tears, I won't have to.

❧

God gives you hope, even though you find it hard to hold back the tears. The Bible says, *"Those who sow in tears will reap with songs of joy."* That means that out of your grief, God will bring the reward of joy which will last for ever.

Sometimes, God, it seems that pain and problems will last for ever. Thank you for reminding me today that tears are only temporary. How I look forward to the day when you will personally wipe away the tears of us all.

Reasoning with the Lord

"Come now, let us reason together," says the Lord. "Though your sins are like scarlet, they shall be as white as snow; though they are red as crimson, they shall be like wool."
ISAIAH 1:18

Have you ever pleaded in prayer? I don't mean if you have ever wrung your hands and cried, although that is a kind of praying, too. To plead with God means to present your case, as in a court of law.

God asks us to plead with Him when He invites us to come and reason with Him in prayer. The Lord is delighted when we arrive at His throne having sought in advance His heart's desire in a matter. He loves it when we are ready to defend our intercessions and petitions, ready to explain why we believe it is His will to do a certain thing or act in a certain way in a situation. When we pray that way, God can see we are attaching importance to our intercessions and petitions.

Before a lawyer presents his case in court, he takes great pains and a great deal of time to think through his petition. The same should be true for us as we approach the Lord in prayer. Before you offer your intercessions and petitions, take time to quietly sit before the Lord and listen. Ask Him to reveal to you His heart's desire in a matter. Only then, when you offer your petition, will you be able to say that you are praying in His will.

Lord, before I pray today, I want to quiet my heart, still my thoughts, and centre my attention on you. I want to listen to you in order to discern your will for me for this day. And thank you for inviting me to think through my petitions and intercessions — I take seriously the prayers I offer before your throne. Thank you for taking them seriously, too.

Work and Pray

If a man cleanses himself from the latter, he will be an instrument for noble purposes, made holy, useful to the Master and prepared to do any good work.
II TIMOTHY 2:21

Jesus worked hard, sometimes so hard that he didn't have a chance to eat or sleep. He was exhausted one crowded afternoon and collapsed in a boat as His disciples pushed off from shore. Even the Christians in the book of Acts laboured so hard that the Church could barely keep up with itself. But one thing is true of both Jesus and those early Christians: they prayed as much, if not more, than they worked. And it was prayer which gave their labours such astonishing success.

I love hard work, too. But I have to be careful that it stays in balance. In other words, I desire to work, work, work like Martha . . . but I also desire to pray, listen, and meditate like her sister, Mary. It is prayer that energizes every task. And even a crowded schedule can be easily managed if undergirded by praise and intercession.

"Work, work, from early until late. In fact, I have so much to do that I shall spend the first three hours in prayer." MARTIN LUTHER

❧

Someone has said, "Every Christian needs a half-hour of prayer each day, except when he is busy, then he needs an hour." Today, cover each appointment, each person you will encounter, with prayer. Now purpose to go through the day in measured moments; don't look at the work you have to do as a marathon. No matter how full your appointment book today, you will have energy . . . if first you pray.

Lord of every labour, thank you for the work you give me to do. Bless you for sanctifying it and making it "spiritual work" as I do my labour to your glory. Thank you for the Spirit-inspired energy you will give to carry me through this busy day!

Tired of Sinning?

So I find this law at work: When I want to do good, evil is right there with me . . . What a wretched man I am! Who will rescue me from this body of death? Thanks be to God – through Jesus Christ our Lord!

ROMANS 7:21, 24–5

I love the Confession in the Book of Common Prayer which reads, "Almighty God, Father of our Lord Jesus Christ, maker of all things, Judge of all men; We acknowledge and bewail our manifold sins and wickedness which we, from time to time, most grievously have committed by thought, word and deed against Thy Divine majesty, provoking most justly Thy wrath and indignation against us. We do earnestly repent and are heartily sorry for these our misdoings . . ."

I love that Confession. But I hate that Confession. Sometimes I get so weary of my sin that I cry, "What a wretched person I am!" I so look forward to the day when I'll no longer recite that Confession or transgress against my loving Lord, when I'll be free from this body of sin and death.

The Puritans prayed, "Oh my Lord, may I arrive where I need no more to weep or watch or be tempted. Where nothing defiles, where there is no grief, sorrow, sin, separation, tears or consuming cares. Where there is personal completeness. Where the more perfect the sight, the more beautiful the object. The more perfect the appetite, the sweeter the food. The more complete the soul, the more happy its joys, where there is full knowledge of Thee."

Lord, please possess me so that all my thoughts and desires rise to you. Soothe my sorrows. Sanctify every success. May I hate my sin as you hate it . . . may I grow to love your law as you do. Brighten my hope that soon there will be no more sin and I will at last find final completeness in you!

Romance vs. Love

This is the message you heard from the beginning: We should love one another.
I JOHN 3:11

T he romance has gone out of my marriage. Instead, there is love. Romance used to say, "I'll do absolutely anything for you," but love goes a step further and says, "Yes, and I'll prove it."

> Romance is fleeting, but love is long.
> Romance is flying, but love is a safe landing.
> Romance seeks perfection, but love forgives faults.
> Romance anguishes as it waits for the phone to ring
> to bring a voice that says sweet things,
> but love is the anguish of waiting for a call
> that assures you someone else is safe and happy.
> Romance is suspense, anticipation and surprise,
> but love is dependability.

Romance is dancing in the moonlight, gazing deep into desired eyes, but love is saying, "You're tired, honey, I'll get up this time." Romance is delicious, but love nourishes.

ANONYMOUS

Loving another person like this is a sure-fire way to become more like Jesus. Move past the romance, the feeling of living on the edge, move past the delicious emotions, and nourish another person with real and lasting love.

Lord, I can see that this kind of love will wage unrelenting war against my self-centredness. Help me to lose myself in loving you and in loving others. May I move past romance and begin laying my life down . . . in love.

Victory Is Mine

There have been many Olympic athletes that have captured the attention of Americans. Jim Thorpe, Carl Lewis, and Mary Lou Retton are just a few. But there is one Olympian who has captured more than our attention. His story has gripped our nation's wonder and imagination. His name is Eric Liddell.

Liddell was a true athlete and a true Christian. He followed his calling to the greatest detail, even to the point of forfeiting a chance for a gold medal when he refused to run on Sunday. It would be his British partner who would win that race, leaving Liddell to win the second race later in the week.

What captures our imagination so is not Liddell's athletic prowess. Eric Liddell was a man who knew the outcome of life's race and ran accordingly. He placed his Master's voice above his coach's advice. God above country and ambition. He even placed his Lord above personal disappointment because he knew that:

". . . In me you may have peace. In this world you will have trouble. But take heart! I have overcome the world."   JOHN 16:33

Eric Liddell was a man at peace with God and the world. Imagine the pressure his fans and peers pushed on him to race just ten mere seconds on that Sunday. But to Eric those ten seconds would bring toil and unrest in his soul.

The victory was not Liddell's to win. Christ had said "I, not you, Eric Liddell, have overcome the world." In that promise, Liddell lived at peace and won a crown brighter than any medal.

Lord, let me see the finish line of eternity and run the race on your terms. Let me play out the race of life as if the tape were across my chest. You have won the victory and I praise you for it.

No Escape

Where can I go from your Spirit? Where can I flee from your presence? If I go up to the heavens, you are there; if I make my bed in the depths, you are there.
PSALM 139:7–8

There's hardly a soul who hasn't wrestled with the overwhelming urge to flee when faced with suffering. Whether it be bad health, bad finances, or bad relationships, people – even Christians – search for an escape. Escape into daydreams. Escape into sleep. Escape into television. And a few even escape into suicide. Sometimes the strongest most stalwart of saints are the most likely candidates.

Even a powerful prophet like Elijah tried to escape his suffering. When the wicked Queen Jezebel heard through the grapevine that Elijah had wiped out hundreds of her prophets, she went after his neck. Elijah got weak-kneed and ran for his life. *"I have had enough, Lord,"* he said. *"Take my life . . ."* Read it for yourself in I Kings 19:1–9.

Circumstances may vary from person to person, but we can draw comfort from the fact that all of us are as vulnerable as Elijah. And if you look closer at how this mighty prophet surfaced out of his despair, you'll see that God Himself took Elijah in His arms and wiped away his tears.

The lesson of Elijah is for you. Just as surely as the angel of the Lord personally gave the prophet a sip of cool water and laid him down to rest, the Lord touches your life through the people He places around you. Elijah was able to turn the corner and get back on the track, thanks to God. And you can, too.

Lord, if I go up to the heavens, you are there. If I rise on the wings of the dawn and settle on the far side of the sea, even there your hand will guide me and your right hand will hold me fast. There's no way I can escape your love . . . I praise you for that!

NOVEMBER

Shaking the Status Quo

Often it's not *what* Jesus did, but *why* He did it. Healing people was, for Jesus, a daily part of His public ministry. But the point behind the following story has to do with *why* Jesus performed the miracle:

Another time He went into the synagogue, and a man with a shrivelled hand was there. Some of them were looking for a reason to accuse Jesus, so they watched Him closely to see if He would heal him on the Sabbath. Then Jesus asked them, "Which is lawful on the Sabbath: to do good or to do evil, to save life or to kill?" But they remained silent. He looked around at them in anger and, deeply distressed at their stubborn hearts, said to the man, "Stretch out your hand." He stretched it out, and his hand was completely restored. MARK 3:1–5

The Lord was deeply disturbed by the indifference the congregation showed toward the handicapped person. He was upset that the people were more concerned about the letter of the law and the proper way to do things rather than meeting the need of a suffering person in their midst. It was their cold stubborn apathy which prompted Jesus to act.

There are many reasons for reaching out to meet the needs of people around you. One reason may be to simply lend a helping hand. Another may be to put your gifts and talents to use. But a valid reason could be that you must take action against the nonchalance and indifference others have toward the needs at hand. Many a church has been sorely convicted when a believer steps out and shakes up the status quo!

Lord, help me to move fellow believers beyond the careless neglect we often show towards those in need. Give me courage to take action against apathy, and may your body become stronger for it.

Pray for All the Souls

Various cultures throughout the world either pray for, or to, the dead. I think I know why. It's because we aren't afraid to say what comes to our mind when we pray to the dead. Their ears are closed. They can't raise their eyebrows. They can't judge. Dead souls tell no tales.

But if we heed God's word, our attention is to be paid to the *live* souls in our midst. And that's where we falter. But consider these words from James 5:16:

Therefore confess your sins to each other . . .

"Aagh! What a terrible thought," we respond. Telling another Christian that we've lied or lusted seems out of the question. "Why would we do that?" Because the other Christian is to . . .

. . . pray for each other . . .

We confess our sins so that our brother can pray for us. Such prayer will assume complete trust, compassion, and acceptance. No judgment of any kind is mentioned by James. In fact, just the opposite. We are to pray for one another so that . . .

. . . you may be healed.

You see, when we sin our soul becomes sick. Just like when you come down with a cold you aren't at full capacity. Prolonged unconfessed sin will eventually gnaw like a cancer and leave us virtually dead, spiritually. And when you feel that you are at the point of no return, look at what James says next:

The prayer of a righteous man is powerful and effective.

Just think if we turned our attention to all the souls in need of confession, prayer, and healing. It would revitalize our churches and draw great numbers into the kingdom.

❧

Lord, make my life one of confession before my brother and sister. Show me my sin that I might go to my brother for his prayers. And make me sensitive enough to pray without judging when my brother or sister comes to me.

An Art Lesson

We know that we have come to know Him if we obey His commands.

I JOHN 2:3

When I'm at my art easel, secondhand information won't do. If I'm working on a painting of daisies, I must have a vase of fresh daisies to study. There's no way a photograph can convey the dark tones of real shadows or the thin transparency of a petal. Recently I finished an art project which included drawings of thirty-eight pairs of hands. I hired a model who could stand next to my easel and pose his hands this way and that. The result? The sketchings of hands look . . . real.

When I fail to study the real thing, my paintings show it. They lack life if I've only worked from photographs or other people's ideas. And what is true for the artist, is true for the Christian. So many believers settle for secondhand information as they seek to know the Lord better. Some only get to know the Lord through other people. They feel energy from a friend's testimony and then attempt to transfer another's experience into their life. It won't work.

If a painting is to shine with life, it must represent the real thing. If a Christian is to shine with the light of Jesus, it will mean taking time to get close to the real thing or, in this case, the real Person. The closer we draw to Him, the more our life will look, feel and be . . . real.

❧

Obedience, according to I John 2:3 is the key to knowing God. When we read the Word, the Spirit speaks to our heart, prompting us to obey. It's the real and only way to know God.

Son of God, I desire to know you. I want to study your life through your Word and listen to your voice when I pray. Forgive me when I copy information in a secondhand way from someone else's experiences. My life will only be changed as I trust and obey you.

Present Age Problems

Ever had a day when everything, absolutely everything, went wrong? It happened to me just yesterday.

I was all ready to go to work and as I powered my wheelchair on to the mechanical lift of my van, I pressed the toggle switch to raise the lift and . . . nothing happened. It broke. My dear friend, who was standing by nicely dressed for work, had to hand-crank the lift with me on it. That was no easy feat.

That was the same day my corset snapped a fastener, two people cancelled important appointments, my computer erased two pages of work, and, I broke a tooth. I went immediately to the dentist, only to have him accidentally crack another tooth right next to the broken one.

Can you identify? The cost of living is sky-high. Interest rates are up. Washing machines don't last as long as they used to. The mice are back in the garage. Parking is becoming a nightmare. Stress is a daily companion and you feel like you're holding the loose ends of your job together by your fingers and toes.

Well, listen to this 20th century prescription out of Romans 8:18:

I consider that our present sufferings are not worth comparing with the glory that will be revealed in us.

Consider what Paul meant by "our present sufferings". When he wrote those words, Christians weren't facing cost-of-living increases, they were counting the cost of their lives. People were living under a cruel system which got its kicks from throwing believers to lions. Talk about stress!

Thank you, Lord, for giving me a "Romans 8:18" perspective on my problems today. The struggles I face are not worth comparing to the trials of the early Church – and I realize that my problems aren't worthy to be compared with the glory that will one day be revealed in me. Thank you for this hope.

Basement Search

An illustration of Guy Fawkes approaching Parliament in 1605 is as subtle in its belief in God's omniscience as the thirty-six barrels of dynamite that were hidden under the building that November day. As you view the scene, you are drawn immediately to one eye in the night clouds with beams of light focused on the heart of Mr Fawkes.

Only God saw Guy Fawkes' heart as he huddled with three matches in the basement. And God's sovereign eye moved His sovereign hand to send Sir Thomas Knevet on a search throughout the basement. As Parliament later proclaimed, it would be a day of "thanks and praise for the wonderful and mighty deliverance" by God.

Oh, that I could remember that searching eye whenever I let sin hide in the basement of my heart. Sin's devious plan threatens to destroy all that I've worked for and believed in . . . with one spark. Some sin I try to hide for more than a night. Even a week. And sometimes more than a year. But the eye of God is relentless. He either finds me out with His Word or lets the stored barrels of my sin explode, just so that I can see the danger of rebellion.

You know my folly, O God; my guilt is not hidden from you.   PSALM 69:5

"It's not worth the pain," God says. "It is folly for you to hide your sin. I know it is there. I know what it will do. Open your heart that I might expose the explosive stuff and grasp the matches you hold in your hand."

Let His eye see and His hand restrain.

℞

Lord, my sin sits ready to ruin me. By your loving eye I ask that it be exposed to me. I dare not take one more step lest the matches of temptation and anger and loneliness strike and destroy this day and our joy.

Triple Trouble

Rather, as servants of God we commend ourselves in every way: in great endurance; in troubles, hardships and distresses.   II CORINTHIANS 6:4

Troubles. Hardships. Distresses. Ever heard that old adage, "Bad things come in threes"? There's no biblical support for such arithmetic, but it happens.

For example, bitterness was a temptation to me in the early days of my paralysis. Deep inside I knew it was wrong, but I justified myself, saying, "Surely God won't mind if I let off a little steam every now and then. After all, I *am* paralysed!"

As if that trouble weren't enough, God added a second hardship. Several months into my hospital stay I had an operation on my lower spine. After the surgery I was forced to lie face down for fifteen days while the stitches healed. "I am sick and tired of this," I complained out loud.

Then, the third distress. I caught the flu. Suddenly not being able to move was peanuts compared to not being able to breathe. I was fit to be tied! But as I thought about it, I understood what God was doing. No longer was my bitterness a tiny trickle; it was a raging torrent that could not be ignored. It was as if God were holding my anger up before my face and saying lovingly, but firmly, "Stop turning your head and looking the other way. This bitterness has got to go. What are you going to do about it?"

The pressure had got so strong that I was either going to give the situation over to Him completely or allow myself to wallow in bitterness. Faced with that ultimatum, it helped me see clearly what a wicked course bitterness would be. Sometimes troubles, hardships and distresses – in threes or more – back us into a corner to get us seriously considering the lordship of Christ.

Lord, when troubles pile on, may I look to you for help and hope.

Hungry for Home

We are looking forward to a new heaven and a new earth, the home of righteousness.   II PETER 3:13

California is beautiful, but there's nothing quite like my home state of Maryland. Whenever I get a little homesick for the land of the Chesapeake Bay, Ken and I drive down to Pico and 25th Street in Santa Monica to visit The Maryland Crab House.

It's just a few miles from the California beach, but you'd never know it. You walk into the restaurant and spot Baltimore Oriole banners and Georgetown University pennants tacked on the walls. When you order hot hard-shell crabs, they spread butcher block paper on the table just like they do at home. Wooden mallets for cracking crabs. Old Bay seasoning and vinegar for dipping crab meat. When I surround myself with familiar things, I get hungry for home.

I do the same thing when I get homesick for heaven. I read Revelation. I corner a friend who loves talking about the Lord's return. I browse through I Corinthians 15 and relish the hope of one day having a body that works. I smile at the signs of the times. I wonder what it means to be clothed in righteousness. In my mind I close the curtain on sin, Satan and suffering and delight in the soon and coming new heavens and new earth.

When I surround myself with familiar things, I get hungry for home.

Are you a little bone-weary of living in a sin-sick world? Surround yourself with a few well-worn verses about heaven or hymns about the Lord's return. Listen to a cassette sermon on the second coming. Daydream about unseen things and you may find yourself hungry for the home of righteousness.

Would you please help me to see heaven as my home, Lord? Make me hungry for heaven so that I can honour you better down here on earth.

God's Will for Your Life

Delight yourself in the Lord and he will give you the desires of your heart.
PSALM 37:4

Ask any young Christian what God's will is for their life and you'll probably hear this: "I don't know, but I sure would *love* to know." Well, we *can* know the will of God in a general sense, for God's will is that we be saved, Spirit-filled, sanctified, submissive and suffering. God's Word makes all this clear.

But what about God's specific will for your life? Which career should you pursue? Which college? I love Dr John MacArthur's advice, "If you are lined up with God's general will, those five basics, then do whatever you want! If those five elements of God's will are operating in your life, who is running your wants? God is! The psalmist said, 'Delight thyself also in the Lord; and He shall give thee the desires of thine heart.' God does not say He will fulfil all the desires that are there. He says He will *put* the desires there! If you are living a godly life, He will give you the right desires."

Simply put, if you are operating in God's general will, you can confidently move forward to pursue the desires God has placed in your heart. And once you are rolling, God can then grab the steering wheel with the strong arms of His will to direct you exactly where He wants you to go.

Finding the Lord's specific will for you may mean pushing down the narrow line until you hit a dead end, but at that point, God will open a door so wide, you won't be able to see around it – only go through it.

Lord, fill me with your Spirit, sanctify me, help me to submit and follow you when I suffer. I can then have every confidence I'm wedged securely in the centre of your specific will.

God's Prerogative

Do not judge, or you too will be judged. For in the same way you judge others, you will be judged, and with the measure you use, it will be measured to you.
MATTHEW 7:1–2

While my husband and I were eating in a fast-food restaurant discussing gardening plans for the afternoon, we overheard a couple at a nearby table having a heated argument. "You dumbbell," the woman hissed, "why don't you ever listen to me?!"

I mentally slammed down the gavel and pronounced the woman guilty. The nerve of her talking like that! However, the sentence we render on others may turn round and condemn us; because when Ken and I were gardening in the back yard that afternoon, I found myself getting irritated with his technique of pruning. I started to complain. I hardly uttered a word when God stabbed my memory with the woman in the restaurant. I felt the gavel come down on me and it hurt.

We must not judge rashly, assuming the worst of people. We cannot judge unmercifully or with a spirit of revenge. Finally, we must not jump to conclusions and judge the hearts of others, for it is God's prerogative to try the heart.

Yes, we ought to weigh between right and wrong. Yes, we should hold our brother accountable to scriptural standards. But judging goes far beyond discerning and carries with it an attitude of condemnation. Let Jesus be the judge of men's hearts and instead of rendering a sentence on others, let's pray for them.

Judge of all hearts, I love your heart of compassion and tender mercy. Thank you that I have been judged at the cross and there is no need for me to pass condemnation on others. Help me to have a compassionate attitude towards those who need your forgiveness. Help me to pray for them rather than pass judgment.

No Dark Pews!

"For this is what the Lord has commanded us: 'I have made you a light for the Gentiles, that you may bring salvation to the ends of the earth.'"

ACTS 13:47

There is a church in England that has no lights. Many people who visit the church are shocked that the architect left out something as important as overhead lighting. But the architect had a plan. The various families who regularly attend the church are given their own pew, as well as a lamp and a book. When a family comes to church, their lamp is lit. If they are not in church, the pew is dark.

What difference can one darkened pew make? "Not much," you might think. But what if several pews were lacking lamps? Then the whole church would be affected. It's obvious. If all are present and in their pews, the church is alive with light. If not, the place becomes dark.

What a beautiful picture of the body of Christ! If any one of us is not using the gifts God has given, there will be darkness; but as we use our gifts, the whole body will be full of light. This is how intimately we are linked one with another. That's why the Lord made it a command – He has made us a light in order to shine for the sake of others.

If one part suffers, every part suffers with it; if one part is honoured, every part rejoices with it.
I CORINTHIANS 12:26

Help me to know, Lord, what it means to be a part of your body, to function with others for the good of all and the glory of the Son. Help me to understand my place in the body, including my responsibility to brothers and sisters around me. Help me to realize that my role, no matter how small, is significant. Shine through me, Lord, so that the lives of my friends and family will be brightened.

We Will Shine

"Those who are wise will shine like the brightness of the heavens, and those who lead many to righteousness, like the stars for ever and ever."

DANIEL 12:3

The other night before I went into the house, I stopped to listen to my neighbour's whistling pines and enjoy the thin slice of moon making a smile on the horizon. The night was a starry dome which took my breath away and before the cold drove me indoors, my heart broke with joy and I whispered to the sky, "Jesus, wait for me, I'm coming home, I belong up there." Stars do that to me.

Symbols of crowns and thrones, crystal seas and stars are found on virtually every page of Scripture. And to some, such symbolism can be off-putting. Just look at today's verse. We will shine like stars? As C. S. Lewis has said, "Who wishes to become a living electric light bulb?"

But wait. Have you ever stood in the night wind and looked up at a blanket of stars? The blazing brightness of the heavens so captures you that words can hardly express the ache in your heart.

Here's the thing. The glory of the stars that captivates you will one day be yours. The ecstasy which enraptures your heart at the sight of a night ablaze with twinkling lights . . . you will one day enter into that same ecstasy. One day you will put on glory like that. It will be yours for ever and ever.

For more reading on this delightful subject, pick up C. S. Lewis' *The Weight of Glory.* When it comes to wrapping reality around heavenly symbols, nobody says it quite like him.

Lord, the next time beauty captures my heart and makes me breathless, help me to remember that such glory is my destiny in heaven. Oh, that one day I shall shine like the stars for ever and ever!

Constant Troubles

We are proud and independent people. Just ask yourself what you would do if, at a street corner, a Boy Scout reached to steady your arm as the walking light turned green. You would surely shake him off. But let's say the walking light and traffic were obscured by a blinding snowstorm. Pride and independence would then be your downfall and you would appreciate the aid of a steady arm.

This is the reason why God fills our lives with so many troubles. Troubles ensure that we will reach for God's steady arm, learning thankfully to lean on Him. "The reason why the Bible spends so much of its time reiterating that God is a strong rock, a firm defence and a sure refuge and help for the weak, is that God spends so much of His time bringing home to us that we *are* weak, both mentally and morally, and dare not trust ourselves to find, or to follow, the right road," says Dr J. I. Packer.

This is why constant troubles such as a chronic health condition or a difficult marriage can be considered advantages in the Christian's life. Constant troubles give the believer a constant opportunity to lean on the strong Rock. A godly habit of resting in divine help can be more easily formed.

We are hard pressed on every side, but not crushed; perplexed, but not in despair; persecuted, but not abandoned; struck down, but not destroyed.

II CORINTHIANS 4:8–9

◄►

No trouble comes my way, Lord, that you haven't decreed. And if my troubles are constant, I acknowledge that your purpose is to have me constantly lean on you. Forgive me when I grumble at hard times that never seem to go away, and teach me to find peace in your perfect will for me. Trials may be constant, but your love is even more constant. Thank you for that.

Our Advocate

We have one who speaks to the Father in our defence – Jesus Christ, the Righteous One.   I JOHN 2:1

An advocate is a person who pleads another's cause. But Jesus, our advocate, adds a twist. He pleads His own cause. And He does so to our advantage.

For instance, picture a throne room with the devil reading a list of charges against you. He throws you an accusing glance and sneers, "This wretch deserves to die. He says he's a Christian but his life stinks. He claims to know Jesus but you'd never be able to tell from the way he acts."

Now picture Jesus stepping forward as your advocate. He speaks confidently and with authority, saying, "This person is mine. I died for every sin he ever committed." That would be enough, but then Christ adds an amazing announcement: "What's more, I've not only erased his debt, but I want you, Father, to credit to his account all of my righteousness."

Jesus, our advocate, would be generous enough in cancelling the debt of our sin on the cross. But He went further. He not only paid the penalty and cleared sin's slate, He gave us His right standing, His goodness. When the Father looks at you, He sees all the good things His Son has ever done.

Such a debt, we can never repay. We can only praise!

"Even now my witness is in heaven; my advocate is on high. My intercessor is my friend as my eyes pour out tears to God; on behalf of a man he pleads with God as a man pleads for his friend."   JOB 16:19–21

Blessed is the man to whom God credits righteousness apart from works: *"Blessed are they whose transgressions are forgiven, whose sins are covered."*
                                                      ROMANS 4:5–7

I kneel in my heart, Lord Jesus, at all that you've given me. Forgiveness of sin. And righteousness with our Father.

Breath of Life

Again Jesus said, "Peace be with you! As the Father has sent me, I am sending you." And with that He breathed on them and said, "Receive the Holy Spirit."
JOHN 20:21-2

I remember some years ago catching a terrible cold during a visit to Aberdeen, Scotland. Within twenty-four hours it settled deep into my lungs – a dangerous thing for me, a quadriplegic. I was able to handle my cold while sitting up in my wheelchair. But at night while lying flat on my back in bed and unable to move, I gasped for breath.

I lay there in the dark, pushing away claustrophobic feelings. *If only I could escape into sleep. If only morning would come. If only I could breathe!* Then it hit me. What I was struggling with for the moment, thousands of people live with every day. I knew then what would relieve my panic: I began praying for every quadriplegic I knew who was hooked up to a respirator.

As I interceded for each one, I prayed that God would breathe on them His breath of life, His peace, calming their frustrations and dispelling their fears. I asked God to give each of them His peace. Before long, I mumbled my last prayer and drifted off into a deep, relaxed sleep.

Sometimes when we are gripped by fear, a good prescription for peace is to pray for others. Especially others who are pressured by circumstances more confining than yours. Think of someone who needs your prayers today and ask the Lord to breathe on that friend His breath of life and peace.

Breathe on me, Breath of God. Fill me with life anew,
That I may love what Thou dost love, And do what Thou wouldst do.

Breathe on me, Breath of God. Until my heart is pure,
Until my will is one with Thine, To do and to endure.

Party Spoiler

When He noticed how the guests picked the places of honour at the table, He told them this parable: "When someone invites you to a wedding feast, do not take the place of honour . . . But when you are invited, take the lowest place, so that when your host comes, he will say to you, 'Friend, move up to a better place.' Then you will be honoured in the presence of all your fellow guests. For everyone who exalts himself will be humbled, and he who humbles himself will be exalted." LUKE 14:7–11

Can you imagine that scene? I'm sure after the Lord spoke no servant moved, no dish clattered. Silence must have hung over the table as the prominent people nervously tried to hide their embarrassment. Jesus spoiled the party.

There is no room in Scripture for a one-sided view of our Lord. Jesus always oversteps the comfort zones of people. He hits the light switch in stuffy rooms of darkness and evil. He barges into our lives, tearing aside the curtains we've tried to pull over secret sins. He heaves His shoulder against the doors we've locked to protect private habits from His scrutiny.

Jesus always "talks out of turn", such as around banquet tables with prominent guests of honour. Always, always He urges some inconvenient, untimely change in people's lives. And how are we to respond? *"He who humbles himself will be exalted."*

Lord, I'm grateful that, when it comes to my sin, you leave no stone unturned. Although it hurts when you expose my impure motives, thoughts and actions, I know you are bringing my wrongdoing to light so that, with your help, I can change my ways. This is difficult to ask, Lord, but keep elbowing in on my comfort zones until I am the spotless, blameless, pure child you want me to be.

In Whose Life Do You Live?

"Remain in me, and I will remain in you. No branch can bear fruit by itself; it must remain in the vine. Neither can you bear fruit unless you remain in me."　　　　　　　　　　　　　　　　　　　　　　　　JOHN 15:4

The university gymnasium is packed, and from the platform I can see every student. The microphone works fine. I can see my notes. But something is wrong. I am only ten minutes into my message, but there's a restlessness in the air. The faces of the students in the front row hold blank expressions. They look as dull as I feel.

I realize I sound hollow. More than that, I feel hollow. Even though I'm sharing powerful truths from God's Word, I know my words lack energy. I'm separated from my message, disconnected, out of gear. Before I embark on my next sentence, I breathe a silent prayer – no more going through the motions.

Within minutes I can sense the difference, between my effort and God's energy working through me. I feel relaxed, free. There is joy in my voice and the faces of the kids on the front row even begin to brighten.

Nothing is more mechanical than when we attempt to live a supernatural life apart from God. I've done it. You do it. When we live apart from Him, prayer becomes dull, witnessing becomes dry, and relationships sag under the weight of selfishness. Our jobs become routine and even performing an act of kindness becomes an unpleasant duty. Our relationship to the Lord even becomes a chore.

In case you're feeling a little self-sufficient, remember that in Him you live, move and have your being. Apart from Him you can't do a thing. So count yourself dead to sin but alive to God in Christ.

Lord Christ, you were raised from the dead through the glory of the Father that I, too, might live a new life. Forgive me when I go through the motions. Let me live through you today, always and only in your power.

Perspective

They will soar on wings like eagles; they will run and not grow weary, they will walk and not be faint.
                                                                ISAIAH 40:31

Birds overcome the lower law of gravity by the higher law of flight. And what is true for birds is true for the soul. Souls that soar on wings like eagles overcome the lower law of sin and death. Hannah Whitall Smith writes, "The 'law of the spirit of life in Christ Jesus' must necessarily be a higher and more dominant law than the law of sin and death; therefore, the soul that has mounted into this upper region of the life in Christ cannot fail to conquer and triumph."

Why is it then that so many Christians fail to conquer? Perhaps it's because we fail to mount up and soar with wings and choose instead to live on the same low level as our trials. Little wonder we blunder when the battleground we choose is on an earthly plane. Christians are powerless there; that is, unless they shift to a higher battleground and choose weapons of warfare that are spiritual.

What we need is perspective. We need to see what birds see. When we soar on wings like eagles, trials look extraordinarily different. When viewed from their own level, trials look like impassable walls; but when viewed from above, the wall appears as a thin line, something easily overcome.

You *have* wings. You don't need stronger, better ones. You don't need more wings, or larger ones. You possess all that you need to gain a heavenly perspective on your trials and thereby overcome. A passive or inactive trust in the Lord won't do. To *use* your wings is to actively trust in God.

Lord, I don't want to trust you in theory or in word only. I want my trust in you to be as active and as strenuous as "mounting up with wings". As I do, thank you for the higher, heavenly perspective you give me over my trials.

Jesus, Son of Man

For there is one God and one mediator between God and men, the man Christ Jesus.
I TIMOTHY 2:5

I love the way Jesus was such close friends with John. Their friendship was intimate and powerful, close and sweet. While on earth, they were inseparable. John was the only man who stayed by the cross.

I also love the way Jesus was such close friends with Mary, sister of Martha. He deferred to her. Lavished accolades on her. He even memorialized her when she wiped His feet with her tears.

When I look at these warm and intimate friendships, my heart fills with praise that Jesus was . . . a man. A man of flesh-and-blood reality. His heart felt the sting of sympathy. His eyes glowed with tenderness. His arms embraced. His lips smiled. His hands touched. Jesus was male!

Jesus invites us to relate to Him as the Son of Man. And because He is fully man, you can relate to Jesus with affection and love. It would be hard to trust God if He were only Prime Mover, First Cause or Source of All with no respect to gender. It would be impossible to love a Lord who was only some vague, hazy theological concept.

The essence of Christianity is knowing Jesus Christ the Lord as priest and king, head and husband, shepherd and life-giver. He is cornerstone of the Church, that is, His body and bride and building. Knowing the Son of Man in all these respects has a relational and affectional dimension – yes, we can love God, and yes, we can love a Man.

Thank you that, as the Son of Man, you understand every human passion, you feel every hurt, and you sympathize with every tear. Oh, Jesus, may your favour of friendship rest upon me.

In the Potter's Hands

"Go down to the potter's house, and there I will give you my message." So I went down to the potter's house, and I saw him working at the wheel. But the pot he was shaping from the clay was marred in his hands; so the potter formed it into another pot, shaping it as seemed best to him." JEREMIAH 18:1–4

On November 19, 1991, Cathe Chermesino was running down South Street, trying to make it to Calvary Baptist School before the late bell rang. On the surface she had it all. She was a beautiful, talented thirteen-year-old who possessed YMCA swimming medals, not to mention a beautiful singing voice. When she ran across the street, she was hit by a fast-moving car and thrown into the air. Immediately Cathe became totally paralysed.

Cathe now goes to school sitting rigid and upright in a bulky wheelchair. She breathes through a ventilator and has to carefully mouth her words so others can lip read.

On the first anniversary of her accident, she gave her testimony at her church. "I'm like the potter's clay," she said. "I'm being reshaped into something that I believe will be far better. What looks harmful for me will actually turn out to be good. Before the accident I was an awful snob, but now God has given me an inner peace. I'm giving my voice a rest until I get to heaven."

Her mother looked lovingly at her daughter and added, "Cathe needs just two things to make it through. A lot of prayer and a little bit of oxygen."

Recently I wrote Cathe and gave her a verse from Deuteronomy 31:8:

"The Lord himself goes before you and will be with you; he will never leave you nor forsake you. Do not be afraid; do not be discouraged."

Lord, if you can help Cathe to rise above her circumstances, I know that with your grace I will rise above mine.

Be Thankful

For since the creation of the world God's invisible qualities – His eternal power and divine nature – have been clearly seen, being understood from what has been made, so that men are without excuse. For although they knew God, they neither glorified Him as God nor gave thanks to Him, but their thinking became futile and their foolish hearts were darkened. ROMANS 1:20–21

What child hasn't been told a thousand times, "Now, be sure to say thank you." It's part of good training. More than common courtesy, expressing gratitude is critical to the development of a child's character.

I painfully learned that lesson when, as a little girl, I failed to say "thank you" to Aunt Kitty after she gave me (under my mother's watchful eye) a charm for my bracelet. The next day I was on the telephone, rubbing my sore backside and apologizing, "Aunt Kitty, you will never know how grateful I really am."

It's an old story: Ingratitude carries serious penalties. Probably the oldest story is out of Romans chapter 1. It says that although men knew God, they failed to give Him thanks. And you know what happened next. God seriously punished them for their thankless hearts.

That should say something to you and me; because if a thankless spirit was the undoing of a generation long ago and far away, is it any different today? In fact, you know God a lot better than those to whom He revealed Himself through creation – that means you have even more to be thankful for!

◈

Look around you. The blessings abound: The smiles of children, the beauty of a glorious sunset, the comfort of a warm bed at night. Small and great, there are plenty of reasons to say to God, "Thank you."

Lord, receive glory today through my thankful spirit. I am so grateful for who you are and what you've done. Show me more reasons today for which I can give you thanks.

It Is Well with My Soul

Why are you downcast, O my soul? Why so disturbed within me? Put your hope in God, for I will yet praise him, my Saviour and my God. PSALM 42:5

H ave you ever started out your day feeling downhearted, a little blue
. . . for absolutely no reason? The psalmist asks a good question.
"Why are you downcast, O my soul?"

Is is the weather? Is it what you ate last night for supper? Is it an annoyance that's been building, or just a vague, hazy dullness of soul that can't be explained? Often there's simply no reason for being downhearted.

That's why the psalmist quickly advises to put our hope in God, and to do it by praising Him. Nothing lifts our spirits quicker or higher than to place our praise at the feet of the Lord Jesus. Why don't you do that right now by saying from your heart (or singing, if you know it) this familiar hymn of praise?

> Though Satan should buffet, tho' trials should come,
> Let this blest assurance control:
> That Christ has regarded my helpless estate,
> And hath shed His own blood for my soul.
>
> It is well, it is well with my soul.
> It is well, it is well with my soul.
>
> And, Lord, haste the day when my faith shall be sight,
> The clouds be rolled back as a scroll:
> The trump shall resound and the Lord shall descend,
> "Even so" – it is well with my soul.

Lord of hope, I place my trust in you and I praise you for making all things well with my soul. Please receive glory as I magnify and adore your name, lifting my soul before you. With you, there is no reason to be downhearted.

A Good Wife

Charm is deceptive, and beauty is fleeting; but a woman who fears the Lord is to be praised. PROVERBS 31:30

Why is it I cringe whenever I read Proverbs 31? Probably because the wife mentioned is more than chief cook and bottle washer. This lady buys real estate, reads *The Wall Street Journal*, designs and sells clothes, keeps a daily exercise routine, runs her household like a fine-tuned machine, is praised by her children, helps the homeless, gives to the poor, then goes to bed late and rises early. I'm exhausted just reading about her.

When I look to Proverbs 31 for inspiration, I find it hard to get past the first verse. Because of my disability, I can't even open a refrigerator door. Push a vacuum cleaner? I tried that once when I had a friend "tie" it to the front of my power wheelchair so I could push and pull it over the carpet. I'm still finding nicks and scratches on my floorboards to this day.

What's funny is that Ken thinks I'm a good wife. Our marriage is good not because I know how much toilet paper is left on the roll, or that I can juggle five bags of groceries when leaving the market. Ken believes I am a good wife because of one tiny verse in Proverbs 31 – I've learned, and am still learning, to fear the Lord.

❧

The fear of the Lord is the beginning of wisdom; and it is wisdom which gives any marriage depth and meaning. You and I may not be able to match the work level of the Proverbs 31 woman, but we can have her character. No matter what we *do*, we can be faithful, supportive, sensitive, kind, observant, creative and loving.

The best way I can love my family and friends, Lord, is to first fear you. May I be faithful and loving today to those whom you've placed in my life.

Stretcher Bearer

Some men came, bringing to Him a paralytic, carried by four of them. Since they could not get him to Jesus because of the crowd, they made an opening in the roof above Jesus and, after digging through it, lowered the mat the paralysed man was lying on.   MARK 2:3–4

The four friends of the paralysed man probably did more than carry the stretcher. Maybe they arrived early at their friend's house to help him get ready. When the group arrived at the home where Jesus was teaching, they most likely placed the paralysed man on the ground to survey the scene. Going through the crowd wouldn't work; they must come up with an alternate plan of action. Eyeing the stairs up the side of the house to the roof, they realized, that's it!

Persistence paid off. A ripped-up roof certainly got Jesus' attention, but the four friends – their faith, creativity and commitment – probably drew more attention. Perhaps as Jesus looked up to see crumbling tiles dropping from the ceiling, He may have thought of His own words, *"Whatever you did for one of the least of these brothers of mine, you did for me."*

Would you be my stretcher bearers, when I can no longer stand?
Would you each pick up a corner of my pallet in your hand?

This burden's just too heavy, I find I cannot bear
Its pain, its grief, its sorrow; and so I chance to dare –

To ask if you would carry me through valleys dark and wide;
Then set me safely down again where peace and hope abide.

God said His yoke was easy and His burden would be light;
That's surely why He sent you each to lead me through the night.

And now I must lift others and the burdens they may bring;
I'll be a stretcher bearer carrying wounded for the King.

BEV ENGELDINGER

Be Still

"Be still, and know that I am God; I will be exalted among the nations, I will be exalted in the earth." Psalm 46:10

One of the best ways to get to know God is to be . . . still. I have learned that lesson from spending years in forced bed rest.

Up in my wheelchair, I can at least flail my arms or shrug my shoulders. But on my bed, gravity works against me and, for that reason, I'm even more paralysed when lying down. Things aren't as distracting when I'm lying still and so I experience first-hand a deeper knowledge of God through prayer.

Sometimes I'm amazed that, from my bed, I can help set into motion the cogs and wheels of God's workings in the world. Through my prayers I may change the destiny of a life or a nation. Lying on my bed, I can hasten the day of the Lord's return. I don't move a muscle while I'm in bed, but I help move the hand of God here and abroad.

~&~

Try praying some time while lying in bed (make sure not to do this when you're tired or you might fall asleep!) Lie very still. Don't move. Invite the Lord to speak to you in the stillness and quiet. Press your weakness up against His strength, your ignorance up against His knowledge. Be still . . . pray . . . and get to know God better.

"An intercessor means one who is in such vital contact with God and with his fellow men that he is like a live wire closing the gap between the saving power of God and the sinful men who have been cut off from that power," says Hannah Hurnard.

Lord, I quiet my soul before you. I am still. I lie down in your love and open my heart and mind to your word. My prayer, this day, is to know you more intimately and personally.

The Old Lamplighter

"You are the light of the world. A city on a hill cannot be hidden. Neither do people light a lamp and put it under a bowl. Instead they put it on its stand, and it gives light to everyone in the house." MATTHEW 5:14–15

Born in 1900, my father loved to tell stories of days as a little boy in Baltimore, Maryland. I heard about the first time the Wright Brothers flew their plane over the city. I heard about the first Model-T to chug down Howard Street, scaring all the horses. And I remember Dad talking about the old lamplighter.

Every evening at dusk the lamplighter would come down Stricker Street where Daddy lived carrying a lantern and a pole. He would make his way back and forth across the street, lighting each street lamp. When the lamplighter disappeared into the twilight, you would always know where he had been by the avenue of light left behind.

An old story such as this communicates a fresh truth for present-day lamplighters. As Christians we have the privilege of leaving a long trail of light behind us as we touch for Christ the lives of those around us. Where we go, darkness is dispelled. Where we minister, people see the lighted path we've left. Where we love, the Light of the World shines.

You, O Lord, keep my lamp burning; my God turns my darkness into light. PSALM 18:28

The lesson of the lamplighter is to touch lives one by one. Saying and meaning "God bless you" to the bag boy at the supermarket. Telling neighbourhood children that Jesus loves them. Listening to the heartfelt pleas of a suffering friend and stopping to pray right there.

May I introduce others to you, the Light of the World, and may their lives be touched with your glory so that they might leave a trail of light, too.

All the Wrong Reasons

The name of the Lord is a strong tower; the righteous run to it and are safe.
PROVERBS 18:10

My sister Jay, as a teenager, was famous around our home for whining, "Daddy, I've got a problem." We knew what that meant. He would laugh, reach for his wallet and say, "Okay, Jay, how much?" It irritated me that she seemed to take advantage of Dad's kindness. But Daddy didn't seem to mind.

That's often the way we are with God. We run to Him for all the wrong reasons. We go to God because someone has snubbed us and our feelings are bruised. We go to God when we've failed and our pride is wounded. We run to God for sympathy, hoping he'll understand our point of view. I know I sometimes run to God because I've procrastinated, forgotten to prepare a message, and I don't want to appear stupid before a whole bunch of people.

None of these are good reasons for running to the Lord. But thankfully, God doesn't hold against us our wrong motives. The Lord doesn't even want us to waste effort trying to clean up our act before we come to Him – that's His responsibility.

Whether it's silly pride or self-centred disappointment, run to the Lord. Come to the cross for all the wrong reasons. It is there God will redeem every impure motive.

❧

Lord, when I have a problem, I know you are the place to go. You are the person to reach for. Thank you for not demanding that I clean up my act before I come to the cross – I trust you will do that for me when I kneel at Calvary, confess my sins, and bow before your will. Bless you that your name is a strong, high tower. Your name gives me safety. I thank you for that.

The Major Problem with Minor Sins

No-one who lives in him keeps on sinning. No-one who continues to sin has either seen him or known him.
                                                                    I JOHN 3:6

"Sin becomes a crime, not against law, but against love; it means not breaking God's law so much as breaking God's heart."
                                                                    WILLIAM BARCLAY

What hurts me most about sin is not that it breaks God's law, but that it breaks His heart. Sin is not weakness or a disease. Sin is a mockery of His mercy and a disdain of His love. Sin grieves God.

That's why our battle against even minor sins is always major. Our sin is an offence to God. The battle may mean putting a lid on backbiting gossip. No more flirting with your best friend's spouse. No more saying one thing to your Christian friends and quite another to your co-workers on the job. It may mean tackling subtle sins – curbing your appetite, reining in your daydreams, and ceasing to make copies of cassettes that say, "Unauthorized reproduction prohibited."

Does tackling small sins seem too minor? If so, remember that any sin is a choice to fellowship with the devil. That's why once the Spirit convicts you of some sin . . . the minor becomes major.

Lord Jesus, I want to delight you. I no longer desire to give my sin a smooth-sounding name and I turn from doing things that displease you. Give me power to obey.

Scaling the High Bar

It is God's will that you should be sanctified; that you should avoid sexual immorality; that each of you should learn to control his own body in a way that is holy and honourable . . . and that in this matter no-one should wrong his brother or take advantage of him.   I THESSALONIANS 4:3–5

God telling me that I should be holy is like Him telling me to scale the high jump at a track meet. But wait. Who's that in front of the high bar? Could it be? Yes, it's the Lord. And He's there to give me a knee-up.

In fact, Jesus even helps me to pace myself as I take a run at the jump. The first step is to *"avoid sexual immorality"*. That means "just say no". Turn on the keys to the ignition and leave. Hang up the phone. Turn off the TV. Cancel the subscription. Having taken this first step, I'm closer to the high bar.

Second, *"Control your own body in a way that is holy and honourable."* In other words, value your body. Call the media a liar when it sells beauty cheap. God did not create body parts. He created you.

Third, *"no one should wrong his brother or take advantage of him."* Don't be a fake. Don't entice others. Be honest with yourself. Admit you can't handle temptation.

Lo and behold, you are up and over the high bar of holy living, all because you paced yourself with Jesus at your side. Don't think that God's will for you to be holy is too high a standard. He's provided graceful steps for you to get a good running start. Now all you have to do is take them.

Lord, take me now to the level of excellence you desire for me. Lift me up. Encourage and empower me to take these small but important steps of obedience in order to more easily scale your high standards.

Where Are the Simons?

A certain man from Cyrene, Simon, the father of Alexander and Rufus, was passing by on his way in from the country, and they forced him to carry the cross.

MARK 15:21

I once read that criminals to be crucified often had to carry to the place of crucifixion their own cross beam, a piece of wood weighing up to fifty pounds. Jesus started out by shouldering His cross, but He had been so weakened from floggings, that a passer-by named Simon was pressed into service.

It's interesting to note that Simon was only *passing by* and that he was *forced* to carry the cross of Christ. I like to imagine, however, the relief Jesus must have felt – after having helped so many others in so many ways, here was a man to help Him!

❧

Often you'll hear suffering and overburdened people say, "This is the cross I must bear." These dear people need burden-bearers. They need help and, in a way, their unspoken plea may be, "Where is my Simon?"

But who will help? Like Simon, you may see yourself as an innocent passer-by being forced into service. Helping an aunt recover from a stroke. Assisting a neighbour who just got out of the hospital. Lending a hand to a co-worker who recently was diagnosed with a terminal illness.

And like Simon, the task may take you unawares, your plans may be interrupted and you may feel put upon. But as you carry the burden of a suffering friend or family member, you may discover your attitude will change – especially when you see that smile of relief and gratitude. You'll discover the privilege of being someone's Simon.

What a privilege it was for Simon to carry your cross, Lord. In a way, I have the same privilege as I bear the burdens and carry the hurts of your body, my brothers and sisters in Christ. Let me be a Simon to someone today.

Too Much of a Good Thing?

Grace and peace be yours in abundance through the knowledge of God and of Jesus our Lord.   II PETER 1:2

My friend Judy makes the tastiest little chocolate eclairs of anyone I know. Once she threw a tea party in my home, laying out her nicest linens, china and silver. My friends and I daintily picked up each little eclair, savouring every bite.

The first eclair was scrumptious. The second was just as good. By the time I got to the third, I just popped it in my mouth. Did I eat a fourth? I can't even remember. All I know is that several days later when I looked in the mirror and saw pimples on my chin, I sighed, "Yes, you can enjoy too much of a good thing."

Well, there is one good thing we can never get enough of. Grace and peace are ours *in abundance* in the Lord Jesus. You can never enjoy too much of the Lord. Some people may call you a fanatic and say you are overdoing it, warning that "enough is enough". But don't listen. You can never pray too much or read God's Word too often.

For instance, three years ago, I decided to shift into overdrive and read the Bible more in order to know Christ better. That meant doing double-duty during prayer time. It meant making an effort to change old habits, including TV at night. And you know what? I can't get enough of the Lord now. The closer I draw to Him, the more overstuffed I am on the abundance of His grace and peace. Yes, I've learned that contrary to popular opinion about chocolate eclairs . . . there are *some* things you simply can't get enough of.

I want to know you better, Lord, for I can never enjoy too much of the abundance of your grace and peace.

DECEMBER

Christic in You

There the angel of the Lord appeared to him in flames of fire from within a bush. Moses saw that though the bush was on fire it did not burn up. So Moses thought, "I will go over and see this strange sight — why the bush does not burn up." When the Lord saw that he had gone over to look, God called to him from within the bush, "Moses, Moses!" and Moses said, "Here I am."

EXODUS 3:2–4

A blazing bush that glows in a halo of fire . . . and yet doesn't burn up? Now *that* was a strange sight. As Moses drew closer, perhaps he thought it was a remarkable new kind of foliage unlike the rest of the desert scrub brush. Then, what a shock to hear the voice of God Almighty speak from the bush.

Weeks later, long after the prophet moved on, I wonder what happened to that bush. I don't think Moses broke off the branches to enshrine them in a little box on an altar. He didn't uproot the bush to memorialize it. No. As Major Ian Thomas has said, "Any old bush would have done. A scruffy, scraggy looking thing or a beautiful looking bush so shapely and fine. The bush is not important — only that *God* was in the bush!"

The burning bush is an Old Testament example of a New Testament truth: Christ in you, the hope of glory. God can set any life ablaze with Spirit-inspired power. A lowly outcast or an honoured aristocrat. An unskilled individual with lack-lustre gifts, or a talented person who is beautiful and bright. The "you" doesn't matter. What does matter is Christ in you.

To them God has chosen to make known among the Gentiles the glorious riches of this mystery, which is Christ in you, the hope of glory.

COLOSSIANS 1:27

❧

Let me burn for you, Lord. Let me shine.

"All Things" as Defined by Paul

And we know that in all things God works for the good of those who love Him, who have been called according to His purpose. ROMANS 8:28

Have you ever wondered what are the "all things" the apostle Paul is talking about? In II Corinthians chapter 11, he lists a few of the "all things" which God uses to work together for his good.

Things like severe floggings. Being exposed to death. Five times lashed with a whip, three times beaten with rods. Another three times stoned. Shipwrecked, constantly on the move and in danger from rivers, bandits and false believers, Paul laboured while tired, hungry and thirsty. "I have been cold and naked," he says, closing out the list.

These are just a few problems Paul must have been thinking of when he penned that powerful truth about God using everything for our good and His glory. Our problems seem to pale in light of Paul's list. For us, "all things" might include a bad medical report, an overdrawn bank account, a flat tyre on the motorway, or a splitting headache that lasts all morning. Even my wheelchair seems small compared to the constant brushes with death which Paul faced.

Sovereign God, I praise you that you work all things for the good of those who love you. Each problem, each trial I face today, fits into your marvellous plan for my life. Forgive me when I complain about my struggles. I'm sorry that I often fail to remember that you are in control, that you hold in your powerful hand all things in my life.

I want to cooperate with you today and trust you that the inconveniences and problems which I will encounter are by no means mistakes. Thank you for the assurance that you will work today's events into a life plan for my good and your glory.

Mercy

Speak and act as those who are going to be judged by the law that gives freedom, because judgment without mercy will be shown to anyone who has not been merciful. Mercy triumphs over judgment! JAMES 2:12–13

Why do we assume that the mercy of God is mainly a topic of the New Testament, while the judgment of God is a topic of the Old? Don't we realize God's mercy is talked about four times as much in the Old Testament? We wrongly think that judgment and anger characterize the God of Israel while kindness and compassion solely belong to the Lord of the spiritual Israel.

True, the New Testament reveals the full blooming of mercy and its triumph at the cross, but it's not like God suddenly had a change of heart or cosmetic surgery on His character. God did not do an about-face between the Old and New Testament. He did not switch to a merciful mood when He saw His Son walking among men. Mercy is not a mood, but a changeless character-quality of God who is eternal.

He is the same, whether in the Old or New Testament. Whenever God appears to men, He always acts like Himself. He is the same God who appeared in the Garden of Eden as in the Garden of Gethsemane. He has always dealt in mercy with man and will always deal in justice when His compassion is despised and rejected.

A good study on the character of God is A. W. Tozer's *The Knowledge of the Holy*. This beautiful classic looks into the eternal qualities of God, giving us a glimpse of how great and infinite the love of God is.

God, you are good when you judge and you are good when you show mercy. How marvellous and beyond our understanding you are! Thank you for being merciful in your judgment, while always judging with complete mercy.

The World, the Flesh and the Devil

For everything in the world – the cravings of sinful man, the lust of his eyes and the boasting of what he has and does – comes not from the Father but from the world. I JOHN 2:16

Look closely at this verse. How would you sum up the cravings of sinful man? With one word: lust. And what about the lust of his eyes? That's envy. And boasting is just another word for pride. They say that virtually every kind of sin can be traced to these three villains – lust, envy and pride.

So how is the battle against those opponents going for you today? Maybe you are toying with daydreams and imagining yourself in the arms of someone forbidden. Perhaps envy is enticing you to spend beyond your means in order to keep pace with the neighbours. And pride may be tempting you to run mental movies of past successes.

Is all this struggling worth the effort? Wouldn't you rather sit ringside and watch someone else go his fair share of rounds against lust, envy and pride? Well, if you are wrestling against these villains today, you are in a better state than many who have no feeling for the struggle at all. You are in a better condition than those who are stagnated in apathy.

Bishop Ryle has said, "The very fact that the devil has pinpointed you as his opponent should fill your mind with hope. For to be at peace with the world, the flesh and the devil is to be at enmity with God."

Lord of the battle, please fit me for conflict today for I constantly face temptation. Rather than lust, I want to desire you. Instead of envy, may I be jealous for fellowship. Instead of pride, I would rather boast in you. Guard me and my loved ones from the world, the flesh, and the devil.

Rejoice!

"Rejoice in that day and leap for joy, because great is your reward in heaven . . ."
LUKE 6:23

It's a word you read a lot in Scripture. Mary rejoiced when the angel announced she would bear the Saviour. Angels rejoiced in the sky over Bethlehem. People rejoiced to see lame men walk and deaf men hear. The women rejoiced as they raced from the empty tomb. Even the apostle Paul commanded, *"Be joyful always."*

But Jesus takes it a step further when He exclaims, *"Leap for joy!"* This is no sedate and dispassionate command. You can't be dignified and demure when you're exclaiming. In fact, scholars note that the word "rejoice" is best communicated with a jump-up-and-down, clenched fist, throw-your-head-back, and yell out loud, "Oh, joy!!" *This* is the power-packed emotion behind the Lord's words in Luke 6:23.

The people in Scripture were not plaster-of-paris saints who uttered their amazements in less-than-amazing tones. When they exclaimed surprise or excitement, you better believe they were bursting with joy. So when you read Scripture, never read the word "rejoice" without a smile. Remember, God's Word is alive and active, full of feeling and brimming with heartfelt emotion.

They will enter Zion with singing; everlasting joy will crown their heads. Gladness and joy will overtake them . . . ISAIAH 35:10

Somewhere in Scripture it says that as a bridegroom rejoices over his bride, so God rejoices over you. That's stupendous. Incredible. There aren't enough adjectives to describe the wonder. God bursts with joy over you. He observes you obeying Him and exclaims, "Oh, joy!" And He will one day crown you with such joy everlasting.

My cup overflows with joy, Lord, when I think of your great and unsurpassing love. May I enjoy you today and delight over you as you delight over your children!

Hold God to His Word

Being confident of this, that He who began a good work in you will carry it on to completion until the day of Christ Jesus. PHILIPPIANS 1:6

"Hold God to His Word." Does that sound a bit cheeky? Well, to the timid person who prays, yes. But how does the prayer warrior feel about holding God to His Word? My, that's everyday praying.

God enjoys it when we bring His Word before Him. He delights to do His will, and that we should expect Him to do it, only delights Him more. Charles Spurgeon put it this way: "You and I may take hold at any time upon the justice, and the mercy, and the faithfulness . . . of God, and we shall find every attribute of the Most High to be, as it were, a great battering ram with which we may open the gates of heaven."

This quote inspired me when I was first paralysed. Back then, I desperately wanted to rise above my depression and get my spiritual act together. When a friend showed me Philippians 1:6, I decided to use the verse as a lever. I would do what it said: Be confident. So in prayer, I held God to His Word and believed that, despite a tragic accident, He would complete His good work in me. And you know what? God is doing it.

Presumptuously holding God to His Word is arrogance. Humbly holding God to His Word is meekness. We can confidently expect God to do what He says He will do in Scripture, but our confidence must be tempered with a lowly and humble spirit. Blessed are the meek, for they will inherit the earth . . . blessed are the poor in spirit, for theirs is the kingdom of heaven.

Today, let me look to your promises with expectancy and assurance. For your Word never returns to you empty, but always accomplishes what you desire. I glorify you for that.

Bold Love

Jesus entered Jericho and was passing through. A man was there by the name of Zacchaeus; he was a chief tax collector and was wealthy . . . He ran ahead and climbed a sycamore-fig tree to see him, since Jesus was coming that way. When Jesus reached the spot, He looked up and said to him, "Zacchaeus, come down immediately. I must stay at your house today." So he came down at once and welcomed Him gladly.   LUKE 19:1-6

Why it is that Jesus singled out the little man in the sycamore tree, no one knows. What's clear is this: The Lord stepped boldly into Zacchaeus' life. Out of the entire crowd, Jesus called him by name. He told Zacchaeus to scurry down from his perch. And the Lord not only invited Himself to his home, He hardly gave the little man time to think twice about it.

Some would say that Jesus was a bit bold to presume upon Zacchaeus. *Telling* a host he must open his home to you? Bold, yes. But it was the boldness of love. Jesus insured that His command would be well received for He inclined the heart of Zacchaeus to welcome Him.

The love of God *is* daring and courageous. But wait. When you consider that it's the Lord of the universe who steps up to the door of your heart and knocks for entrance, only a fool would refuse Him entry. Like Zacchaeus, Jesus invites Himself into your life, bringing His own joy and welcome. And just as He did with Zacchaeus, He tells you not to hesitate.

"Here I am! I stand at the door and knock. If anyone hears my voice and opens the door, I will go in and eat with him, and he with me."   REVELATION 3:20

◆

I can learn something from Zacchaeus, Lord. I can throw open the door of my heart to you and say, "Welcome!"

I'm Dying to Know . . .

Those who belong to Christ Jesus have crucified the sinful nature with its passions and desires.   GALATIANS 5:24

We use words in strange ways. Take the word "dying". Your daughter in tenth grade says she's dying to know the football captain of the neighbouring high school. Your son in Little League might be dying to meet the national baseball commissioner. Or perhaps you are dying to know what the loud quarrels next door are all about.

It's an exaggeration, to say the least. You're not really willing to kick the bucket in order to find out about your neighbour's problems. But there is one use of the expression that is no exaggeration at all. Are you dying to know the Lord?

The apostle Paul spoke of this when he said, *"I want to know Christ and the power of His resurrection . . . becoming like Him in His death."* Paul realized that in order to know Christ fully, it meant crucifying the old man. Mortifying his sinful nature with all its passions. Nailing worldly affections to the cross. Reckoning himself dead to sin and alive to God.

We say we want to know the Lord's love, to feel His favour, to experience His joy and peace. We want to know His presence and His smile. But could we say we are dying to know Him? If so, Jesus asks you to meet Him at the cross.

~

What does it take to know Jesus in an intimate and personal way? The Bible calls it being crucified with Christ, but you could call it "saying no to sin". Ask the Lord to give you His resurrection power and help you squelch anger, stifle gossip, and put a lid on those mind games.

The power of your resurrection, Lord, is what I need when I say "no" to sin. Let me become like you in your death, crucifying every passion that displeases you. I want to know you. I am dying to know you.

Sweet Hour of Prayer

Then He returned to His disciples and found them sleeping. "Simon," He said to Peter, "are you asleep? Could you not keep watch for one hour?"

MARK 14:37

> Sweet hour of prayer, sweet hour of prayer,
> That calls me from a world of care,
> And bids me at my Father's throne
> Make all my wants and wishes known.

God invites us to make all our wants and wishes known to Him. It's not only a marvellous invitation, but it's what prayer is all about. God wants you to tell Him your problems so He can comfort you. He wants to hear about your longings so He can purify them. Tell Him about your temptations so He can help you conquer them.

Talk to God about everything that's in your heart. And when you do, remember that prayer is also the chance to hear the heartbeat of God. He desires to make known to *you* His wants and wishes.

When you pray this way, you may discover that a whole hour – an entire hour of sweet communion – has just flown by. Time races away all too quickly when you're spending it in intimate conversation with your dearest friend.

> And since He bids me seek His face,
> Believe His Word, and trust His grace,
> I'll cast on Him my ev'ry care,
> And wait for thee, sweet hour of prayer.

Lord, you are my friend and I want to tell you about my wants and wishes. More so, I want to hear you share your heart with me. As I open up your Word, speak to me. And as your Spirit opens up my heart, may my prayer be honest and real. Lastly, tell me, Lord, how much time I am to spend with you in prayer.

There Remains a Rest

There remains, then, a Sabbath-rest for the people of God; for anyone who enters God's rest also rests from his own work, just as God did from His. Let us, therefore, make every effort to enter that rest, so that no-one will fall by following their example of disobedience.   HEBREWS 4:9–11

O ne day we will enter into God's seventh and final day, the Sabbath-rest of eternal joy and peace. We will discover many wonderful riches in heaven, and will also discover the absence of some dear helps. We will finally rest from petitioning God because there will be no necessity. We will rest from fasting and watching. No more preaching. No baptism or memorial of the Lord's Supper. The harvest will be gathered in. The tares will be burned.

And there is one more thing from which we will rest. Evangelizing. There will be no more need to share the Gospel with unsaved people because the kingdom will have been completed. "What? No more witnessing?!" you say?

That's right. There will be plenty of singing and praising, serving and rejoicing. There will be worship and adoration, but no more opportunity to share the good news with unsaved loved ones.

That fact, if anything, should make you get moving down here on earth. There's work to be done. Unsaved friends and neighbours need to know Christ. The lost in your community need to hear the Gospel. Whole nations need to be evangelized. People are on the brink of perishing and the end is fast approaching.

There will be plenty of time to rest in heaven. Now is the time to evngelize.

Forgive me for shuffling my feet when it comes to sharing your Gospel with those who don't know you, Lord. Today, lead me to someone who needs to hear about you.

Immanuel

I hated school when other kids created trouble. Do you remember the feeling? You'd be falsely accused of calling someone a name. Or other kids wrote nasty notes about your hair or clothes. Or the bully towered over you, ready to punch your lights out. For those moments, the world might as well have ended. You couldn't imagine how life could go on.

I imagine Joseph felt like that when he heard of Mary's pregnancy. His engagement was not going according to classroom rules. People started talking. Whispering. Giggling. Sneering. And who knows, perhaps Mary had an older brother that would have beaten the life out of Joseph.

But notice what the angel tells Joseph: *"The virgin will be with child and will give birth to a son, and they will call him Immanuel – which means, 'God with us'."*　　　　　　　　　　　　　　　　　　　MATTHEW 1:23

God with us. What wonderful words Joseph heard. It made all the difference.

Remember those tough days at school? What a relief it was when the teacher showed up at just the right moment to make things right. To stop the talking. To halt the fight. The teacher was in the room and all was well. Whew! So, too, God would be with Joseph and Mary.

But that's not all, I imagine. God was not only going to be there, He would be on their side. Just like the teacher who says, "I'm with *you*, son. The rest of you, run along."

God's promise must have emboldened Joseph because the next day he took the less travelled road and married Mary. Such was his confidence in God's presence and God's defence.

❧

Lord, life has not presented itself in a pretty package each day. But I know you are with me. And I know you are on my side. How can I fail? Give me courage to take roads less travelled because you are mine and you are there.

He Leads

"He calls his own sheep by name and leads them out. When he has brought out all his own, he goes on ahead of them, and his sheep follow him because they know his voice." JOHN 10:3–4

Ever get the feeling you're somewhere out in front of God as you move through your week? You bump up against a trial, and you know from Scripture that God is going to work all things together for good, but somehow you have the idea He's *behind* you, armed with a dustpan and broom, ready to do a cleanup job on you and your problem.

Or perhaps you imagine God standing a few paces back with a bottle of glue, ready to pick up the broken pieces of your life and paste them back together. Or do you imagine Him with hammer and nails ready to follow after you and do a patch-up job should things fall apart?

If you feel as though God's principal activity in your life is to follow behind you and throw a rope after you've fallen headlong into a trial, then you need to memorize our verse for today. A shepherd never follows his flock, he leads them. Jesus Himself says that *He goes on ahead*. He blazes a straight path and charts the way.

Never is God surprised by your trials. Never does He push you out ahead and back you up with a dustpan and broom. God is out in front. In fact, God totally encompasses you, front, side, and rear guard. As it says in Psalm 139:5–6:

You hem me in, behind and before; you have laid your hand upon me. Such knowledge is too wonderful for me, too lofty for me to attain.

Thank you for leading me, Lord. Thank you for charting all of my days, planning every event so that it fits miraculously into a pattern of good for my life.

God's *Omiages*

"When He ascended on high, He led captives in His train and gave gifts to men."
EPHESIANS 4:8

Some gifts you give because it's expected. Other gifts are spur-of-the-moment surprises. Such are the gifts Ken enjoys presenting to me. He calls them *"omiages"*. In Japanese, it means "a little gift which you are not required to give, as for a special occasion".

When I'm on a trip, I have fun picking out *omiages* for my husband. Once it was a tie from Ohio, another time it was a tee-shirt from New York City. When I came home from Texas, I presented him with a jar of chili sauce. Little, unexpected gifts. Ken is always so pleased because he knows that an *omiage* doesn't have to be given. That makes it all the more special.

That's the way Jesus is with us. He's not obligated to give us gifts. He's not rquired to shower us with blessings. He owes this utterly rebellious planet absolutely nothing, and that's why His gifts are all the more special.

He who did not spare His own Son, but gave Him up for us all – how will He not also, along with Him, graciously give us all things? ROMANS 8:32

❧

Thank God for His *omiages* the next time you are blessed by the sound of pattering rain on the window. Or a ray of sunshine on your kitchen floor. The smell of pine on a cold December day. The clattering of horses' hooves on cobblestones. The cooing of pigeons in the park.

God gives gifts simply because He wants to. To top it off, they are generous gifts, not little *omiages*, but big ones. What gift has God given you today? Praise Him for His blessings, small and great.

Lord and giver of life, thank you for being so generous. Today I will count my blessings and be mindful to turn to you often and say, "Thank you!"

Sin's Deceitfulness

See to it, brothers, that none of you has a sinful, unbelieving heart that turns away from the living God. But encourage one another daily, as long as it is called Today, so that none of you may be hardened by sin's deceitfulness.

HEBREWS 3:12–13

Some time ago I pulled into my driveway after stopping at the local gas station for a fill-up. When I got out of my van, I noticed my gas cap was missing. The attendant had forgotten to put it back on. *Oh bother!* I fumed. Exasperated, I drove back to the station to inquire about my cap.

"Is this yours?" the attendant asked as he held up a stainless steel gas cap. I told him "yes" but, when I watched him screw the cap on my van, I took a closer look. It wasn't mine.

I felt guilty, but not guilty enough to keep me from driving around for a few days with the hot gas cap. *Hummph! they were the ones who lost it in the first place . . . why shouldn't I take one of theirs?* I regarded my straight-faced lie to the attendant as less sinful than it actually was in the sight of God.

A few nights later I stumbled across Hebrews 3:12–13 in my devotions. The next morning found me at an auto supply store to purchase a new cap to give to the gas station attendant. He refused to take it, saying it wasn't important. I wish he had realized the whole experience was more for my sake than his. Until recently, I had a sun-faded, never-opened boxed gas cap on my dash to remind me just how deceitful sin really is.

Lord, forgive me when I emasculate my sin, and make great-sounding excuses for it. I am sorry that I try to rationalize my wrongdoing. Let me never become hardened by sin's deceitfulness.

Serve Wholeheartedly

Serve wholeheartedly, as if you were serving the Lord, not men, because you know that the Lord will reward everyone for whatever good he does, whether he is slave or free.   EPHESIANS 6:7

When it comes to serving the Lord, some people sigh and shuffle their feet. They feel tired and drained, wishing someone else at church would volunteer for the responsibility.

Christian service sounds like backbreaking work with little reward. There are those who even find service distasteful, the very people to whom they minister, a turn-off – such as teaching a rowdy group of twelve-year-olds who squirm through Sunday School. *"This* is the sort of thing for which Christians will be rewarded?" you wonder as you dodge a spit ball.

Whether a Sunday School teacher or a choir member, a preacher or a secretary, no church worker is immune from weariness and tiresome routine. So if your witness has no warmth and your preaching, no power, then double-check to see *who* it is you are serving. For it is not the rowdy group of pre-teens that you are ministering to, so much as the Lord Jesus Himself. When we serve with our focus on the Lord, we are able to draw on His energy. Only then can we serve wholeheartedly.

Perhaps you feel manacled to a desk with just enough slack in your chain to reach the filing cabinet, the tea kettle and the washroom. Or maybe you feel chained to the kitchen sink or a vacuum cleaner, a computer, or a study carrel in the lonely back corner of a library.

No "Five Easy Steps to Serving Enthusiastically" will do the trick. Only when your focus is on Jesus can you put passion into your service. He must not only be the One we serve, but the one from whom we draw power.

Lord Jesus, in your power I will serve you today!

Post-blizzard Promise

" 'He is like the light of morning at sunrise on a cloudless morning, like the brightness after rain that brings the grass from the earth.' "

II SAMUEL 23:4

Roaring winds, the spray of sleet and snow, dangerous and slippery ice. Remember those storms when you were a child? I sure do. I'd shiver under my quilt, listening to the creaking branches outside my bedroom window. Would the house survive? Would I?

Moaning winds made me feel lonesome. I hoped sleep would let me escape the night, but every time I'd nod off, rattling windows would shake me awake. I watched the twisted shadows of branches jerk madly across the bedroom wall. Would morning ever come?

Yes, but with it, a different picture. I awoke to soft rays of sun warming my bed covers. The howling had ceased and only an occasional gust would swirl powdery snow off the sill. Quiet called me out of bed and to the window where I gasped at the dazzling white landscape. It was . . . beautiful.

There are days when my soul feels windblown, raw and exposed – times when I'm tossed in a blustery tempest with everything breaking loose. But the God who brings beauty out of blizzards promises to bring peace after the storm. And when the beauty dawns, I hardly remember the fright of that stormy trial.

❧

If you sense storm warnings, hold on to a couple of "winter watch" verses from Scripture. Recall how near and present the Lord really is. Cling to His promise of peace. Remember that joy comes in the morning. Let Him cover your fear with His love, like a blanket of snow, soft and gentle.

You are the Lord who calmed the storms and brought peace to fearful hearts. Praise you for being the light of morning at sunrise. Thank you for being the brightness after rain.

Two Trees in the Garden

In the middle of the garden were the tree of life and the tree of the knowledge of good and evil . . . And the Lord God said, "The man has now become like one of us, knowing good and evil. He must not be allowed to reach out his hand and take also from the tree of life and eat, and live for ever."

GENESIS 2:9; 3:22

It's an old, old story. The serpent beguiled Eve, she and her husband ate from the tree of the knowledge of good and evil, and death, sorrow and disease became a fact of life.

Some people think God was unkind in banishing Adam and Eve from the Garden. But not so. God was just. Not only that, God was kind for *"After he drove the man out, he placed on the east side of the Garden of Eden cherubim and a flaming sword back and forth to guard the way to the tree of life."* GENESIS 3:24

How good and merciful of God to keep diseased and sin-sick man from eating of the tree of life. Had Adam and Eve done so, it's likely mankind, in his sad and sorry state, would have lived for ever. Who wants to live for ever in a body of sin and death? Not me.

Far from being a story of heavy-handed, cruel justice, the real story in the Garden is one of God's wisdom and compassion.

◦ۀ

The tree of life not only grew in the Garden of Eden, but it will one day grow in the new heavens and new earth. Revelation 22:2–3 says, *"On each side of the river stood the tree of life, bearing twelve crops of fruit, yielding its fruit every month. And the leaves of the tree are for the healing of the nations. No longer will there be any curse."*

Thank you for showing such mercy in the Garden of Eden, Lord. And thank you for eternal life free from sorrow and sin.

How Good and Pleasant

How good and pleasant it is when brothers live together in unity! . . . it is as if the dew of Hermon were falling on Mount Zion.   PSALM 133:1, 3

I grew up with three sisters and we were the perfect picture of unity at all times. Hah! I wish. Like any other family we had our differences. But there were many times when Psalm 133 seemed like a family motto. It made us regret the times of conflict.

Perhaps at this moment you're in the midst of a great struggle to resolve conflict in your family or in the family of God. You know the pain and sleepless nights such conflict causes.

As David ruled his kingdom, I have no doubts that he saw division and conflict among his people. And so whenever peace and unity came, his joy was deep and heartfelt. In Psalm 133, he pictures just what such unity meant to him.

Israelites lived in an arid climate. But Mount Hermon to the north provided refreshing mists in the morning that quenched the thirst of the land. It refreshed one's dry skin and made the day bearable. Struggles between you and another brother or sister can create a desert-like feeling in your soul. Everything about your life seems lifeless and dry. But when that moment of agreement in the spirit comes, your body literally feels refreshed.

If you are trying to resolve a conflict, it's almost worth dropping everything else to bring about peace. Only then can your soul – and the soul of that brother or sister – be at rest. Unity is good. It is pleasant. It is refreshment.

⊱∞

Lord, may my life be a refreshment to another saint in Christ. May my words refresh and my actions heal. Thank you for times of miraculous refreshment and healing when unity seemed impossible.

His Purpose for You

*The Lord will fulfil His purpose for me; your love, O Lord, endures for ever —
do not abandon the works of your hands.* PSALM 138:8

God always finishes what he starts. He never begins a project only to
leave it half-done. He never writes a run-on sentence. He never walks
away from a mesy workbench. Unlike us, God never carried over items
on His "To Do" list from one eternity to the next. He always completes
what He begins. That includes you.

He started working on you years ago, long before you became a
Christian. Take heart today that the blueprint for your life is still spread
before Him. He won't stop working on you until He reaches His goal.
By the way, His goal is summed up in Romans 8:29 and His purpose
is that you might *"be conformed to the likeness of His Son . . ."*

Read Psalm 138 to see how God accomplishes His work in your life. He
fulfils His purpose in you with love and faithfulness (verse 2). Part of His
goal is to make you fearless and stouthearted (verse 3), humble (verse 6),
and confident in His ability to preserve and protect you (verse 7).

For more evidence of God's "finishing what He starts", be encouraged
by Philippians 1:6. He will never abandon or forsake you. His goal is to
make you more like Jesus and He won't stop working on His goal for
you until you are complete.

*I am grateful, Lord, that you promise you will fulfil your purpose for me. Thank
you for not abandoning your work in my life when I am stubborn or disobedient.
Today, I want to be willing to cooperate with you. I want to agree with your
purpose in my life. I want to desire the same goals you have for my life. I praise
you that you always finish what you start.*

Things that Last

So we fix our eyes not on what is seen, but on what is unseen. For what is seen is temporary, but what is unseen is eternal.   II CORINTHIANS 4:18

This year Ken and I spent a little extra to buy the fattest, bushiest tree we could find on a California Christmas tree lot. Its outdoorsy fragrance fills our living room and I can close my eyes and catch a whiff of the High Sierras. We unearthed our box of Christmas ornaments from the garage, carefully unwrapping each decoration we've collected over the years.

There's a little wooden horse. There are hand-painted clothes-pin angels, soldiers and shepherds. A polar bear made out of bread dough. A little cornhusk doll. A bell from my sister. Each ornament is treasured, each has its honoured place on our tree.

Silver icicles, lights and cellophane – the sparkling, temporary stuff – has little meaning. When Ken and I untrim our tree, the icicles and fluffy angel hair will be dumped in the trash. But the ornaments will be treated with special care.

Things that have meaning last. Things that hold no meaning, although shimmery and eye-catching, are soon forgotten. It's like that in life, too. There are many dimensions to our lives – some that have lasting value, and others, though they add sparkle, that quickly fade.

What are the lasting things in your life this Christmas? Are you accumulating treasured memories, as you would old and lovely family tree ornaments? Does your first love for the Babe in the manger last in your heart through the years? Does your desire for God's Word quiet you during the frantic rush of the holidays? When you take away all the temporary glitter, I hope you find real love in your heart and in your home – that's what Christmas is all about.

Lord, may you be my lasting treasure all year round!

At the Breast of the Lord

Ah, a child's life, wrapped in a warm blanket, sleeping peacefully in his mother's arms with hardly a care in the world. Worries aren't his responsibility. A baby seems to know that Mother will always be close by tending to every need. No wonder a baby sleeps soundly.

Do you ever wish your life were like that? Flip through the pictures of Baby Jesus on your Christmas cards, sleeping peacefully, and you might think, "If only my life were that simple."

This Christmas season God has a reminder for you:

"I will extend peace to her like a river, and the wealth of nations like a flooding stream; you will nurse and be carried on her arm and dandled on her knees. As a mother comforts her child, so will I comfort you; and you will be comforted over Jerusalem."   ISAIAH 66:12–13

That's an odd description for our heavenly Father, but God paints this tender picture in order to make an important point. He wants to remind you that His breast is a place of comfort. In Him, you can be satisfied. You, too, can rest peacefully knowing that someone will always be close to you, tending to every need. The Lord is your father, friend, husband and brother. And according to Isaiah 66, He is also your mother. He is everything to you, just as a parent is to a child.

So during this fast-paced holiday season when everything seems a little out of control, a little crazy, if you are feeling the heavy burdens of being an adult, take a moment to talk to the Lord as would a child. He longs to pick you up and wrap you tenderly in His care. And in His arms, you will find rest.

Lord, I lie against your breast, my place of comfort. Today I honour you as my father, mother, my everything.

God's Sovereign Timetable

*In those days Caesar Augustus issued a decree that a census should be taken of
the entire Roman world . . . And everyone went to his own town to register.*
LUKE 2:1, 3

Unpleasant circumstances often have a way of being the best part of
God's most magnificent design. Performing their civic duty under
the census posed a great inconvenience to Mary and Joseph.

The distance between Nazareth and Bethlehem was no short hike over
sixty miles of rugged terrain. Despite Joseph's attempts to make the trip
comfortable, it must have been extremely difficult for Mary, into her ninth
month of pregnancy, to make the three-day journey. But God decreed
to have His Son born in the city of David and He used an external
circumstance – the census – to get the Holy Family from point A to
point B. Despite the headache and hardship, God's sovereign timetable
was ticking off right on schedule.

Sometimes we make the mistake of thinking that only the right things,
the comfortable things, are a part of God's design. A good job, an adequate
home, and money in the bank give us the impression that we must be
doing something right. Then when inconvenience or hardship hit, we
wonder what went wrong.

Maybe nothing has gone wrong. Maybe we just need to realize that
our most unpleasant circumstances, much like Mary and Joseph's, often
have a way of being the best part of God's most magnificent design. God's
sovereign timetable is working in the life of your family, too.

*Oh, help me to see, Lord, that every unpleasant circumstance in my life is, indeed,
part of your wonderful design for my life. I thank you for the example of Joseph
and Mary who did not complain over the inconvenience of a census, a rough road,
a cold night, or a crowded inn.*

What Child Is This?

"You will be with child and give birth to a son, and you are to give him the name Jesus."   LUKE 1:31

If you ask the man-in-the-street what he thinks of the Babe of Christmas, you'll be surprised at the answers. Just look at the folks who were there when it happened.

The innkeeper was downright indifferent – a census had come to town and he was busy ringing up the cash register. Then there was Herod – he tried to destroy everything connected with the Christmas celebration. Consider the shepherds in the field – only after the angels bent over backwards to explain the celestial fireworks were their fears finally put to rest.

The wise men were curious, poking here and there with questions until they found answers that satisfied. Still others, like Simeon in the temple, waited. Other people hoped, like Anna the prophetess. Then there were those who, like Mary and Joseph, worshipped the newborn King.

People haven't changed much since Bible times and the man-in-the-street responds in much the same way. Are you, like the innkeeper, indifferent? Too busy? Are you still searching, looking for answers? Or maybe you're frightened because the Baby in the manger asks too much of you. Stop and think how *you* would have responded had you been the man on the streets of Bethlehem that night.

There are a thousand different ways to respond to the news that a Saviour has been born to deliver man from his sins. But the fact remains that until a Child was born, this world was cloaked in utter darkness, abandoned, hopeless and lost. But for unto us, a Child is born, a Son is given! There is only one response: Worship and joyous praise!

Lord Jesus, I only have one response to your birth: Joy! No more let sin and sorrow reign, nor thorns infest the ground! For you have come to make God's blessings known far as the curse is found!

Christmas in the Stable

While they were there, the time came for the baby to be born, and she gave birth to her firstborn, a son. She wrapped him in cloths and placed him in a manger, because there was no room for them in the inn.   LUKE 2:6–7

I leaned on my elbow looking out the farmhouse window while my mother and sisters cooked food and set the table for Christmas Eve dinner. As the snow fell in light, dry flakes, a soft haze made our barn almost disappear.

During the late afternoon, I pulled on my jacket, stuffed a few carrots in my pockets, and hiked to the stable. I felt sorry for the horses and goats in the barn. All of us were going to open presents that evening, and I didn't want the animals to feel left out.

It was quiet in the stable with the smell of hay, the cosy odours of horses' coats, and a peaceful feeling that warmed me to the heart. The sound of horses crunching carrots. The quiet of my own breathing. I sighed, feeling protected and loved. Maybe it was the beauty of solitude contrasted against the bustling cheer inside the farmhouse, but in some way God spoke to me that afternoon. I felt His love in the solitude.

Maybe you don't live on a farm. Perhaps when you look outside, you see the back yard of your next-door neighbour. Or you might live in an apartment. Or a trailer. You could be in a hospital or a nursing home. Not many of us live near a stable. But you know what I'm talking about. Find that place to be apart. A place of quiet and solitude. It could be a walk to a nearby park, or the cool quiet of an upstairs bedroom.

Wherever it is, make time to be alone today. With Him.

Speak to my heart, Lord Jesus, I am quiet and still before you.

Step Outside

It was a chilly night in Bethlehem. People escaped the cold, damp air and crowded into the little inn at the end of the street. They had left their donkeys and camels in the back stable, had shut the door, and were now laughing and chattering with distant relatives they had not seen in years.

Family ties were renewed over bowls of hot soup and goblets of wine. People broke bread together, swapping stories about their long journey. A teenage boy strummed his lyre and several fathers clapped their hands in time to the music.

While balancing a tray of meats and breads, the innkeeper answered a knock at the door. A man calling himself Joseph stood outside with his cloak pulled tightly around his head. It was late, cold, and he and his young wife who was heavy with child needed a room. The innkeeper could barely hear Joseph speak with so much background noise, but he managed to explain that there was no room. Only an empty stall or two in the back stable.

The innkeeper quickly apologized and slammed the door shut against Joseph. Outside, Joseph stood and listened to the laughter behind the door. He sighed deeply, turned, and quietly led Mary to the stable. While a celebration of music and feasting continued behind the warm walls of the inn, yards away, the Son of God quietly entered history.

Sometimes the most special moments of Christmas happen not during a crowded party, but in cool, quiet silence. In the midst of bustling activity, God seeks out the quiet heart.

What a contrast between the serene stable and the busy inn. If only someone had taken the time to peer out a back window, or leave the party to check on his donkey, just think what he would have discovered! Perhaps he would have seen the angels, the shepherds, and yes, even the Son of God.

Come into my heart Lord Jesus, there's room in my heart for you.

Eternity's Boxing Day

Picture yourself as a housekeeper going about on Boxing Day in London during the 18th century. This is a special day and you are expecting a tip for your annual service. But on this particular Boxing Day, your master doesn't remember anything that you have done. "Did you clean our house *today?*" he asks. "Why should I reward you for something you did in the past? I don't remember you cleaning our house last week."

That's not how Boxing Day is supposed to work. Every good master knows that a servant's reward needs to be based upon the service rendered during the entire working relationship.

Our service for Christ is likewise evaluated upon our entire relationship and not based on our most recent work. And such service has its due reward. Christ is not a chancy master who's going to short-change you on the greatest of all Boxing Days. No. His promises of reward are as trustworthy as His predictions of judgment against sin.

If any man builds on this foundation . . . his work will be shown for what it is, because the Day will bring it to light. It will be revealed with fire . . . If what he has built survives, he will receive his reward.

I CORINTHIANS 3:12–14

～

Our Lord is not cheap, according to Paul. Rewards will be granted to those who have pleased God and have built upon the foundation of Jesus Christ. Every deed or word outside of the compelling belief in Christ is doomed to burn. What a relief to know that our falterings will burn and our faithfulness remain.

Have you built upon your faith in Christ? Such things will not burn. And when the ashes clear, you'll wear them in your crown as brilliant reminders of a trustworthy master.

Lord, I commit each word and deed as service rendered for you. Thank you for calling me to your service. Thank you for your promise of reward. Your calling is more than I deserve. Your promise more than I can imagine.

After Christmas

Let us fix our eye on Jesus, the author and perfecter of our faith, who for the joy set before Him, endured the cross, scorning its shame, and sat down at the right hand of the throne of God.　　　　　HEBREWS 12:2

One of my favourite days of the holiday season is 27 December. The rushed conversations and frantic last-minute purchasing is over. Between Christmas Day and New Year's Eve, I take a day or two off, sleep in, get up to a relaxed breakfast, and breathe a sigh of relief.

Later in the morning, we collapse on the couch in front of the fire, play board games or reopen gifts to take a longer, closer look. We read books and flip through photos. We nibble leftover Christmas pudding and keep a warm pot of coffee for anyone who may happen to drop by. For supper that evening, the menu is more leftovers, perhaps sandwiches of turkey and stuffing. It's casual, homey and relaxed. But most important, it's simple.

It's a deliberate kind of simplicity. Demands and distractions may have sidetracked us before, but December 27th is reserved for peace and quiet. There's plenty of time to meditate on what the good news of our Saviour's birth really means. There's time to ponder the future and pray. There are more than enough quiet moments to relax in the love of the Lord.

This week, aim for simplicity. The last few weeks may have been filled with baking, shopping, concerts, gift wrapping and dinner parties, but today, celebrate simplicity as you fix your eyes on Jesus.

Lord Jesus, this week people around the world heralded your birth and celebrated your gift of love. May the wonder of your birth remain with me all through this day as I fix my eyes on you. I quiet my heart, I relax my mind, I slow my pace so that I may meditate on your love, so pure and simple.

Grandma Grace's Bible

Jesus Christ is the same yesterday and today and for ever.   HEBREWS 13:8

When I travel with my friends, Bev and Francie, we always enjoy heading back to our hotel room after a busy day of appointments and speaking engagements. We put on our pyjamas, pile into bed together, and open up the Bible for devotions.

One evening it was Francie's turn to lead the hymns and Scripture reading. She rummaged through her suitcase and brought out an old, tattered Bible. "This is my Grandma Grace's," she smiled as she snuggled between Bev and me.

Francie cracked open the old Bible. The binding was torn and she carefully turned each delicate page. Francie tilted the book so we could read Grandma Grace's faded scribbles in the margin. In old-fashioned script, we got an up-close look at this elderly woman's love for the Lord Jesus. Her words were nearly a century old, but the love of which she wrote was anything but obsolete.

As Francie read aloud her grandmother's personal notes, I felt as though this woman shared the rhythm of my heart. We were kindred spirits. We could have been best friends. And her notes weren't reminiscent of dusty days gone by, for each word was a powerful and poignant reminder that Jesus *is* the same yesterday, today and for ever.

❧

There's nothing old or worn out about the love of God. His love has not yellowed with age. It is neither fragile or ragged at the edges. God's love is as current now as it was a century ago, as fresh today as it will be tomorrow. Today, praise the Lord that He *is* the same, always loving, always merciful, and that with Him there is no shadow of turning.

Jesus, I'm amazed that you never change. You are always faithful. Your promises are time-tested. Together with the saints of the ages, including Grandma Grace . . . I praise you!

The Desert of Solitude

But when God, who set me apart from birth and called me by His grace, was pleased to reveal His Son in me so that I might preach Him among the Gentiles, I did not consult any man, nor did I go up to Jerusalem to see those who were apostles before I was, but I went immediately into Arabia and later returned to Damascus. GALATIANS 1:15–17

"Others may, but you cannot." That was not only a cross-stitched proverb I once saw hanging in someone's hallway, but it was the direct and personal word of the Holy Spirit to me. I saw many of my Christian friends enjoying all sorts of wonderful activities, but if I ventured into the same, I felt out of place and a little uncomfortable. Not wanting to trouble my friends, I kept these feelings to myself and quietly retreated, not from my loved ones, but from the activities. My spirit felt better for it, but I was also lonely.

Those became marvellous times of fellowship with the Lord Jesus. Having forfeited activities that were, for the most part, morally neutral, I was more free to pursue a pure-hearted devotion to God. My loneliness became that which drove me deeper into the heart of my Saviour.

Distancing yourself from something that once held your heart can be a kind of withdrawing into the desert of solitude where desires can be purified. It's a way of detaching your desire from the magnetic pulls of this world in order to attach it more firmly to Christ.

The love of God constrains us all, but it more tightly constrains some than others, making the soul restless until it finds its desires fulfilled in the Lord and in the Lord only.

Make me sensitive to your constraining love, Lord, and if you are calling me into a desert of solitude, please give me the courage to follow.

In God's Eyes

"You are the God who sees me."   GENESIS 16:13

When I was a teenager, rushing out of the house to meet my friends, I would invariably be stopped at the door by my father who'd say, "Joni, I want you to act as though someone were always watching. Don't forget you're an Eareckson."

That irked me. I didn't want someone peeking into my life, observing everything I was doing. There were private teenage things I wanted to keep hidden. What an embarrassment to have some friend of my father's encroach on my Saturday night turf to say, "Hi there, how's your dad doing?"

But now, many years later, I'm comforted by the idea that I ought to live as though someone were always looking. It's an incentive to live an honest, responsible life. Besides, someone *is* watching. Your life and mine is an open book before the Lord.

If you love the works of darkness, that idea will embarrass you. If you love the light, the idea that God never takes His eyes off you will be a comfort. For those who are obedient, the watchful eye of God will seem tender and protecting. For those who disobey, the open book of your life incites resentment and embarrassment.

Nothing in all creation is hidden from God's sight. Everything is uncovered and laid bare before the eyes of Him to whom we must give account.

HEBREWS 4:13

Fear must never be an incentive to obey for it will only breed burdensome rule-keeping behaviour. Please don't fear the watchful eye of God, but draw comfort from His scrutiny into your life. Let Him protect you, let Him guard you with His eye.

See me, Lord, and know my every thought and action. I invite you to look into everything I do today, everything I decide or say. Watch me, please, and may your steady and loving gaze be my incentive to love you steadily in return.

Take Inventory

Where did this year fly to? Just when I get into the groove of writing the correct year, I've got to learn a new one. It's hard to keep track any more.

That's why right now is a great time to take inventory. Go back over the year and ask yourself: Did I meet all of my goals, or at least some of them? Did I keep all my promises, at least those I remember? Have my relationships strengthened with family and friends? Did my life in the Lord Jesus deepen and grow? If I were to ask a close friend, would he say that I've changed for the better over the last year?

I'm not asking you these things to make you feel guilty. It's just good to close out the old, to tie up all the loose ends, and to bring closure to one year before you begin a new one.

So set aside a few minutes right now and take inventory. Consider each question and turn it into a prayer as together we stand on the threshold of a new year.

≈§

Did I commit myself to do something yet fail to do it? *Lord, give me the courage to make amends with those I failed. Help me to be a promise-keeper and make good on my word.*

Did I testify as a Christian in my place of work? *Lord, help me to stand up for the faith where I work because I want to be salt and light to the people around me.*

Did I show appreciation to family and friends? *Lord, forgive me for unresolved conflicts and arguments left hanging. Help me to deepen my friendship with each family member and each person you've placed in my life.*

Did I enjoy being alone with the Lord this past year? *Lord, keep reminding me that quiet time with you is the source of my strength. As I commit myself to a special time of prayer and the study of your Word, hold me to my vows. May I glorify you in the year to come!*

New Testament

⤳ ACKNOWLEDGEMENTS ⤳

The author and publisher acknowledge with thanks permission to reproduce copyright material as listed below:

The Banner of Truth Trust, Pennsylvania, for the extract from *The Valley of Vision* by Arthur Bennett, which appears on 16 March.

Christian Fellowship for the Disabled magazine, New Zealand, Issue No. 58, November 1992, for the extract by Joy Gregory, which appears on 10 November.

Contemporary Books Inc., Chicago, for the poem by William Herbert Carruth from *One Hundred and One Famous Poems*, Ed. Roy J. Cook, 1985, which appears on 23 June.

Fleming H. Revell Company, Old Tappan, New Jersey, for the extracts from *The Christian's Secret of a Happy Life* by Hannah Whittal Smith, 1976, which appear on 31 May and 17 November.

Guidepost magazine for the story reproduced on 18 January.

HarperSanFrancisco for the extracts from *The Knowledge of the Holy* by A. W. Tozer, which appear on 19 and 20 February.

Hope Publishing Company, Illinois, for the text from "Wonderful Grace of Jesus" by Haldor Lillenas, 1918, which appears on 27 February.

Inspirational Press, USA, and HarperCollins*Publishers*, UK, for the extracts from *The Business of Heaven* published in *The Inspirational Writings of C. S. Lewis* in the USA, and *The Business of Heaven* in the UK, 1984, which appear on 13 March.

InterVarsity Press, Illinois, for the extract from *Knowing God* by J. I. Packer, which appears on 12 November.

Kregal Publications, Grand Rapids, Michigan, for the quotation from Matthew Henry in *Psalms* by C. H. Spurgeon, 1976, which appears on 8 July.

The Reformed Episcopal Publication Society, Philadelphia, for the prayer from *The Book of Common Prayer*, 1932, which appears on 28 October.

Tyndale House Publishers Inc. for the extracts from *Draper's Book of Quotations for the Christian World*, by Edythe Draper, 1992, which appear on 24 January, 6 February, 17 April, 16 June, 20 August, 14 October and 24 November.

Victor Books, Wheaton, Illinois, for the extract from *Found: God's Will* by John MacArthur, 1977, which appears on 8 November.

Word Publishing, Waco, Texas, for the extracts from: "I Am His, and He Is Mine" by George W. Robinson, which appears on 21 April; "No One Ever Cared For Me Like Jesus" by Charles F. Weigle, which appears on 22 April and 7 October; "O Love That Wilt Not Let Me Go" by George Matheson, which appears on 29 June; "Near the Cross" by Fanny Crosby, which appears on 24 July; "There Is A Fountain" by William Cowper, which appears on 23 August, and "Sweet Hour of Prayer" by William W. Walford, which appears on 9 December. All published in *The Hymnal*, 1986.

World Wide Publications for the extract from *Wondrous Power . . . Wondrous Love*, which appears on 20 May.

Zondervan Publishing House, Michigan, for the extract from *The Saving Life of Christ* by Major W. Ian Thomas, 1961, which appears on 1 December.